MW01438999

The Pathway: Color Picture Photo Edition

THE PATHWAY

COLOR PICTURE PHOTO EDITION

Bruce Davidson

DAVID AND BATHSHEBA OF THE HEBREW BIBLE

The Pathway: Color Picture Photo Edition

Copyright © October 24th, 2024 Bruce Davidson

All rights reserved. No part of this book may be used or reproduced by any means (graphically, electronically, or mechanically), including photocopying, recording, taping or by any information storage retrieval system without written permission of the publisher.

ISBN - 9798344291253

Printed in the United States of America

First Edition (2024)

Amazon Publishing Company USA (Headquarters)
Kindle Direct Publishing (KDP)
410 Terry Avenue. N.
Seattle, Washington 98109-5210
206-266-1000

The Pathway: Color Picture Photo Edition

*This novel is dedicated to the memory of
Jacqueline Bouvier Kennedy,
The most gracious lady who ever lived.*

The Pathway: Color Picture Photo Edition

THE DAVIDSON CENTER
IN JERUSALEM, ISRAEL

The Pathway: Color Picture Photo Edition

TABLE OF CONTENTS
CHAPTERS TO THE NOVEL,
"THE PATHWAY: COLOR PICTURE PHOTO EDITION"

Foreword by Congressman Jo Congressman Bonner	7
Introduction	10
Chapter One I Would Be True	13
Chapter Two The Battle of Gog and Magog	61
Chapter Three The Marriage of David and Bathsheba	93
Chapter Four The Hypnotic Moon	124
Chapter Five Solomon's Temple Rebuilt	143
Chapter Six Jacob's Trouble	197
Chapter Seven The Battle of Armageddon	238
Chapter Eight The President of the United States Address to the Nations of the World	252

TABLE OF CONTENTS

Chapter Nine	257
The Coming of the Israeli Messiah	
Chapter Ten	276
Every Stone of the Temple Shall Be Thrown Down	
Chapter Eleven	291
The Millennial Temple	
Chapter Twelve	310
The Rightful Place for the Ark of the Covenant	
Chapter Thirteen	315
The Restoration of the Throne of David	
Chapter Fourteen	322
The Grand Reunion	
About The Author	327
The Star of David	329

The Pathway: Color Picture Photo Edition

FOREWORD BY CONGRESSMAN JO BONNER

Bruce Davidson combines his love for the people of Israel with his considerable talents as writer, actor, and orator to bring us his long-awaited novel, "The Pathway: Color Picture Photo Edition."

A popular fixture in Mobile and along all of Alabama's Gulf Coast for many years, Bruce has literally devoted the past several years to bringing this important story to life.

He and I first met when I was still representing the people of South Alabama in the United States Congress. Looking back, it is not unusual for a Congressman to meet with constituents who are passionate about the many challenges and obstacles to attaining lasting peace in Israel and throughout the Middle East.

But few people come to such a meeting with the kind of determination — and actual zeal — that Bruce has for this subject. And without a doubt, Bruce may be the only person I know who feels so strongly about this subject that he, actually, made a tremendous sacrifice in both time and effort to put pen to paper to bring his story to life. Believe me, this has been a calling for Bruce Davidson in every sense of the word.

After visiting Israel, myself, back in 2005, I remember returning to the United States with a much greater appreciation for just how special this place really is. I was also struck by how small Israel is and by how close, in proximity, the people in The State of Israel are to everyone else.

This point was highlighted when our delegation traveled one day from Jerusalem to the Golan Heights. There, standing seemingly in the middle of nowhere, was a directional sign pointing in kilometers to the distance to Jerusalem, Amman, Haifa, Baghdad, Damascus and Washington, D.C.

There was also a directional arrow pointing to the Israeli Prime Minister's Office.

It was all a stark reminder of just how close to danger everything is in Israel.

The Pathway: Color Picture Photo Edition

While attaining a lasting, permanent peace in Israel has been elusive to many of our world's greatest minds, perhaps the best way to make this goal a reality is to speak more to the heart than to the head. If this is, in fact, possible, then perhaps Bruce Davidson's newest work, "The Pathway: Color Picture Photo Edition," is the best place to

Josiah (Jo) Robins Bonner, Jr.
Member of the U.S. Congress (2003-2013)

INTRODUCTION

QUEEN BATHSHEBA, THE ROSE OF SHARON
SONG OF SOLOMON 2:1

"The Pathway: Color Picture Photo Edition" is a novel that expresses the impetus and urgency of the complete restoration of Israel. The question is how that fruition may be accomplished and come to term, a process that officially began when Israel became a State in 1948. Israel has walked a pathway that started when Abraham was appointed by God to be the eternal father of a chosen nation. That path delivered the Israelites from the bondage of Pharoah in Egypt only to lead them through the wilderness for forty years. Then, the journey went on to Joshua's conquest of the Promised Land, to David bringing Jerusalem under his control, to the construction and loss of Solomon's Temple resulting in captivity of the Jews in Babylon, to the Crucifixion and Resurrection of Jesus Christ, the travesty and atrocity of the Holocaust in World War II, Israel becoming a nation once again in the 20th century, and all the wars fought since then to maintain Israel's dignity and sovereignty.

Yet an Eternal Promised Land is directly ahead. And it would be no small feat for the Jews and ultimately the world to realize what direction to take to finally reach their destination.

And just as much as the people of Israel in olden days clamored for a king and queen to establish a monarchy, so too it was meant to be in a modern time, with all its advanced technology and current international events, that Israel would insist on having a worthy king and queen to lead them to victory.

"And all the Elders of Israel gathered themselves together and came unto Samuel, the Prophet, and said, 'Now, make us a king to judge us like all the nations.' And the Lord said unto Samuel, 'Hearken unto the voice of the people in all that they say unto you and show them the manner of the king that shall reign over them.'" I Samuel 8:4, 7, 9

"And the people of Israel said to Samuel, the Prophet, 'We will have a king over us. That we also may be like all other nations. And that our king may judge us, and go out before us, and fight our battles.' And the Lord God of Israel said to Samuel, 'Hearken unto their voice, and I will make them a king.'" I Samuel 8:19, 20, 22

The people of Israel urgently wanted a king and queen that they could see with their eyes. And so it would be that the God of Israel raised up a king and queen of a democratic monarchy who would be inspired by the Israeli Messiah to safely, yet not without many complications, blaze the way to Camelot. And they were going to be no ordinary king and queen, but fearless warriors as well, making the hard, fast, and continuous decisions to create the most opportune circumstances conducive to successfully bringing restoration about in its purest form.

There would be no weak link in this royal couple's chain that binds them to each other and the people of Israel. The modern-day king and queen of Israel were always meant to be.

The Hebrew Bible speaks of the good king, Josiah, who lost his life in a ferocious battle (The Battle of Megiddo) which resulted in a humiliating defeat. And Josiah had to forfeit his kingdom. But both the Hebrew Bible, that is, the Old Testament, and the New Testament state loud and clear of a contemporary war taking place at Megiddo, the war to win or lose all wars, the Battle of Armageddon. Revelation 16:16

"The Pathway: Color Picture Photo Edition" is a novel rendering the hope that peace is not merely a pipe dream and offers the expectation that there may be a shot of Camelot being restored rather than lost forever.

Most sincerely,

Bruce Davidson
Song of Solomon 4:7
Song of Solomon 2:1

The Pathway: Color Picture Photo Edition

CHAPTER ONE
"I WOULD BE TRUE"
by Howard Arnold Walter

DAVIDSON HIGH SCHOOL
MOBILE, ALABAMA USA
SOMETIME IN THE 21st CENTURY

The Israeli State And American Coalition, better known by its acronym, I.S.A.A.C., is a military exchange program agreed upon mutually by the United States and Israel. Israeli soldiers were transferred to bases all throughout the United States to be stationed and trained, while American troops, both officers and enlisted, were assigned to bases all throughout Israel. The success of this program, in terms of world security and protection, proved to be phenomenal, as the proximity of alliance between the two countries proved to be even more intimidating to those enemies who diametrically opposed the democratic comradery of the United States and Israel. The demographics of each country noticeably changed as well, as both nations got a good taste of each other's culture in the process.

BROOKLEY AIR FORCE BASE/BATES FIELD
THE MOBILE AEROPLEX AT BROOKLEY
MOBILE, ALABAMA USA

One way the United States expressed its eagerness for the I.S.S.A.C. military exchange program with Israel was to reopen, renovate, and expand the old Brookley Air Force Base in Mobile, Alabama (USA). The base had been phased out in 1969 by the current Defense Secretary, Robert McNamara, and the biggest event to occur since its closing was the Airbus plan to assemble A319, A320 and A321 aircraft at the Mobile Aeroplex at Brookley Air Force Base. The landscape and dimensions of the base were greatly enlarged. The front gate of Brookley Air Force Base used to be close to the top of the ramp at Michigan Avenue, where drivers got off at Interstate 10. But now, the new front gate extended out miles further reaching all the way to Government Boulevard. In fact, expansions were made on all sides of the base, to make it one of the largest United States Air Force Bases in America. The United States government bought acres and acres of houses along all the streets of Michigan Avenue, in between Interstate 10 and Government Boulevard. New acreage was procured all the way around the original base. And the brand-new improvements made, coupled with the latest and greatest fighter jets flying in and out, along with the top-notch personnel who transferred to become stationed at Brookley, all combined to make the upgraded base one of the greatest marvels in the United States. The additional square mileage acquired made Brookley Air Force Base, also referred to as the Mobile Aeroplex at Brookley, impressively massive. All the aerial activity caused Mobile to become a very noisy city, but considering how much the economy had improved by leaps and bounds once the base was complete, no one complained very often. And the fine people of the Port City of Mobile, Alabama definitely felt more protected. They, certainly, weren't overly concerned about radical terrorists parachuting in.

Lieutenant Colonel Jesse Hartman, an Israeli Department Commander and Aerial Defense Combatant, was one of the first to enthusiastically endorse the I.S.A.A.C. Program and see it become a reality. He brought his son, David Hartman, to the base on the very first day he reported to Brookley. David was in his senior year of high school. The move from Israel to the United States inspired David to make Harvard University in Cambridge, Massachusetts (USA) the college he set as a goal to go to, rather than the Hebrew University in Jerusalem, Israel. David also planned on majoring in aeronautical engineering at MIT as well, in pursuit of a career as a fighter jet pilot, just like his father. All of David's ancestors were military men, and many of them were genuine Israeli heroes. They participated in the war that made it possible for Israel to become a State in 1948. They engaged in the Six-Day War of 1967 and the Yom Kippur War of 1973. David had relatives involved in conflicts prior to Israel becoming a State as well as other battles afterward. David's father was a decorated Israeli hero, and David had the very same ambitions. David's 6-foot, 2-inch tall, muscular build, with rugged features, handsome looks, jet black hair, deep brown eyes, and focused demeanor made him fit the part too. David had been going to Hartman High School in Jerusalem, an Orthodox Jewish school affiliated with the Shalom Hartman Institute. His developed ability at soccer, also referred to as football in Israel, had served to make him so athletic and agile that Coach Crenshaw at Davidson High School told David that he would give him a shot at trying out for the football team, home of and known as the Davidson Warriors. David was looking forward to becoming Americanized. So, not going to the Hebrew University after high school would not be a big disappointment for him. Harvard University, along with MIT, would fit his plans perfectly. And now, David was on a field trip with his father, inspecting the latest model fighter jets and their flight performance. For David, it was a glorious day being at the newly modernized, restructured, and expanded Air Force Base in Mobile, Alabama.

DAVIDSON HIGH SCHOOL
MOBILE, ALABAMA USA

The climate can be quite humid in the Port City of Mobile and along the Gulf Coast, especially during the hurricane season. One of the major pastimes in Mobile, other than fishing, hunting, and frolicking on the beach at Dauphin Island and Gulf Shores, Alabama under beautiful blue skies, is dodging Category 1 to Category 5 hurricanes. It's just like the old cliché that's said in Mobile: "If you don't like the weather in Mobile, stick around. It'll change."

The Israeli military and the American military had been working together on a top secret training program for fighter pilots, in conjunction with I.S.A.A.C. goals. And with every waking day, David aspired to follow in the footsteps of his father to one day become a fighter pilot himself. David wanted to excel at making his father and all of Israel proud of him.

The multi-colored leaves of orange, green, red, and brown were already being carried across the roads and yards of homes by the seasonal fall wind as one clear indication that the classes at Davidson High School in Mobile were resuming. David is strolling down the hallway as a shuffle of students, from freshmen to seniors, race past him in between classes. David stops at the locker of an attractive senior, with an athletic build equal to his own, in a feminine counterpart manner, and said, "Can I buy you lunch, Bathsheba?" Bathsheba Rosenberg, whose military parents had also been transferred from Israel, slowly closed her locker with books in her arms, and turned contemplatively to look up at David. She was wearing a pink angora sweater with a matching flannel skirt. Bathsheba had auburn hair, deep emerald-green eyes, and an athletic, olive tone color hardbody. Bathsheba is an Ann Margret look-a-like, as portrayed in the Elvis Presley movie, "Viva Las Vegas."

With a frisky look on her face, Bathsheba responded, "What's on the menu?"

David said, "I'm not sure. I'm hoping it's a hamburger with some fries. I'm getting a little burned out on Kosher food.

" Bathsheba laughed out loud and said, "You are funny, David!"

David and Bathsheba got their trays of food in the Davidson High School Cafeteria and sat at the table against the wall where the windows provide a view of Pleasant Valley Road, the main street out in front of the school that leads to both Azalea Road and Montlimar Drive. After they began eating, David exclaimed, "Bathsheba, I want to read something to you. It's a poem by Harold Walter Arnold:

"I would be true, for there are those who trust me.
I would be strong, for there is much to suffer.
I would be pure, for there are those who care.
I would be brave, for there is much to dare."

After David finished reading, Bathsheba looked back at him with an astonished look on her face and said, "David, it is just unbelievable that a guy like you, who has the scientific aptitude you have, is such a major poet!"

"Well, I just love both literature and science, I suppose." David said.

"No, David. I mean it. You are a genuine poet. You've had a poet's heart ever since I've known you, when we were children. It's something that helps to give you reason in life." Bathsheba responded, with her eyes squinting and mouth half open. Bathsheba was dazzled by David, and the feeling was quite mutual of David's perspective of Bathsheba.

"Whoever loved that loved not at first sight? William Shakespeare. Romeo and Juliet." David quipped.

David was the one sitting at the table with the view of Pleasant Valley Road, and out of nowhere, Jonathan Diamond rushed closely to David's right side, sat down at the cafeteria table, and blurted out, "David! You're not going to believe it! You and I are on the roster to play football for the senior team! You're even being considered for quarterback, and the coaching staff is thinking about placing me in the position of tight end!"

David couldn't believe it.

"Have you been drinking some Mogen David Wine or something, Jonathan?" David retorted, half-way looking around like he was a little embarrassed, as Bathsheba giggled on the other side of the cafeteria table.

"I'm not kidding, David," Jonathan confirmed. "Coach Crenshaw thinks we've both got what it takes, and he wants to win the championship really bad this year."

Jonathan was, hands down, David's best friend. Jonathan's parents also had transferred from Israel to participate in the I.S.A.A.C. Program. Jonathan, like David, was a handsome, athletic young man with dark features, and hazel eyes. David and Jonathan were unquestionably destined to follow similar paths in life.

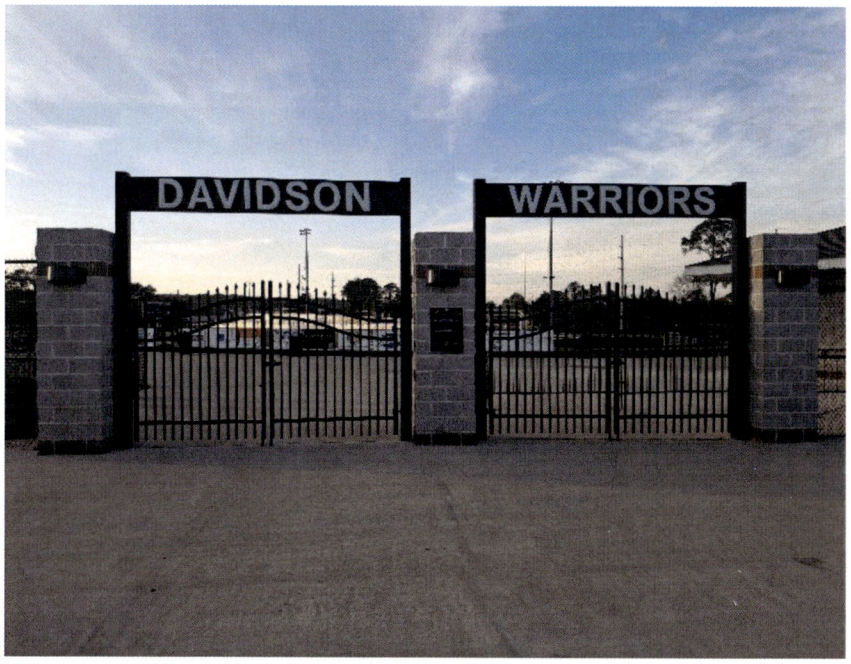

THE DAVIDSON HIGH SCHOOL WARRIORS ENTRANCE TO
THE ON-CAMPUS STADIUM IN MOBILE, ALABAMA USA
FRIDAY NIGHT

It was the big game to determine which high school team in the area would go to the State Championship. Coach Crenshaw, the Head Coach for Davidson High School and all of his staff were most proud of the Davidson High School Warrior Football Team uniformed in the school colors of gold and black, especially where David and Jonathan were concerned. Coach Crenshaw's hunches had paid off, and he felt that the blend of David Hartman and Jonathan Diamond was a winning combination for his team. Some of the American boys resented the Israeli guys moving in and "taking over," but Coach Crenshaw didn't care what anyone thought. They were playing the McGill-Toolen Catholic High School Yellow Jackets, whose colors are orange and black. The Yellow Jackets were a formidable team, a respected rival, and had knocked the Davidson Warriors out of the State Championship way too many times. This time, Coach Crenshaw was not taking any chances, and David and Jonathan were his ace in the hole.

FRONT BLEACHERS TO THE NEW DAVIDSON HIGH SCHOOL ON-CAMPAS STADIUM

It was a close football game all the way through. Now, it had gotten down to the wire of the game. The score was 14 to 17 in favor of the Yellow Jackets with 12 seconds on the clock in the fourth quarter. Davidson was on the 47-yardline of McGill-Toolen. The Davidson Warrior Football Team came out of the huddle for what possibly could have been the final play of the game. David, the quarterback, just happened to look over to the sideline, and noticed that Bathsheba, the head cheerleader, was giving David a timeout sign with her hands, as the other Davidson cheerleaders were yelling, "Go Warriors!" and making full use of their pom-poms. David relented, and signaled a timeout sign himself. The referee blew his whistle, as David ran in Bathsheba's direction, with coaches and football players grumbling on both sides of the field and spectators wondering what in the world was going on.

SIDE VIEW OF THE NEW DAVIDSON HIGH SCHOOL ON-CAMPUS STADIUM

It was a close football game all the way through. Now, it had gotten down to the wire of the game. The score was 14 to 17 in favor of the Yellow Jackets with 12 seconds on the clock in the fourth quarter. Davidson was on the 47-yardline of McGill-Toolen. The Davidson Warrior Football Team came out of the huddle for what possibly could have been the final play of the game. David, the quarterback, just happened to look over to the sideline, and noticed that Bathsheba, the head cheerleader, was giving David a timeout sign with her hands, as the other Davidson cheerleaders were yelling, "Go Warriors!" and making full use of their pom-poms. David relented, and signaled a timeout sign himself. The referee blew his whistle, as David ran in Bathsheba's direction, with coaches and football players grumbling on both sides of the field and spectators wondering what in the world was going on.

David made it to the sideline where Bathsheba was standing. She looked at David with tears in her focused eyes and said, "You only make a play for me, right, David?"

David paused for just a second, as he tenderly looked at Bathsheba and said, "That's right, Bathsheba, just for you. I only make a play for you."

Tears began streaming down Bathsheba's face.

"That we may choose something like a star to stay our minds on and be stayed, David." Bathsheba recited from her heart.

David nodded his head in affirmation, "'Choose Something Like A Star.' That's my favorite poem by Robert Frost. My Star would just so happen to be you, Bathsheba." David responded, feeling inspired, as he fought back showing his own emotions.

GO DAVIDSON HIGH SCHOOL WARRIORS!

With that, David turned around and headed toward a newly formed huddle. Bathsheba immediately went back to twirling and throwing up her baton in an alluring and most impressive manner. Then, the ball was hiked, and David went back, as Jonathan ran in perfect form down the right sideline. David hurled the ball, a Hail Mary pass, as Jonathan curved inward toward the middle of the field, out-dodging Yellow Jackets left and right. Jonathan leaped to successfully catch the ball in mid-flight at the 21-yardline, only to then zigzag close to the left sideline of the field, out maneuvering two more tacklers before darting with great agility into the endzone, to secure the victory leading to the championship game. Davidson had just enough time left to kick the extra point, winning the game 21 to 17. The Davidson High School Cheerleading Team, led by Bathsheba, was joyfully rooting their team on to victory from the sideline. So, the Davidson High School Warriors went to the State Championship that year. And they made Coach Crenshaw very proud, winning the championship with a score of 42 to 35. After the game, Coach Crenshaw made the remark to the entire football team: "You guys have sure made me look good today!" Yet everyone, especially all the Davidson Warrior students, understood perfectly that they had won the game because David stayed his mind on Bathsheba, and Bathsheba stayed her mind on David, exactly as Robert Frost's poem. "Choose Something Like A Star," depicts.

THE DAVIDSON HIGH SCHOOL PROM AT THE LEWIS COPELAND AUDITORIUM LOCATED AT DAVIDSON HIGH SCHOOL

Bathsheba accepted David's invitation to go to the Davidson High School Prom with him, which was to take place at the Lewis Copeland Auditorium, located right on the Davidson High School campus. She wore a beautiful, blue dress, the same shade of sky-blue as the star and stripes on the Israeli flag. Bathsheba knew David would make a comment about the color. David loved America, and was proud to be a citizen, but he missed the country of Israel at times. The fact that Bathsheba was still with him in the United States practically signified that he was capable of taking the most important part of the country with him. And Bathsheba would continue to be with him, because they were both awarded academic scholarships to Harvard, with David also receiving a double scholarship to also go to the Massachusetts Institute of Technology, better known as MIT. The opportunity to go to Harvard University and MIT gave David "a meant to be sensation," especially since Bathsheba and Jonathan would be there with him as well. Neither one of them regretted not attending the Hebrew University in Jerusalem.

David thought that Bathsheba looked absolutely stunning in her new prom dress when he picked her up in his red sports car. "My new dress was quite expensive, David. Do you think it was worth it?" Bathsheba asked, fishing for a compliment. "Worth dying for, seeing you wear it, Bathsheba!" David responded, as he opened the passenger side of his car to let her in. Bathsheba rendered a belly laugh and pushed David slightly on his chest out of jest, as David politely helped her into the car seat. "You look very handsome in that tuxedo, David." David closed Bathsheba's door, came around to the driver's side, got in, and asked, "You don't think I look too formal, do you?" Once again, David scored another sincere giggle from Bathsheba, as she looked up at him affectionately, and responded, "No." David leaned over, pinned a white rose corsage to the front of Bathsheba's new blue dress, gave her a kiss and said, "Now, with your new perfect-shade-of-blue dress and the white rose, you look just like the Israeli flag."

DAVIDSON HIGH SCHOOL AUDITORIUM

The Lewis Copeland Auditorium, named after a highly esteemed, distinguished, very prominent, former Davidson High School principal, had been greatly expanded since it was originally built. The building was extended all the way down to the Davidson High School Warriors On-Campus Stadium and enlarged all the way out to the fence adjacent to the student parking lot on the right side of the auditorium. There was a large open area created within the back of the newly built structure, which more than accommodated the entire senior student body for the Davidson High School Prom. And what was once the lap track is where the Davidson High School Warriors On-Campus Stadium now stood.

THE LEWIS COPELAND AUDITORIUM
DAVIDSON HIGH SCHOOL IN MOBILE ALABAMA

    David and Bathsheba entered fashionably late to the Lewis Copeland Auditorium. They both had become such high school celebrities that their absence up to the time they arrived had been noticed. And when the two suddenly appeared, you could almost hear a grasp, because the picture of the two of them coupled next to each other in their prom garb was most striking.

    The large, designated room for the prom was moderately dark. There were strobe lights flashing different colored balls of light to create a soothing mood, as couples were slow dancing when David and Bathsheba entered in. The Disc Jockey in the back of the room was in his booth playing different requests of songs that were made of him, mostly by the ladies present. The DJ whole-heartedly congratulated the senior class for reaping the hard-earned rewards of their fervent, passionate work, in between his musical renditions that entertained everyone.

SIDE OF THE DAVIDSON HIGH SCHOOL AUDITORIUM

All of a sudden, as David went to the punch table to get Bathsheba and himself some punch, the Disc Jockey decided to play the all-time favorite song of both David and Bathsheba, "Gypsy," sung by Stevie Nicks of Fleetwood Mac. It wasn't a coincidence. Bathsheba managed to make a request of the song while David was getting the punch and socializing with the principal of Davidson High School and his wife. Nevertheless, it caused chills to go up both David and Bathsheba's spines, considering the setting they were in, and that they were both prompted to seize the moment at hand.

"Oh, listen, Dear. It's our song!" David exclaimed. "May I have this dance?" He requested, as they set their punch glasses down on their table, and David led Bathsheba to the dance floor with a noticeable flair. The couple quickly became the center of attention. The song, "Gypsy," was not only David and Bathsheba's favorite song, but the video by the same name was their favorite musical video, highlighting Steve Nicks dancing in ballerina style and performing the Tango with Lindsey Buckingham. David and Bathsheba had every dance move of that video totally memorized, and they were mimicking each one of those moves in top form under the colored balls emitting from the strobe lights, moving all around the prom night dance floor, and demonstrating that they had more than their fair share of practice doing the tango together. There were couples on the dance floor who stopped dancing, just so they could focus on watching David and Bathsheba. Many of the girls sitting down were swooning, some with goosebumps, because it looked so romantic.

BACK OF THE DAVIDSON HIGH SCHOOL AUDITORIUM

David and Bathsheba, ever since they arrived at Davidson High School, had exhibited that they were quite an item. But observing them now, dancing so much in sync with each other and so dressed up, was quite a phenomenon to behold. They looked like professional dancers, and the people observing could not take their eyes off of them. It was mesmerizing. David was twirling Bathsheba around, and then, bringing her back close to him for an embrace. David was so dapper, debonair, and stylish in his bearing and composure. And with every motion, Bathsheba met David with an intense, sultry gaze. They looked like a prince and a princess portrayed in a movie. It was a moment that the entire Davidson High School senior class on prom night got caught up in and would never forget.

And at one very special moment in the dance, when David could not be possibly dancing any closer to Bathsheba, he said, looking directly into her eyes, "I've never seen anything so beautiful in my life."

To which, Bathsheba responded, in an attractive manner, "You are all fair, my Love. Be careful what you ask for, David. You just might get it."

"Harvard, here we come, Bathsheba!" David replied.

"And who knows where after Harvard, David!" Bathsheba ventured to declare.

WHEN THE STUDENT IS READY, THE TEACHER WILL APPEAR

Harvard University in Cambridge, Massachusetts was founded on September 8th, 1636. The Ivy League College was named after its first benefactor, clergyman John Harvard, although the school has never been affiliated with any denomination. Harvard University is the oldest institution of learning in the United States and the most prestigious college in the world. Harvard's library has the world's largest academic library system, and its muti-billion dollar endowment is the largest of any academic institution. Harvard has three campuses. The university's 209-acre main campus is centered on Harvard Yard in Cambridge, about three miles west-northwest of downtown Boston, and extends into the surrounding Harvard Square neighborhood. Including all three of Harvard's campuses, the university grounds have grown to 21 million square feet.

HARVARD UNIVERSITY
IN CAMBRIDGE, MASSACHUSETTS USA

Established in 1879, Radcliffe College was a Women's Liberal Arts College that functioned as the female counterpart institution for the all-male Harvard University. In 1946, Harvard classes became co-ed. In 1977, there was a merger of Harvard and Radcliff's admissions. And then, in 1999, the female body of students merged completely into Harvard, and Radcliffe College became the Radcliffe Institute for Advanced Study. What used to be Radcliffe College is less than a one-minute drive away from Harvard University.

The Massachusetts Institute of Technology, better known as MIT, in Cambridge, Massachusetts, was founded on April, 10th, 1861 by its first president, William Barton Rogers, who had worked for years to organize an institution of higher learning devoted entirely to scientific and technical training. MIT was established in response to the increasing industrialization of the United States, and stressed laboratory instruction in applied science and engineering. MIT has been crowned the best university in the world for graduate employability. It has been named the number one university in the world. MIT is two miles away from Harvard University via Massachusetts Avenue. Many of those going to MIT become trained aeronautical engineers in preparation of becoming experienced pilots.

Since 1945, Hanscom Air Force Base located in Bedford, Massachusetts, about a twenty-five mile drive from Harvard, emerged as the center for the development and acquisition of electronic systems, with key importance focused on radar. Yet in cooperation with the I.S.A.A.C. Program, the United States Air Force collaborated with Harvard and MIT in developing students to become fighter jet pilots. This program was a tremendous success, and the Aerial Combat Training at Hanscom Air Force Base had become so effective that it enhanced the careers of cadets desiring to be fighter jet pilots even more than the United States Air Force Training Academy. Hanscom Air Force Base also, unbelievably, surpassed the excellence of Luke Air Force Base, the Air Education and Training Command Center (AETC), located fifteen miles west of Phoenix, Arizona.

Both David and Jonathan were given the opportunity to attend the United States Air Force Academy just north of Colorado Springs, Colorado. But they wanted to go to Harvard and MIT and participate in the I.S.A.A.C. Program at Hanscom Air Force Base, combining Officer Training School (OTS) and Fighter Jet Instruction. David and Jonathan were both awarded academic scholarships to Harvard and MIT, majoring Aerospace Engineering at Harvard and working toward their Bachelor of Science Degree in Aeronautical Engineering at MIT. Of course, David also was very enthusiastic about Harvard's enriching Liberal Arts curriculum, with a serious emphasis upon English and Literature. Bathsheba, along with many other Israeli students, was awarded an academic scholarship to Harvard as well.

David's very first freshman class of the fall semester, in fact, was an English Literature Class at Harvard's Barker Center at eight o'clock on a Thursday morning. He would be coming to this particular class on every Tuesday and Thursday. David noticed on his schedule that the professor teaching the class was the very well known man about campus, Dr. Samuel Goldstein. David made his way to the classroom, managed to find a seat close to the front and waited along with the other students for the professor to arrive.

Eventually, an older gentleman, very distinguished looking, rather thin, of average height, with graying hair, and a mustache walked into the classroom wearing very impressive quality slacks and a vest. He had a book under his arm, took a seat at the front of the class, fully intending on making himself comfortable. He spoke in a firm, yet joyful manner: "Good morning to you, one and all, and welcome to Harvard. I know this must be your initial class at the university, considering this is a freshman course, this is our first day of attendance, and it's eight o'clock in the morning. I'm Dr. Samuel Goldstein, and I'll be your host over the next few months, exploring with you the wonderous world of English Literature. We'll save the amenities for another time, as I am quite certain we will, in the course of this adventure, become acquainted with each other very well. So, for right now, please turn with me in your English Literature book to page 187."

As Dr. Goldstein made the page request, he stood up from his desk, and began walking around the room, with a stack of papers ready to be distributed, as he spoke: "This syllabus that I am providing each of you clearly outlines what will be expected of you each and every time you come to class in the course of this semester. It may seem in your view somewhat random of me to begin our curriculum today on page 187, rather than page 1, but I find immense satisfaction in introducing my students to this course of English Literature with a poem from Rudyard Kipling. He was awarded the Nobel Prize in Literature in 1907. Dr. Goldstein proceeded to discuss the life of Rudyard Kipling in an intriguing fashion. And as David was observing Dr. Goldstein, his mind began to inexplicably flashback to a time that gave him very powerful impressions of déjà vu. David's mind uncontrollably altered back and forth between the classroom where Dr. Goldstein was teaching that morning and a period of time that could easily be described as Before Christ (B.C.). And David, who knew his Hebrew Bible, had a particular verse that kept coming to mind from the First Book of Samuel: "Then, Samuel took the horn of oil, and anointed him in the midst of his brethren. And the Spirit of the Lord came upon David from that day forward." I Samuel 16:13

Then, the alternating finally stopped. But David was no longer in Dr. Goldstein's English class. He was, obviously, over two millenniums back in time. David was a young shepherd boy in this vision (Joel 2:28, 29; Acts 2:17, 18), and Samuel, the Israeli Prophet, who looked exactly like Dr. Goldstein, was anointing David to be king over all of Israel. And for that moment, David's mind was not even close to being in an English class at Harvard. For that intense, real instant, David perceived that the God of Israel had just anointed him to be king in another era. Then, Samuel said to David: "The Lord God of Israel has sought him a man after his own heart, David, and you are that man, and he has commanded you to be Captain over his people, Israel." David was living in that moment, as he had once before. He was there again, without question. He was in a place that was fully recognizable. And the realization of reliving that life more than implied that a new cause, a new purpose would be just ahead. And as much as David, back in another time, immediately, went on to defeat Goliath after his first anointing, so would it be that David would straightaway find his imminent destiny after this renewed anointing in a modern day world. And the Spirit of the God of Israel came upon David from that day forward. It was God's intention to use David to beat down the foes of Israel, and to establish the Throne of David forever, as the God of Israel had always promised. Just as much as David and Jonathan swore an oath to each other, God had sworn an oath to preserve David and Jonathan, and to maintain a man on the Throne of David from one generation to the next. Just as much as David of the Hebrew Bible was used in the preparation of building the first Temple, it was God's desire to use David of a more contemporary time to restore the Temple on an appointed day in the near future, an event that would come to pass in the God of Israel's perfect timing. It was an expectation whose time had come.

I HAVE FOUND DAVID, MY SERVANT. WITH MY HOLY OIL, I, THE GOD OF ISRAEL, HAVE ANOINTED HIM. PSALM 89:20

Then, once David had completely absorbed what had occurred, he began fading back to the classroom, with Dr. Goldstein's voice practically serving as a beacon: "So, in conclusion of today's meeting, as promised," Dr. Goldstein said, "I would like to share with you a special poem by Rudyard Kipling, that I intentionally wanted you to remember on your first day of class at Harvard University, a poem that you may very well carry with you as a keepsake in life. The poem is entitled, "IF ---." And it goes something like this, as I will be paraphrasing here and there:

'If you can keep your head, when all about you are losing theirs and blaming the situation on you. If you can trust yourself, when all men doubt you. If you can wait and not be tired by waiting. Or be lied about, and not deal in lies. If you can be hated, and not give way to hating. And yet not intend to look too good in the eyes of others, nor talk too wise. If you can dream, and not make dreams your master. If you can meet with triumph and disaster and treat those two impostors just the same. Or watch the things you gave your life to become broken, and stoop and build them back up with worn out tools. If you can make one heap of all your winnings, and risk it on one turn of pitch-and-toss, and lose, and start from the beginning, and never breathe a word about your loss. If you can talk with crowds and keep your virtue. Or walk with kings, and not lose the common touch. If neither foes nor loving friends can hurt you. If all men count with you, but none too much. If you can fill the unforgiving minute with sixty seconds worth of distant run, yours is the Earth and everything that's in it.'"

Dr. Goldstein concluded the poem with just one final comment: "With that, ladies and gentlemen, you are dismissed. Welcome to Harvard!"

David remained seated for a moment as the other students made their way out of the classroom. He had a laser beam focus on Dr. Goldstein. Eventually, David got up, and walked over to Dr. Goldstein, who was organizing his desk. David looked at him in amazement and said, "I know you!"

Dr. Goldstein looked up at David, with a wise, joyful, grandfatherly expression on his face, "I'm fully aware of that, David."

David responded, "But, how can this be? I've never met you before today. But something --- something is really happening!"

Dr. Goldstein concurred, "Yes. Something is happening, indeed, and we need to talk about it, that is, you, myself, and of course, Jonathan Diamond and Bathsheba Rosenberg."

"You're familiar with Bathsheba and Jonathan?" David asked, exclaiming. "Wait a minute! You're Israeli, aren't you?"

"Born and raised in Israel, my boy," Dr. Goldstein confirmed. "Let's just say that this is perfect timing for us to cross paths, you and I."

"Perfect timing," David mumbled to himself, "I can sense that it's important for us to talk, all four of us together."

"Not to sound too urgent, David, but it's critical that we all discuss some matters. Are you familiar with Harvest Restaurant?" Dr. Goldstein asked.

"Yes. I recently heard about it," David said. "It's just off campus in Harvard Square. I understand it's quite a nice place."

"It's a superb restaurant for you to take Bathsheba on a regular basis during your journey here at Harvard. There's a very romantic quality about Harvest Restaurant," Dr. Goldstein relayed, with David appreciating the inside tip. "Shall we say this Saturday evening at seven-ish? I'll make the reservations. They know me all too well at Harvest. I have a special table there that I frequent. The restaurant has a very relaxing atmosphere. Let Bathsheba and Jonathan know that it'll be my treat."

"Sounds great!" David said. "I know this is right on target."

"And David," Dr. Goldstein said in a serious tone, "I want you to keep something in mind until we all meet Saturday night. It can be summed up in five very powerful words."

David stood there before Dr. Goldstein in total suspense.

"Everything has come full circle," Dr. Goldstein emphasized, as he took David's hand to shake it. "Everything has come full circle, young man. I look forward to seeing you all Saturday night. Here's my telephone number just in case you need to call me." Dr. Goldstein handed David a card with his other hand. "Dress business casual. It's going to be intriguing!"

As David turned to walk out the door, he took a glance at the card:

Dr. Samuel Goldstein
Harvard University English Department
Barker Center, 12 Quincy Street, Cambridge, MA 02138
617-495-6070, Ext. 777
"Be ashamed to die until you have won
some victory for humanity."

THE HARRY ELKINS WIDENER MEMORIAL LIBRARY HARVARD UNIVERSITY

Camelot Lost. Camelot Restored. (King Arthur and his Court)

It would be a couple of days before David would be seeing Dr. Goldstein again. And before the semester got fully cranked up, he wanted to pay a visit to Harvard's main library, the Harry Elkins Widener Memorial Library, part of the Harvard Library System. There are over seventy different libraries on Harvard's campus, but David wanted to check out the main library first. The total number of libraries collectively comprise the Harvard Library, a most impressive system that carries the largest research collection anywhere around the world in print and digital formats, incapable of being matched by any other library.

David's main topic of interest was United States President John F. Kennedy. And what better place could there be for David to learn more of this great man that he admired so much other than Harvard University? After all, this was the very college where the Thirty-Fifth President of the United States had graduated.

David read a choice selection of books and various references regarding the highlights of the 35th President's life, which included John F. Kennedy's upbringing, his stay in England when his father, Joseph P. Kennedy Sr., was appointed by President Franklin Delano Roosevelt to be Ambassador to England, JFK's education, his military service during World War II as Commander of PT-109 in the United States Navy, the tragedies involving his brothers, Joseph P. Kennedy, Jr., Robert Francis Kennedy (Bobby), and Edward Moore Kennedy (Teddy), his sister Kathleen, better known as "Kick," who died in an airplane crash, his rise to the United States Congress and Senate, taking Jacqueline Lee Bouvier to be his wife, and his entire presidency. David watched many of the documentaries of the president on a monitor and absorbed the words of JFK into his very soul, serving to greatly inspire him.

The humor of John F. Kennedy dazzled David, including a quote made by JFK in his youth: "A life of complete leisure is the hardest work of all."

JOHN F. KENNEDY

David also watched portions of all four presidential debates between JFK and Vice President Richard M. Nixon, who had served under President Dwight D. Eisenhower for the past eight years. They were the very first televised presidential debates in United States history. They are now referred to as the Great Debates. The one single moment that caught David's attention the most in the fourth debate was Kennedy's response to Nixon, when the Vice President remarked that JFK had a responsibility to be right in his criticism of the country, and that he was downgrading America by "running her down." The next future president slightly turned toward Nixon and said: "I really don't need Mr. Nixon to tell me about what my responsibilities are as a citizen. I've served this country for fourteen years in Congress and before that in the service. I have just as high a devotion, and just as high an opinion. What I downgrade, Mr. Nixon, is the leadership the country is getting, not the country."

David concurred with JFK's attitude about some of the dreams he wanted to inspire and accomplish during his presidency, like seeing peace in the world, by stating: "I'm an idealist without illusions."

David admired the social skills Kennedy possessed and the connections he had with so many Hollywood celebrities, like when, on May 24th, 1961, he and the First Lady, Jacqueline Bouvier Kennedy, entertained Princess Grace Kelly, the former Hollywood movie star, and her husband, Rainier III, Prince of Monaco, at the White House.

David viewed another video, where on May 25th, 1961, before a joint session of Congress, John F. Kennedy boldly shared a vision destined to come to pass in July of 1969, stating: "I believe that this nation should commit itself to achieving the goal, before this decade is out, of landing a man on the Moon and returning him safely to the Earth."

And there was, of course, the Cuban Missile Crisis that shocked the United States and the world, when the Soviet Union (Russia; referred to as Rosh in the Bible) transported missiles to Cuba, just off the coast of Florida. David was dazzled by JFK's handling of this dangerous situation and hung on to every word he said in his televised speech of October 22nd, 1962, especially when he challenged the Russian dictator: "I call upon Chairman Khrushchev to halt this clandestine, reckless, and provocative threat to world peace and to stabilize relations between our two nations." Rather than initiate a full-scale retaliatory nuclear war against Russia as his military advisors insisted, President Kennedy, with his brother,

Attorney General Robert Francis Kennedy, by his side, chose to verbally confront the Russian Chairman in an incredibly dangerous poker game with the entire world at stake. And in the end, Khrushchev folded, detouring all the nuclear warheads away from Cuba that he had sent.

David became very enamored and awestruck with President Kennedy when he met with the current Israeli Labor and Foreign Minister, Golda Meir, in Palm Beach, Florida on December 27th, 1962. It was on this occasion that JFK expressed his devotion to Israel, when he said: "Israel was not created in order to disappear. Israel will endure and flourish. Israel is the child of hope and the home of the brave. Israel can neither be broken by adversity nor demoralized by success. Israel carries the shield of democracy, and Israel honors the sword of freedom." Golda Meir went on to become David's favorite Prime Minister of Israel. Her first term began on March 17th, 1969.

Although David was training to become the best fighter jet pilot he could possibly be, he shared President Kennedy's views concerning all weapons of war:

"Mankind must put an end to war, or war will put an end to mankind."

"The weapons of war must be abolished before they abolish us."

This included the day when JFK addressed the General Assembly of the United Nations on September 25th, 1961, and stated: "Every man, woman, and child lives under a nuclear sword of Damocles, hanging by the slenderest of threads, capable of being cut at any time by accident, or miscalculation, or madness."

And with all the worldwide civil unrest that was taking place in David's contemporary day, he felt that the diplomatic words in JFK's televised speech on June 11th, 1963 were most applicable to his own time. Even in the modern, super technological period that David lived, there were horrible upheavals in society that existed, created by civil chaos and racial tension. Pandemonium was created by the riots that were breaking out, and civil rights protesters were filling the streets worldwide on a regular basis. The entire planet was on edge. And it didn't appear that any progress had been made in regard to achieving social justice since the time of President Abraham Lincoln or the calamity of President John F. Kennedy's Administration. Mankind had not grown to learn a single thing concerning equal rights for all, not only in the United States but around the world as well.

Yet unlike the world leaders of David's day, who lacked the ability to offer sympathetic comfort in the midst of this ongoing crisis, the words that President John F. Kennedy incorporated in a televised speech served to appease the nation, even in the midst of a pandemic. The plague of inequality was even exceeding the turmoil of the pandemic at hand. The words that JFK rendered came from his heart and soul, and still prevail to this day:

"Good evening, my fellow citizens. I hope that every American, regardless of where he lives, will stop and examine his conscience. This nation was founded on the principle that all men are created equal, and that the rights of every man are diminished when the rights of one man are threatened.

Today, we are committed to a worldwide struggle to promote and protect the rights of all who wish to be free. It ought to be possible, in short, for every American to enjoy the privileges of being an American without regard to his race or his color. In short, every American ought to have the right to be treated as he would wish to be treated. This is not a sectional issue. Nor is this a partisan issue. This is not even a legal or legislative issue alone. It is better to settle these matters in the courts than on the streets, and new laws are needed at every level, but laws alone cannot make men see right.

We are confronted primarily with a moral issue. It is as old as the Scriptures and as clear as the Constitution. The heart of the question is whether we are going to treat our fellow Americans as we want to be treated. And this nation, for all its hopes and all its boasts, will not be fully free until all its citizens are free. Now, the time has come for this nation to fulfill its promise. The fires of frustration and discord are burning in every city. We face, therefore, a moral crisis as a country and a people. A great change is at hand, and our task, our obligation is to make that revolution, that change, peaceful and constructive for all.

My fellow Americans, this is a problem which faces us all. It seems to me that these are matters which concern us all, not merely Presidents or Congressmen or Governors, but every citizen of the United States. This is one country. It has become one country because all the people born here and all the people who came here had an equal chance to develop their talents. Therefore, I am asking for your help in making it easier for us to move ahead and to provide the kind of equality of treatment which we would want ourselves. This is what we are talking about, and this is the matter which concerns this country and what it stands for. And in meeting it, I ask the support of all our citizens. Thank you very much."

After hearing this speech, David considered that mankind's general response to remedy civil unrest (in the last days), even in the midst of a pandemic, appeared to be worldwide violence in the streets.

David was amazed that the civil unrest occurring during Kennedy's presidency was not so much different than the days in which he lived, and that no progress seemed to have taken place on this vital issue. So, civil unrest persists to this very day. Because social justice will not come until there is a strong component of trust for our respective world leaders. And those leaders must be trustworthy enough for the people to honestly believe that these elected officials have the best interests for the people at heart, leading their constituents with at least some degree of understanding. And that, somehow, all people would be willing to make it their number one priority to be in harmony with each other.

And then, just a little more than two weeks after President Kennedy's speech on civil rights, he delivered David's favorite speech of all time to the people of West Berlin, Germany on June 26th, 1963:

"You live in a defended island of freedom, but your life is part of the main. So, let me ask you as I close to lift your eyes beyond the dangers of today to the hopes of tomorrow. Beyond the freedom merely of this city of Berlin or your country of Germany to the advance of freedom everywhere. Beyond this wall to the day of peace and justice. Beyond yourselves and ourselves to all mankind.

Freedom is indivisible, and when one man is enslaved, all are not free. When all are free, then, we can look forward to that day when this city will be joined as one and this country and this great Continent of Europe in a peaceful and hopeful globe. When that day finally comes, AS IT WILL (Matthew 24:27, 30, 31), the people of West Berlin can take sober satisfaction in the fact that they were in the front lines for almost two decades."

And it was on June 10, 1963, at a Commencement Address at American University in Washington D.C., President John Fitzgerald Kennedy spoke no truer words concerning international affairs:

"No government or social system is so evil that its people must be considered as lacking in virtue. For in the final analysis, our most basic common link is that we all inhabit this small planet. We all cherish our children's future. And we are all mortal. Confident and unafraid, we labor on --- not toward a strategy of annihilation, but toward a strategy of peace."

The assassinations of John F. Kennedy, Robert F. Kennedy, and Martin Luther King, Jr. in the 1960's were also pivotal in bringing the world to such an ominous place of difficult times. These assassinations carried a ripple effect that were even affecting so many people and international events in David's modern era.

No one summed up the situation more appropriately than JFK's wife, Jacqueline Kennedy, concerning the loss of one of America's greatest presidents, when she said:

"Now, I think I should have known that he was magic all along. I did know it, but I should have guessed that it would be too much to ask to grow old with him and see our children grow up together. So, now, he is a legend when he would have preferred to be a man."

HARVEST RESTAURANT
CAMBRIDGE, MASSACHUSETTS

David, Bathsheba, and Jonathan arrived at Harvest Restaurant promptly at 7:00 P.M. David and Jonathan both looked dapper wearing dress slacks, sports coats, and shirts with an open collar. Bathsheba was looking especially sensational in an exquisite, classic style evening dress. The maître d' was expecting them and knew exactly which table to escort them to, as he had known Dr. Goldstein for many years, and had frequented him to the same cozy corner of the restaurant on a number of occasions. As David walked to the table, he couldn't help but be reminded of the five immortal words that Dr. Goldstein had stressed to him: "Everything has come full circle."

"Thank you for coming. Your presence here tonight is a statement that we are all on the same page or, shall we say, wavelength." Dr. Goldstein said. "Using the word, 'page,' is far too much of a pun coming from an old English professor such as myself. Please make yourselves comfortable."

"Well, this restaurant, certainly, is everything you said it would be," remarked David. "What a great atmosphere!"

"Yes. I like it. It's the atmosphere of Harvest Restaurant that has prevented me from going anywhere else for quite some time now," Dr. Goldstein responded enthusiastically. "And of course, you are Bathsheba and Jonathan. What a joy it is to meet you and have all three of you dine with me on this divine appointment! And Bathsheba, you are just as beautiful in person as I knew you would be. You and David make such a handsome looking, delightful couple together."

"Thank you, Dr. Goldstein," Bathsheba graciously replied, most impressed with his charming, courteous demeanor.

Jonathan acknowledged what a pleasure it was to meet Dr. Goldstein, having heard so much about him from David. He, as well, was very impressed with how much of a refined, distinguished gentleman Dr. Goldstein appeared to be.

DR. SAMUEL GOLDSTEIN'S COZY LITTLE CORNER (NOOK) AT HARVEST RESTAURANT CAMBRIDGE, MASSACHUSETTS

"All three of you are getting settled here at Harvard I trust. That is, has it been a smooth transition for you?" Dr. Goldstein enquired.

"Oh, yes!" Bathsheba said, beating David and Jonathan to the response, thinking how nice it was of Dr. Goldstein to ask such a considerate question. "I know this is going to be a wonderful experience."

All four of them chatted casually for a while, and then, decided to order their meals.

Dr. Goldstein summoned Abagail, his favorite waitress, over to the table, and introduced her to David, Bathsheba, and Jonathan. After the amenities with Abigail, leaving no room for doubt of her affability, they were all ready to order.

"I'll have the New England Seafood Boil and the Roasted Beets and Apples as an appetizer." Bathsheba requested, with David ordering the same entrée.

"Excellent choice for both of you." Abigail said.

"I'll go with the 14-ounce Brandt Prime Beef Sirloin with Roasted Brussel Sprouts." Jonathan said.

"And I'll have my usual, Abigail," Dr. Goldstein stated, which meant that he also wanted the 14-ounce Brandt Prime Beef Sirloin, like Jonathan, but with Buttermilk Mashed Potatoes as his side order.

"Very good," Abigail responded, and then, focused on Dr. Goldstein's guests. "I hope you three realize that you're in the hands of an exceptionally fine host. He is good company. Trust me, especially when he's in the relaxing domain of Harvest Restaurant. I'd like to officially welcome all three of you as our special guests."

David, Bathsheba, and Jonathan all nodded in appreciation.

Dr. Goldstein, then, paused for a few seconds after Abigail had left, as if to gather his thoughts, "Well, David has probably mentioned to you that, just like yourselves, I was born and raised in Israel. While I do have a great inclination and imagination for written works, as you know, being David's English Literature professor, I also have an aptitude for music, and have served as a cantor in the synagogue for many years. I've even married a number of couples, having the authority to do so. I consider myself to be an Orthodox Jew, but of course, I'm very well read, and I have an open mind. I happened to get wind of David and Jonathan's victory for the State Football Championship when you were students at Davidson High School, not terribly long ago. It's quite an extraordinary story how I came across the article, as I was doing some research on an unrelated topic. And go Davidson High School Warriors, by the way! Rah, rah! But when I say that I have an open mind, I am mostly referring to very deep topics.'"

"Yes!" Bathsheba exclaimed, in support of David and Jonathan, most impressed with Dr. Goldstein's knowledge of them. "I suppose you can safely say that they are not only all-Israeli boys, but also all-American boys as well."

"Yes, the very best of both worlds, Bathsheba." Dr. Goldstein concurred. "Of course, all four of us, having been born in Israel, are of a unique and special kindred spirit. But let me ask all three of you, at the risk of opening a serious discussion: "Have either one of you ever heard of the Restoration of the Throne of David?"

"I think I can speak for all three of us, Dr. Goldstein." David replied. "We all know what you mean. It concerns Israel with the coming of the Israeli Messiah, Mashiach ben David, to build his Temple and establish his kingdom once and for all. Ever since the second Temple was destroyed in 70 A.D., the Israelis have desired to see the Temple built again."

"Very good, my boy!" Dr. Goldstein exclaimed, as his face lit up. "And of course, I'm sure you're fully aware where the Temple must be built and the hindrances that are keeping it from being built."

"Yes," Jonathan quickly spoke up. "It is absolutely imperative that the Temple be built on the Temple Mount. The Temple Mount would need to be ritually sanctified before the Temple would be allowed to be built."

"My goodness! It's quite apparent that I'm in good company tonight. There's no doubt that control over the Temple Mount is the single most important factor in determining the destiny of our planet." Dr. Goldstein interjected. "That fact is universally conceded. There have been peace proposals, plans, agreements, and accords considered and attempted, but alas, a formal, lasting peace between all the parties involved in the Middle East has apparently remained an impossibility. Perhaps, it should be submitted that only the Israeli Messiah will be successful in bringing about everlasting, never-ending peace to the Middle East and the world. Any and all efforts of mankind have fallen through and miserably failed. And everlasting peace will not be witnessed when Solomon's Temple is rebuilt. Genuine peace will only be documented in history seven years later, after the Tribulation, when the Millennial Temple is built by the Israeli Messiah, and the Messiah alone. Both the major and the minor prophets in the Hebrew Bible," Dr. Goldstein elaborated, "have prophesied that the Millennial Temple will be built. And it's abundantly clear that there will be two Temples built after Israel becomes a State, which, of course, gloriously occurred in 1948. The fulfillment of the prophecy of Israel regaining control of her country again gave us good cause to celebrate the confirmation that the rebuilding of the Temple is within reach. This will be Israel's third Temple, otherwise referred to as Solomon's Temple Rebuilt, that, in turn, becomes the Tribulation Temple, and is destroyed at the end of the Seven Year Tribulation. Then, at that point, the Millennial Temple will be created by the Israeli Messiah, without any need of assistance from human hands. In fact, there are a number of prophecies that have come to pass since Israel was formed as a nation. And there are not many prophecies remaining to be fulfilled before Solomon's Temple is rebuilt. The destructive psyche of human depravity is a component of mankind that makes war an inevitable reality. The Israeli Messiah will make it possible for the Jews and their allies to rise above that depravity and reach out for peace. That may be the very reason why the Messiah is referred to as the Pearl of Great Price. God's plan for the Temple was first revealed to Moses at the foot of Mount Sinai. Out of the thunders of Mount Sinai, the God of Israel revealed his plan by which the Tabernacle of God would be constructed. The connection between the Tabernacle, the first and second Temples, and the two latter-day Temples is unmistakable. The God of Israel said to Moses: "Let them construct a Sanctuary for me that I may dwell among them." And the Israelis today are more than ready to rebuild Solomon's Temple, despite the fact that the third Temple is marked in the Hebrew Bible as doomed, according to Daniel, the Prophet. The Israeli people believe that the two Israeli Temples of the future, Solomon's Temple Rebuilt and the Millennial Temple, must be built on Mount Moriah in Jerusalem, which, of course, is equivalent to the exact location of the Temple Mount. It is also the same place where Abraham, the father of the Jews, built an altar, and where King David bought a parcel of land in high hopes of the Temple being built on that very spot. Mount Moriah is interpreted as the mountain of God's inheritance. Even Moses predicted the Messiah alone would build the Millennial Temple to secure the Israelis, when he said: "You shall bring your people in, and plant them in the mountain of your inheritance, in this place, O, Lord, which you have made for yourself to dwell in the Sanctuary, which your hands have established." And Zechariah, the Prophet, in the Book of Zechariah (Zechariah 6:12, 13), clearly affirms that it will be the Israeli Messiah alone who builds the Millennial Temple, ruling upon his throne under a banner of peace. The Temple, as you know, David, Bathsheba, and Jonathan, is extremely important to Israeli nationality. The Temple is essential to establishing and preserving the national and international unity and integrity of Israel. The Temple is a representation of Israel's national sovereignty. And the Temple brings about a unique measure of stability for the Israeli people. Yet while there are, certainly, many peace-loving Muslims in the world, the radical Muslims advocate a very dangerous brand of Islam. As you said Jonathan, the elimination of Israel is a prerequisite for the emergence of a global Islamic state, from the viewpoint of all radical Muslims and those supporting their cause. Therefore, there is a realistic question as to whether or not the Jewish Temple can be built on the Temple Mount, that is, without the possibility of annihilating the entire world."

"Excuse me, Dr. Goldstein," Abigail said, "I hate to interrupt you, but I have your entrees." Abigail had already slipped the appetizers in, during their conversation. She had expedited the meals for Dr. Goldstein's table.

"All right, the New England Seafood Broil for David and Bathsheba, and the 14-ounce Prime Beef Sirloin for Jonathan and Dr. Goldstein," Abigail politely said, being a superb, first-class waitress. "I trust that Dr. Goldstein is keeping his guests well entertained."

"Oh, yes. Dr. Goldstein is fascinating." Bathsheba confirmed eagerly.

"That's right. I'm not surprised one bit," Abigail said. "He and I have engaged in some very enlightening discussions through the years. He's been a very good friend to me. Okay, you continue to mingle, mingle. Enjoy your meals and let me know if I may assist you in any way."

"She is quite academic herself," Dr Goldstein said after Abigail had left. "Now, let's shift gears somewhat, and focus on Israel's solution to this matter. We have made reference to the Restoration of the Throne of David. As you had mentioned, David, the Jewish Messiah is Mashiach ben David. The existence of our modern-day State of Israel today, formed against all odds, is the number one exhibit of evidence that all the other prophecies of the prophets, great and small, of the Hebrew Bible, concerning every single issue of the end time, are expected to, literally, be fulfilled. As mentioned, the Jewish people's return to the Promised Land of Israel is one of the single most significant fulfilled Biblical prophecies of all time. It, certainly, serves to signify the greatest sign that the latter days are upon us. The entire world observed the Jew's return to Israel in awe as the prophecies of the Hebrew prophets unfolded in high drama in 1948. Many Israelis felt that this occurrence would, in and of itself, usher in the appearance of the Israeli Messiah, but other prophecies need to be fulfilled first. The first great miracle of fulfillment occurred on May 14th, 1948, when the United Nations officially recognized Israel as a State. The loss of the second Israeli Temple in 70 A.D. brought about an ongoing threat concerning Israel's continued national existence. Yet now, hope has been renewed that all the other prophecies, especially concerning the Temple, will follow suit in fulfillment. The Millennial Temple becoming a reality in the future at the hand of the Messiah will be the ultimate proof that the prophets knew what they were talking about, and that they genuinely were inspired. The Israelis and all our ancestors cannot, by any means, reach their proper spiritual status without the Temple being rebuilt on the Temple Mount in Jerusalem. The Temple, of the last days, will be the supreme statement of Israeli sovereignty. There will be a new level of spiritual attainment achieved through the building of the Millennial Temple. And the Millennial Temple will shine as a beacon to the entire world. The Restoration of the Throne of David is dependent upon the building of the Millennial Temple by the Israeli Messiah alone. As it is written by Zechariah, among others: "The Jewish Messiah shall build the Temple, and he shall sit and rule upon his Throne." And Zechariah also made it clear that the trademark of the Messiah's reign will be peace, everlasting peace. Isaiah, the Prophet, pointed out that the Messiah is the Prince of Peace, and that the increase of the Messiah's government and peace will have no end upon the Throne of David and his kingdom, and that he will establish his kingdom forever."

"The Israelis have returned and resettled in their own land for good. They will never be removed again." David firmly said with confidence.

"It's interesting that you would be the very one to point that out. I'm very proud of you, David. I can see that my English Literature class this semester is going to be a wonderful growth experience for both of us." Dr. Goldstein said, once again in a protective, grandfatherly fashion. "With a population approaching a considerable number of Israelis around the world, modern-day Israel has harnessed political, military, and economic ties with the world's democratic superpowers, and has an arsenal that includes an incredible number of nuclear weapons, especially in consideration of the size of our country. It appears, on the surface, that the State of Israel will continue to exist. Despite the fact that Israel's enemies have acquired nuclear and chemical weapons, that they either produced themselves or smuggled in through the black-market. Israel remains one of the world's strongest military powers. And more often than not, we've been victorious in battles facing insurmountable odds, such as the classic Six Day War and the Yom Kippur War, that allowed us to gain back a lot of our land and then some, to extend our borders. And God has just begun the process of expanding the borders of Israel. The Israeli victories thus exhibited is a show of strength that has been nothing short of miraculous. The fact that the God of Israel has intervened to secure these victories is what gives Israel the edge on being unmatched militarily. The Book of Ezekiel makes it quite clear that the Israelis will dwell in their own land, the Eternal Promised Land. This is referring to the land that our ancestors, and their children, and their children's children were intended to abide in forever. This will serve to be a glorious conclusion. And that the God of Israel's servant, David, will be their prince forever (Ezekiel 37:25-28). Ezekiel, the Prophet, goes on to say that God has devised a Covenant of Peace. And it's this very everlasting Covenant of Peace that God fully intends to put in place in the not-too-distant future. We are destined to enter into the Eternal Land of Promise. The God of Israel desires to set up his Sanctuary, the Millennial Temple, in the midst of us forever. You see, the Israeli Messiah is of the lineage of David. He is a descendant of David. And yet, paradoxically, he has been around since prior to the very foundation of the world as well."

"Is everything okay?" Abigail broke in and asked.

"Everything is just fine," Jonathan quickly responded. "It couldn't be better."

Everyone was nodding in accord.

"The food is absolute cuisine!" Bathsheba added.

"And I couldn't help but notice that Dr. Goldstein has your undivided attention," Abigail said cheerfully. "He's had me spellbound a number of times. He can be quite dazzling."

"You're too kind, Abigail." Dr. Goldstein said, seeming a little embarrassed with a red face. "You folks would think that Abigail is one of my nearest kin, rendering compliments like that. But she, literally, is like family to me. You are very special to many people who are patrons of Harvest Restaurant, Abigail."

"I feel that same way about you." Dr. Goldstein." Abigail sincerely responded. "You are special to all of us here at Harvest Restaurant. All of us here are your family! Is there anything else that I can get for any of you? May I entice you with some dessert? The Coconut Chocolate Mousse Cake is incredible."

"No, thank you," Bathsheba responded. "That sounds a little too divine for me, calorie-wise. Everything is just fine."

"She's trying to maintain that girlish figure of hers. I would entice Bathsheba to have the Coconut Chocolate Mousse Cake. The way to Bathsheba's heart is through her sweet tooth." David said, with Bathsheba giving him an innocent glare."

"Well, she's certainly managing to do that," Abigail responded. "How about the rest of you?"

"I'm good," Jonathan said.

"The same here. Thank you for everything." David concurred.

"We're all fine, Abigail," Dr. Goldstein added. "As usual, you've been a superb waitress and a joy to see."

"Thank you," Abigail said with a beaming smile. "Be sure to come again. It's been a wonderful pleasure meeting all of you."

"What I'm leading up to concerning the Restoration of the Throne of David is that since the throne is going to be restored, then, people are being restored as well." Dr. Goldstein stressed emphatically. "The Prophet, Joel, said that the Israeli Messiah would restore his people and raise up his great army, of which the Messiah would designate David to lead the way as his commander. David, of the end time, will be just as much a man after God's own heart as David was in the Hebrew Bible. We shall know that the Messiah is in our midst, and he will put his Spirit upon us, that we may be empowered. And you must know that I can say with total assurance that you are the Restored David, Bathsheba, and Jonathan. I am not referring to reincarnation or anything mystical of that nature. It's just like I mentioned to you when we first met in my class, David. Five words that sum it all up: 'Everything has come full circle.' And you three, among many, many others as well, of course, are obviously most special in the eyes of our God. That is, certainly, no exaggeration in your case."

"I've had flashbacks about this --- recollections --- glimpses. Just like in your class, when I pictured you anointing me many years ago." David said, without doubting one bit that Dr. Goldstein was absolutely correct. It all made perfect sense to David.

"There is much more to say along these lines to verify what I'm saying." Dr. Goldstein added. "David, you and Jonathan are, indeed, the Two Anointed Ones mentioned in the Hebrew Bible, who will be empowered by Moses, Elijah, and the Israeli Messiah. You are also referred to as the Two Olive Trees and the Two Olive Branches. Some will try to say that the Two Anointed Ones are Zerubbabel, who built the second Temple after the Jews were released from Babylonian captivity, and the High Priest, Joshua, but that belief is in error. Zechariah, the Prophet, states that these two will not be operating in their own strength or power, but strictly by their God's power. Also, according to the eleventh chapter of the Book of

Revelation in the New Testament, the Two Anointed Ones of the Book of Zechariah in the Hebrew Bible are referred to as the Two Witnesses, the Two Prophets, and the Two Candlesticks. In all reality, these two are, indeed, the Restored David and Jonathan of the last days, who are expected to be great heroes for Israel, especially in the final week of the Seventy Weeks of Years, commonly referred to as the Seven Year Tribulation mentioned in the Book of Daniel. Moses and Elijah will, at a critical point, converge upon the Restored David and the Restored Jonathan of the latter days. These two men will have the power, as Elijah did in the Hebrew Bible, to shut the skies so that no rain will fall, and also like Moses, having the power to turn rivers and oceans into blood, and to send every kind of plague upon the Earth. These Two Anointed Ones will have the power to perform the same miracles of Elijah and Moses, plus much more, considering the task at hand ahead of them. David and Jonathan, who have a sacred, eternal oath with each other, reinforced by God, are, indisputably, the Two Anointed Ones in our modern time. The Ark of the Covenant is also mentioned in the eleventh chapter of Revelation, the exact same chapter where the Restored David and Jonathan are referred to in the New Testament of the Bible. This fact is highly significant, especially for David. The prophets of the Hebrew Bible foresaw many, many years ago that the latter-day David and Jonathan would blaze the way for Israel's restoration. And David and Jonathan themselves solidified the prophecies of the prophets by making an oath with each other, in the Book of First Samuel 20:42, that God, in his name, would abide between David's descendants and Jonathan's descendants for all time, until everything comes full circle, and they unite again in person. And I know it's safe to say that the God of Israel is honoring that oath between David and Jonathan this very evening. And by the way, since I've been making reference to the Book of Revelation, I should mention that no one needs to remind me that any Jew who advocates the New Testament is regarded by many other Jews as not being a legitimate Jew. But as I said, to make a very long story short, I've been around the block with all this, and it's forced me to have an objective, open mind."

"Wow!" Bathsheba reacted.

"There's more," Dr. Goldstein continued. "In the Book of the Song of Solomon, that is, Song of Solomon 6:10, there is a reference made in regard to Bathsheba: 'Who is she that looks forth as the morning, fair as the Moon, clear as the Sun, and terrible as an army of banners?' This is a highly significant verse referring to you, Bathsheba. David is a military man, as predicted in Ezekiel 37:10 to lead Israel's army in the end time, after God raises his army to life. Bathsheba is the wife of an Israeli military man, and she herself is a woman of spiritual war. And the warfare that you, David, and the Restored Solomon, your son, will be engaged in is guaranteed to be most intense. The Twelfth Chapter of the Book of Revelation speaks of a woman appearing as a great wonder in Heaven. She is described as being clothed with the Sun, with the Moon under her feet. A crown of twelve Stars, symbolic of the Twelve Tribes of Israel, is upon her head. This lady is referring to none other than the Blessed Virgin Mary. She is pregnant with a male child who is destined to rule the nations of Earth with a rod of iron. This, of course, is a reference being made of Mary's son, Jesus, who has been born without sin as clearly stated in II Corinthians 5:21. Revelation Chapter Twelve goes on to say that the devil, described to be a Red Dragon, is ready to pounce upon the child as soon as he is born. The devil also spews out a flood of destruction toward the woman, but the Earth opens to swallow this flood of lies and chaos. She is given two wings of a Great Eagle by the God of Israel, who equips her with his Spirit and power like the eagles mentioned in Isaiah 40:31, to escape the devil's relentless pursuit. Also, it is not a coincidence that Mary, a lady of boundless grace, is mentioned in the chapter immediately after Revelation Chapter Eleven, where Moses and Elijah converge upon David and Jonathan to reinforce Jesus Christ enduing them with power. And it should be noted that just as Jesus was caught up unto God and to his throne in Revelation 12:5, so too will David and Jonathan ascend up to heaven as revealed in Revelation 11:12. Now, I'm going to play outright Prophet here to render a prophecy concerning Bathsheba. It will be at an extremely critical moment that the Blessed Mary will make a visitation to

Bathsheba, a formidable woman of spiritual warfare, out of concern for her welfare. The woman of Song of Solomon 6:10, written in her honor by her son, Solomon (Song of Solomon 3:11), will have a direct encounter with the woman of the Twelfth Chapter of the Book of Revelation. The Queen of Heaven will make herself known to the Queen of Israel. And with that having been said, I've managed to reveal yet two more prophecies concerning Bathsheba."

"I'll say it backwards. Wow!" Jonathan exclaimed.

"I believe I've said enough for now." Dr. Goldstein said. "But I should emphasize, without just blurting it out in an insensitive manner, that the three of you are in grave danger. The main reason for all the imminent peril will be the rise of a madman, who will come to be known as the false messiah. As civilization speeds toward its final destiny, a powerful world leader will emerge to the center stage of international affairs and assume his much-desired place."

Dr. Goldstein went on to conclude, without skipping a beat: "With this soon to come maniac, the false messiah, emerging into the world picture, only to bring a devastating amount of war, destruction, and bloodshed to the Earth, all optimistic hopes and dreams of the future will one day smolder in the ashes of a world gone crazy. He will appear in between the period after the Battle of Gog and Magog and the rebuilding of Solomon's Temple and make his move. He will operate in what he considers to be his own perfect timing, mocking God's perfect timing. He will arise promising lasting peace in the Middle East. But the feigned peace that this villain delivers will be pseudo. He will be one of the people signing a seven-year treaty with Israel, involving negotiations with Israel's harshest enemies. The Bible predicts this treaty between the enemies of Israel and this powerful world leader will bring about a misleading, deceptive, fraudulent peace and prosperity between the country of Israel and her surrounding enemy nations. It will seem like the false messiah is intervening on behalf of Israel. This peace will be short-lived, and only last for three-and-a-half years, that is, the first half of the Seven Year Tribulation. Then, this world leader will break his covenant with Israel. He will, then, go on to violently persecute the people of Israel for the next three-and-a-half years. The last three-and-a-half years of the Seven Year Tribulation will mark the Great Tribulation or "Jacob's Trouble" as prophesied in the Book of Jeremiah, the Book of Daniel, the Book of Revelation and the Book of Matthew by the Israeli Messiah, Jesus Christ. In the midst of the Seven Year Tribulation, the false messiah will cause the sacrifices and offerings at the altar of the Temple to cease. He will blaspheme the God of Israel in the Holy of Holies, proclaiming that he is the Most High God, as prophesied by Daniel, Jesus, Paul, the Apostle, and John in Revelation 13:12-18. The chaos created will pave the way for him to rise as a new world leader. Satan has battled Israel at every turn throughout history, waiting for the right moment to indwell the right person as his final masterpiece. The false messiah will be the absolute embodiment of evil and carry out his dirty work throughout the world. He will establish the New Roman Empire, equivalent to a modern-day Babylon. He will do whatever it takes to destroy God's people, Jewish and non-Jewish, and prevent the Millennial Temple from being built by Mashiach ben David."

Dr. Goldstein hesitated for a moment, as if to gather his thoughts just one more time for the evening, and then, proceeded.

"And as a priority, keep this in mind: Don't be misled by modern-day false prophets making fallacious claims as to when the Messiah is coming. The countless number of souls who died waiting for the Great and Terrible Day of the Lord, that is, believing that the brightness of the Coming of the Lord Jesus Christ will take place, will suddenly find themselves in the Eternal Promised Land of Israel at last!" Dr. Goldstein said emphatically. "And keep in mind that the terminology of 'The Rapture' is not found anywhere in the Bible. The concept of 'The Rapture' was made up by a nineteenth century theologian by the name of John Nelson Darby in the 1830s."

"My rapture is derived from training to fly my fighter jet and keeping company with Bathsheba, not necessarily in that order." David quipped.

"There goes that disarming charm of yours again, David." Bathsheba reacted, with a big smile.

"Bathsheba is the only one who laughs at my jokes." David said sincerely, although others did appreciate David's sense of humor and levity.

"Yes. You two have a fascinating rapport with each other." Dr. Goldstein said, seeming just as amused with David's remark.

"Now, also of great importance is that you be aware that the false messiah will be more than merely a comrade of the devil." Dr. Goldstein elaborated. "The false messiah will be the devil incarnate. Successfully destroying the false messiah would be the direct equivalent of annihilating Satan. And of course, this is an extremely precarious situation which entails many risks, because we don't know the intricate details. Only Almighty God knows. But one thing I do know: Defeating Satan cannot be done without the assistance of the Israeli Messiah. And I also know that our world will not have a chance of procuring peace as long as the false messiah has his way. So, take this as a nugget of wisdom and perspective: Satan may be able to discern when the Seven Year Tribulation is forthcoming, and act accordingly with his plans, but the devil does not possess all the complex information as to how matters will come to pass. Satan is left to speculate on many issues that the God of Israel already had figured out before anyone else came along. A good example of us knowing the broad details is the fact that all four of us are aware that the Ark of the Covenant will somehow be restored to the Millennial Temple after the Messiah builds it. I would venture to say that the responsibility of getting the Ark back to its rightful place has been laid upon your capable shoulders in a large respect, David. Israel can count on you to successfully carry out that task in top form."

"Well, despite all the myths and theories, such as the Knights Templar possessing the Ark and bringing it to Scotland to the Rosslyn Chapel, the Ark being hidden in a cave on Mount Nebo from where Moses saw the Promised Land, the Church of Our Lady Mary in Aksum, Ethiopia preserving the Ark, that the Ark is sealed in a Qumran cave near the Dead Sea, and so forth, Dr. Goldstein." David replied. "I, honestly, know exactly where the Ark of the Covenant may be found."

"I don't doubt that one bit, David, my boy!" Dr. Goldstein said enthusiastically. "Of all the people who are living today, I am not at all surprised that you are privy to having information concerning the Ark. You, certainly, qualify in the God of Israel's eyes. The Ark of the Covenant disappeared after the first Temple and Jerusalem were destroyed by the Babylonians. It is absolutely imperative that the Ark of the Covenant be restored to the Millennial Temple. But we do not want to allow the Ark to enter the Tribulation Temple, that is, Solomon's Temple Rebuilt, because it's been prophesied by Daniel, the Prophet, in the Book of Daniel, that it will be unavoidable to keep the false messiah from blaspheming our God from the location of the Holy of Holies, where the Ark is usually in place. This event will be referred to as the Abomination of Desolation, as predicted by Daniel and by Jesus Christ in the twenty-fourth chapter of the Book of Matthew. We don't want the Ark to be in place when this horrible event of the Abomination of Desolation occurs. And considering that the Abomination of Desolation is a legitimate Hebrew prophecy, then, we can more than assume that it, very unfortunately, is something that will actually occur. But there is sound assurance, according to the prediction of Daniel, that a time will come when the God of Israel's kingdom will destroy all the contrary kingdoms of the world. Daniel also prophesied that the God of heaven will set up a kingdom that will never be destroyed. And from that point in time on, no one is going to ever conquer it. God's kingdom is fully expected to shatter these evil kingdoms into nothingness, and his kingdom will stand forever. We know the overall blueprint, but we do not know the complicated, intricate details. The appropriate place for the Ark of the Covenant will be the Millennial Temple. The Millennial Temple will serve as the permanent, intended home and final resting place for the Ark."

"Wouldn't all these factors open things up for us to play with destiny?" David said. "We can't outguess an omniscient God."

"That's the million-dollar question, David. Is God even in control of all the smaller specifics, or are we making decisions on our own, subject to error, to the extent that our mistakes are fatal enough to cause us to lose the victory and plummet the world into eternal darkness?" Dr. Goldstein responded.

"That's deep! Considering that so many lives are at stake." Jonathan noted, out of sheer alarm.

"There are so many people involved in this big picture who have passed away, such as, our forefathers who looked forward to the day when all of the prophecies of the Bible would come to fulfillment. There are people from all different backgrounds counting on the Eternal Promised Land to be within their grasp." Dr. Goldstein said in closing. "I must, indeed, admit that the entire scenario is a very terrifying prospect. And David, Bathsheba, and Jonathan, while all four of us may have an idea of the overall picture and scheme of things, we are still at a loss to know everything that's going to be necessary to fill in the gaps. Therefore, how do we know there is any guarantee of success, other than including faith into the equation? There are plenty of misguided souls out there who remark that they will get into heaven should they be found worthy. Well, the good news is that we can have a lot more confidence than that about gaining access into heaven, because we are only found worthy through Christ and the foundation that he alone procured, as mentioned in the New Testament in I Corinthians 3:11. Jesus is Mashiach ben David, the undisputed Messiah and gift to the world. Our fate is in the hands of Jesus Christ alone."

"And with all that having been said, Dr. Goldstein," David responded, "considering that your three guests this evening here at Harvest Restaurant represent the Restored David, the Restored Bathsheba, and the Restored Jonathan of the last days, then, it would, apparently, follow suit that you are the Restored ..."

David was interrupted. Dr. Goldstein quickly addressed David's astute, logical deduction.

"That's exactly right, David. The Restored Samuel, the Prophet." Dr. Goldstein interjected, confirming what David, Bathsheba, and Jonathan had already surmised.

CHAPTER TWO
THE BATTLE OF GOG AND MAGOG

The Hebrew Bible states that an attack against the tiny country of Israel will come from all sides, from a vast network of enemy nations. To say that Israel's army will be greatly outnumbered would be the understatement of the twenty-first century.

This is an impending reality, and it will occur suddenly and without warning. A literal interpretation of biblical prophecy of the people of Israel returning to the Promised Land has been fulfilled (the State of Israel was established on May 14th, 1948). And one prophecy that remains to be fulfilled is the Battle of Gog and Magog, a war that originated from the War on Terrorism. This particular war serves as one of Ezekiel's most dramatic prophecies from over 2600 years ago.

The Battle of Gog and Magog is known by a number of different names including the North-Eastern Invasion, the Russian-Islamic Invasion, and the Gog and Magog Invasion. This war involves a huge conglomeration of nations with anti-Semitic regimes designed to destroy the State of Israel, with Russia out in front. A shared anti-Semitic and anti-God obsession will be enough to override any and all existing differences between the Arabs and the Russians. Their hatred of the Jews and all those with an affinity for Israel will be more than enough to motivate the formation of their union with each other.

The events of the horrific day well known to all as 9/11 came as the official warning that the Battle of Gog and Magog was imminent. Even in the period when the modern-day Restored David and Bathsheba lived, the memory of the travesty of 9/11 remained fresh on everyone's mind. The indelible atrocity was an incident that every human being in the world learned from. Most children were taught to heed the evil of this pivotal day. Others, quite tragically, were taught to advocate its terror.

The Pathway: Color Picture Photo Edition

On September 11th, 2001, 19 Muslim radicals (extremists), on a suicide mission, hijacked four American commercial passenger planes and intentionally flew two of them into the World Trade Center Twin Towers, in New York City (New York, New York; USA), resulting in the 9/11 Disaster. Three thousand Americans lost their lives as terrorists successfully targeted the Twin Towers, the Pentagon, and unsuccessfully aimed at the White House. The two planes positioned on a trajectory to crash into the North and South Towers of the World Trade Center complex in Lower Manhattan were American Airlines Flight 11 and United Airlines Flight 175 respectively. Both American Airlines Flight 11 and United Airlines Flight 175 had departed from Logan International Airport in Boston, Massachusetts bound for Los Angeles International Airport. The two planes were both Boeing 767's. Within an hour and 42 minutes after the impact, both 110-story towers collapsed, killing 2,799 and injuring more than 6,000 others. In the meantime, hijackers on board American Airlines Flight 77 deliberately crashed the plane into the Pentagon in Arlington County, Virginia, killing all 64 people on board, as well as 125 people at the Pentagon. American Airlines Flight 77 was scheduled to travel from Dules International Airport near Washington, D.C. to Los Angeles International Airport. American Airlines Flight 77 was a Boeing 757-223. United Airlines Flight 93 was a domestic scheduled morning passenger flight that was hijacked by terrorists on board, as part of the September 11th attacks. United Airlines Flight 93 had departed from Newark International Airport in New Jersey bound for San Francisco International Airport in California. United Airlines Flight 93, a Boeing 757, was intended by the terrorists onboard to make a direct hit on the White House as a target, but it crashed into a field in Somerset County, Pennsylvania, during an attempt by the passengers and crew to regain control of the cockpit. The devastation of these horrendous assaults sparked an international War on Terrorism.

In November of 2001, Osama bin Laden (who eventually was killed by United States Special Forces in Operation Neptune Spear on May 2nd, 2011 in Pakistan) along with the terrorist group, Al-

Qaeda, took credit for the 9/11 terrorist attack. The rationale of bin Laden's despicable deeds can be traced directly to his hatred of democracy, capitalism, free enterprise, the United States, and Israel.

There has been a significant increase in the number of terrorist attacks and major threats since 9/11 (the travesty of September 11th, 2001).

Intensified kinds of wars, famines, plagues (pandemics), and cataclysmic weather, predicted by biblical prophecy, began their fulfillment and intensification in the first part of the twentieth century, escalating to the ultimate fulfillment of other forecasts to take place in the future.

And while there have been many earthquakes, tsunamis (super tidal waves), hurricanes, climate changes causing famines, and other various natural disasters throughout all of history, the frequency of these earthquakes, weather phenomena, and so forth, and the amount of destruction they cause, have increased tremendously since the early part of the twentieth century. Even as climate change has caused global temperatures to rise, there also seems to be an ever-growing number of increasing human conflicts around the world.

The continuous attacks directed toward Israel have shown such a deep embedded hatred, derived from Israel's enemies, that it doesn't seem possible to bring resolution through diplomatic protocol. It appears that the only way that Israel will survive and have ultimate, unprecedented victory will be through the power of military force.

Israel's next war would be a most decisive battle. With those enemies who chose to confront Israel, it would be a winner take all situation. This would not be a world war, but it would involve Israel's foremost enemies. And just as much as these nations desired to acquire the land of Israel, so too would the nation of Israel need to develop an attitude of conquering new territories.

The Battle of Gog and Magog would not be the war to end all wars, but it was a prominent war that has been prophesied by the Israeli Prophet, Ezekiel in the Hebrew Bible:

"'Therefore, Son of man, prophesy against Gog, and say, Thus says the Lord God of Israel: Behold, I am against you, O Gog, the Prince of Rosh. And I will turn you around and lead you on, bringing

you up from the far north, and bring you against the mountains of Israel. You shall fall upon the mountains of Israel, you and your troops and the people who are with you. And I will send fire on Magog. So, I will make my holy name known in the midst of my people, Israel. Then, the nations shall know that I am the Lord, the Holy One in Israel. Behold, it is coming, and it shall be done,' says the God of Israel. 'This is the day of which I have spoken.'"
Ezekiel 39:1, 2, 4, 6-8

"Gog" refers to an individual and identifies him as coming from "the land of Magog," and that he is "the Prince of Rosh" (The Leader of Russia). "Gog" is mentioned a number of times in the 38th and 39th chapters of the Book of Ezekiel. He is the tyrant who will ruthlessly initiate, along with a deadly coalition of nations, an invasion from the north, reclaiming former Soviet republics for a start, as he makes his way to Israel. This invasion perpetrated by Russia will come on top of Israel being threatened by other hostile enemies. This intended assault will be launched just prior to the Seven Year Tribulation.

Gog is the leader of Magog and is identified as "the Prince of Rosh." Ezekiel 38:2 Rosh is a common Hebrew word. Rosh is an identification of Russia. Rosh is a derivative, root word accepted by many expert scholars to be the correct translation of Russia, occurring about 750 times in the Bible. The grammar of the Hebrew Bible (the Old Testament) supports the translation of Rosh (Rus) as a proper noun denoting the geographical location of Russia. Rosh was the ancient name of Russia, once called Rus. There are many who believe that Russia (Rosh) and Magog are one in the same. Gog's advancement to claim new territory and reclaim former Soviet satellite countries (as part of his agenda to, ultimately, invade Israel) will be totally based on propaganda and lies. And another major concern will be China joining forces with Russia.

While the tearing down of the Berlin Wall on November 9th, 1989 and the fall of the Soviet Union on December 25th, 1991 did much for the advancement of freedom, radical Muslims attempted to undermine that freedom by taking control of the former Soviet controlled republics. Six out of fourteen of these republics are, now, under Islamic influence: Turkmenistan, Kyrgyzstan, Tajikistan, Azerbaijan, Kazakhstan and Uzbekistan. The remaining eight of the former Soviet republics include: Ukraine, Belarus, Moldova, Estonia, Georgia, Armenia, Lithuania and Latvia.

The modern nations listed in Ezekiel 38:2-6 are threats to Israel and supportive of the Arab-Islamic agenda. Today, Magog, ruled by Gog (The Prince of Rosh), is comprised of Russia and the six former Soviet republics that are under Islamic influence. Also, Gog's allies include Meshech and Tubal (territories in Turkey), Gomer (Germany), Togarmah (Turkey), Persia (Iran), Cush/Ethiopia (Sudan), and Put (Libya). This contemplated attack against the tiny country of Israel will be plotted from all sides, involving a vast network of enemy nations extending all the way from Russia to the north, Iran to the east, Sudan to the south, and Libya to the west of Israel.

Russia (Rosh) has become economically dependent on the Arabs. Russia's current financial condition and political instability have led their country to forge alliances with Islamic powers that continually call for Israel's destruction. And the government of Russia is selling nuclear, chemical, and biological weapons to Arab countries as black-market items with one single focus in mind: The annihilation of Israel, leading to the emergence of a global Islamic state.

Israel's survival, in the midst of a sea of anti-Semitic hostiles, had been nothing less than miraculous. History has reported one conflict after another in the Holy Land. The issue of who controls the Promised Land of Israel, especially in regard to the Temple Mount, is still the most volatile issue in international affairs.

Ezekiel Chapters 38 and 39 uniquely details a future invasion perpetrated upon Israel by a huge alliance of foreign nations. This prediction, given by God to the Prophet, Ezekiel, is one of the most dramatic prophecies found in the Hebrew Bible. The prophecy foretells of an attempted attack on Israel by a multitude of nations and ends with the supernatural downfall of Israel's enemies through God's direct intervention. Many of the nations, mentioned in these two chapters, are sworn to oppose Israel. Ezekiel Chapters 38 and 39 depict the most detailed prophecy found in the Hebrew Bible, in regard to outlining this future war. The fulfillment of the prophecy, that is, history written in advance, is clearly stated to take place in the "latter years" or "latter days," that is, the last days or the end time. This forthcoming plot to attack Israel, meticulously detailed by Ezekiel, is bearing down. It is predicted that this battle will take place just prior to the Seven Year Tribulation.

The conflict of Ezekiel Chapters 38 and 39 will drastically alter the world. It is most appropriate to say that the Battle of Gog and Magog stems directly from the War on Terrorism. According to prophecy, it is sometime after the Jews return to Israel from the Diaspora (that is, the dispersion/scattering worldwide of the Jews from their homeland due to persecution) and rebuild the land to establish the State of Israel, that the War of Gog and Magog is expected to follow. One primary motive for the war being fought will be to win possession of Jerusalem, Israel and the Temple Mount. But overall, these radical Muslim dominated nations have the shared focus, goal, purpose, and obsession to destroy the State of Israel.

Long time sworn enemies of Israel will ultimately be part of a vast coalition. Many of these countries have been aggressive in pursuing nuclear programs specifically designed to destroy the nation of Israel. Larger countries with adverse economic conditions have not been able to control their arsenals of nuclear, chemical, and biological weapons, allowing their stockpile of weapons to become black-market items. This has contributed to Israel's worst enemies arming themselves with the most dreadful Weapons of Mass Destruction (WMD). These larger countries (especially Russia/Rosh/Magog) have also been sending military advisors to provide training and intelligence to the very nations listed in the thirty-eighth chapter of Ezekiel. And a number of these governments opposing Israel routinely use the billions of dollars in annual profit they derive from the sale of oil drilled in their countries to purchase weapons, rather than to help their own needy people.

But the rogue leaders of these nations were not just acquiring missiles and other nuclear weaponry from larger nations through the black-market. Billion-dollar deals are being signed to sell weapons of mass destruction to these enemies of Israel, and the more sizable nations are also building their own nuclear power stations. To make a military attack upon one of the smaller countries radically opposed against Israel, you might as well be attacking the larger country as well. Many nations have chosen to rise up against the one nation of Israel.

Larger nations have signed accords worth hundreds of billions of dollars with nations who have sworn to obliterate Israel. This marks the beginning of relationships between major trade powers with smaller evil regimes, resisting to agree to strong United Nations sanctions, and flagrantly displaying antagonism toward the United States and Israel.

And while the Battle of Gog and Magog would not involve all the nations of the world, the boiling cauldron of tension it creates is enough to engulf the entire planet, especially because it brings everyone to the brink of nuclear conflagration. To say that there are enough nuclear, chemical, and biological weapons in the world to annihilate all of civilization is the understatement of the twenty-first century. And those who are proponents of the elimination of Israel think that nuclear holocaust is worth the risk. Every known various weapon of war devised by mankind has been utilized.

NATO, the North Atlantic Treaty Organization (North Atlantic Alliance), an intergovernmental, military alliance between united member countries agreeing to mutual defense in response to an attack by any external party, will be limited in preventing Russia (Rosh/Magog) from advancing with schemes of hostile takeover.

HATZERIM AIRBASE
THE ISRAELI AIR FORCE FLIGHT ACADEMY
TOP GUN TRAINING
BEER SHEVA, ISRAEL
44 MILES SOUTHWEST OF JERUSALEM

Before leaving Hanscom Air Force Base in the United States, David Hartman and Jonathan Diamond participated in a special ceremony there to receive their fighter pilot call signs. David was designated the call sign, Soaring Eagle, because he flew his fighter jet as gracefully as an eagle soars across the sky. Observing David rising so effortlessly in his F-22 Raptor Stealth Fighter Jet was just like watching someone breaking free of every troubling care in life. And Jonathan was given the call sign, Greased Lightning, because he loved to fly so fast in his F-35 Lightning IV Stealth Fighter Jet, propelled by the Spirit of God. Jonathan glided upon the wind, causing onlookers to somehow recapture the simplicity of God that escapes man. It was as if David and Jonathan were both reaching for the Eternal One, Yahweh, in flight. The interaction of this charismatic duo, soaring together in such a synchronized fashion as Fighter Wing Leader and Wingman, was an infinite mystery that couldn't be explained away. It was a vivid phenomenon of two men revealing God's own unique purpose in their lives, that is, the kind of meaning that most people search for without end.

As people in Israel stood and stared upwards at the sky day by day, they were inspired with the sensation that David and Jonathan had somehow miraculously discovered the secret of where all new-born life originates, beyond what human intellect was capable of reasoning. There was no more of a glorious sight on Earth. And these two respective call signs would follow them for the duration of their flying careers, and that, of course, was no less true when they transferred to Hatzerim Airbase in Beer Sheva, Israel, after being accepted into the Israeli Air Force Flight Academy for Israeli TOP GUN Jet Fighter Training.

Both David and Jonathan graduated with honors from Harvard and MIT and excelled in their education to become Israeli TOP GUN Fighter Jet Pilots at Hanscom Air Force base in the United States. And their dream came true to be accepted to the Israeli Air Force Flight Academy in Israel to receive training to compete to be the best of the best as Israeli TOP GUN Fighter Pilots.

And the hard-fast-and-continuous Israeli TOP GUN Fighter Jet Training at Hatzerim Airbase was intense. There was a review of the basic instruction of aerodynamics, tactics, and maneuvers, and of course, there was a great deal of advanced learning. Even during training in regard to simulated combat test flights, David, Soaring Eagle, and Jonathan, Greased Lightning, were making an indelible impression upon their Israeli TOP GUN comrades.

F-22 RAPTOR
COMMANDER DAVID HARTMAN

F-35 LIGHTNING IV
COMMANDER JONATHAN DIAMOND

One big reason that David was given the call sign, "Soaring Eagle," as a fighter pilot, other than the obvious rationale of David flying graceful and fast, is that the other student pilots at Hanscom Air Force Base were well aware that David knew his Hebrew Bible. They all knew that David's favorite book in the Hebrew Bible was the Book of Isaiah. And Jonathan confided to them that David's all-time favorite verse was Isaiah 40:31, hence: "But they that wait upon the God of Israel shall renew their strength. They shall mount up with wings of eagles. They shall run, and not be weary. And they shall walk and not faint. Appropriately, this was David's favorite verse."

The Pathway: Color Picture Photo Edition

DAVID'S CALL SIGN OF "SOARING EAGLE" – ISAIAH 40:31

JONATHAN'S CALL SIGN OF "GREASED LIGHTNING"

Jonathan flies a Lockheed Martin F-35 Lighting IV Stealth Fighter Jet, hence, the call sign, Greased Lightning.

"And the fire was bright. And out of the fire came forth lightning." Ezekiel 1:13, Matthew 24:27

Jonathan was dubbed "Greased Lightning" simply because he was so fast and agile at the helm of his Lockheed Martin F-35 Lightning IV Fighter Jet that he was thought by many people of not only being reckless, but also out of control. But Jonathan, was to everyone's amazement, most effective, and also at the same time, kept his cool. Nevertheless, the TOP GUN Training Commanders firmly told him to fly by the manual. For the most part, Jonathan complied, and flew his fighter jet strictly by the book. But he would always align his F-35 Lightning IV Fighter Jet on the cutting edge.

Of all the instructors and mentors who David and Jonathan would draw from, Commander Major Ariel Rosenberg stood out as an outstanding model for the young pilots to emulate. He was a genuine Israeli hero, and his style of teaching stood out from all the rest. Physically, he towered over most men being six foot, four inches tall, with a muscular build and rugged features. Of course, another big factor that specifically stood out to David was that Commander

The Pathway: Color Picture Photo Edition

Rosenberg was Bathsheba's father. He was also a very good friend of David's father, Commander Jesse Hartman. One statement made by Commander Rosenberg at the very beginning of Israeli TOP GUN Training that really stood out to both David and Jonathan was: "Aggressiveness, determination, patience, and a cool head has distinguished the successful pilot from all others throughout the history of aerial combat. The pilot who makes the fewer gross mistakes is the pilot who wins."

It was pointed out that there are major rules of engagement in Israeli Military Science. There is an official approach and diplomatic protocol that must be abided by. Just as there had been a need for the Haganah, Hebrew for "The Defense" of Israel (from 1920-1928), the establishment of Israeli TOP GUN had proven to be a vital component of the Israeli Defense Forces (IDF). Israeli TOP GUN had become designed and tweaked to protect the citizens of Israel. And these newly commissioned officers were there to learn how to become strategists.

Israel has the most technologically advanced military on Earth. And more than any other country that gathered information from all around the world, Israel had to rely on the Mossad, Israeli Intelligence, to provide a regular, ongoing, never-ending collection of international, confidential knowledge for its very survival, most of it being top secret.

It would be in Israeli TOP GUN Fighter Jet School that the more experienced pilots would emphasize that aerial combat at such a high level, with all of its risks, is the most dangerous game in the world. It would be here the students would learn resilience, versatility, and agility in order to maneuver according to circumstance. And they would come to understand how to make split second decisions instinctively. It would be here they would learn to master detail without wallowing it or being overwhelmed by it. It would be here they would learn how to encounter and survive every kind of hazard and opposition known to mankind.

Some of the Israeli TOP GUN Fighter Jet Training included: Israeli TOP GUN Tactics and Maneuvers, mathematical solutions for even the messiest of fighter jet battle engagement problems, fighter jet physics, modern-day dog fights, when to use guns and when to use missiles, Guided Rockets and Unguided Rockets, Aircraft Center of Gravity, the various fighter jets flown by TOP GUN Pilots, Lead Angle, Time-of-Flight, Velocity Vector, Line-of-Sight, cockpit devices such as the display unit, a gyroscope, and the computer, tracking targets by holding the pipper steady in relation to the saddle, Air-to-Air Missiles, Surface-to-Air Missiles, Heat Seeking Missiles, Radar Guided Missiles, Cruise Missiles, gun firing situations that include Tracking Shots and Snapshots, the dangers of overshooting your jet in relation to the target, the rate of G increase, avoiding games of chicken, not allowing an enemy aircraft to get in firing range from behind, judging the changing flight path of a Guided Missile, Thrust-to-Weight Ratio, Guard Frequency, Nuclear Warheads, Atomic and Hydrogen Bombs, Tracking Radar Systems, Fire-Control Computers, Angle of Attack, Jet Thrust Drag, Break Turns, Rolling Turns, Missile Guidance Trajectory, the physics and techniques of primary maneuvers, Pursuit Curves, Lag Pursuit, Lag Rolls, the High Yo-Yo, Turn Radius, Evasive Maneuvers, the Flat Scissors Maneuver, Vertical and Oblique Turns, Radical Acceleration being the vector sum of Load Factor and Gravity, Angles Fight Tactics, Energy Fight Tactics, the Zoom Climb Tactic, Basic Fighter Maneuvering (BFM), Section Engaged Maneuvering (SEM), the End Game of Engagement, Reengaging, Lead Turns, Vertical Maneuvering Speed, the Diving Spiral, the 180 and 360 Degree Rolls, Horizontal and Vertical Maneuvering, Rear-Quarter Shots, the Beautiful Lookup Shots, Lift Vector, Turn Performance, Instantaneous Turn Performance, Sustained Turns, Maximum Turn Performance, G Capability, Turbocharged Fighter Jets, Pure Pursuit, Supersonic Fighter Aircrafts, Hit-and-Run Tactics, Ballistic Flight Paths, Quantum Mechanics, the Theory of Relativity, the electrodynamics of moving bodies, Brownian Motion, Hovering V/STOL fighter aircrafts such as the British Harrier and the Boeing AH-64 Apache Attack Helicopter, Thrust Vector in Forward Flight, Fighter Wing Leaders, Wingmen, the Double Attack, Maneuvering Flexibility, the Offensive Spilt, the Defensive Split, the High/Low Split, Vertical and Horizontal Splits, not to engage unless you have the advantage, Cross Turns, Split Plane Maneuvering, Calculated Risks, Padlocking, the various aircraft formations, Fighter Jets escorting bombers, handling sensory overload, communications with Air Traffic Control, communications with Ground Control, communications with Israeli Command (Code Name: Joshua) and communications with other Fighter Pilots, Maximum Altitude Advantage, utilizing radar to detect targets in heavy clutter, Internal Radar of a fighter jet, Spins, Electronic Surveillance, Reconnaissance, Radar Jamming, Afterburners, the Bracket Attack, the Hook, the Sweep Tactic, Lift Limit, True Airspeed, Kinetic Energy, Potential Energy, Nuclear Physics, Mach Drag, Sustained G Capability, Acceleration Performance, Lift-to-Drag Ratio, Lift-to-Weight Ratio, the effect of gravity on Turn Performance, Roll Performance, Aerodynamic Roll Controls, and Star Wars Nuclear Missile Interception from a fighter jet, also known as the Strategic Defense Initiative, as proposed by United States President Ronald Reagan. And the Israeli TOP GUN Pilots were also entrusted with a great deal of top secret details.

Some of the Israeli TOP GUN Training was a review of what David and Jonathan had picked up at Harvard, MIT, and at Hanscom Air Force Base, but most of what they were learning was brand new. The bottom line to everything was to instill a second nature for making accurate, split-second decisions.

It's one thing to have all the knowledge required to be an equipped Israeli TOP GUN Fighter Jet Pilot. It's quite another thing to be capable enough to effectively make the hard decisions of exactly how and when that valuable knowledge should be applied, employed, and implemented.

The timing of David and Jonathan returning to Israel and embarking on their Israeli TOP GUN Training could not have been more significant. Anti-Semitic tensions were escalating among Israel's enemies toward the nation of Israel, and it was quite apparent that war was on the horizon.

HATZERIM AIR BASE
BEER SHEVA, ISRAEL
PRE-FLIGHT DEBRIEFING ROOM
COMBAT READINESS

An urgent, top secret military mission briefing had been called by top-ranking Israeli Commanders. The entire Israeli fleet was on high alert, and Israel's allies were clued in. There was a serious problem. And the meeting would entail bearing the facts of the issue at hand, analyzing the trouble, discussing the alternatives, and coordinating a course of action. Commander Ariel Rosenberg stood to address the military assembly.

"Our intelligence agency, Mossad, has very recently informed us of a plot by certain surrounding countries of Israel to initiate a complete hostile take-over of our nation." Commander Rosenberg, Bathsheba's father, said to open his statement to all Israeli TOP GUN Fighter Pilots and other distinguished members of the Israeli Defense Forces, with trusted American Commanders joining in who were deeply involved with the I.S.A.A.C. Program. American troops and other allies were on red alert as much as the Israeli troops.

"Based on the information we have, Israel does not have a second to lose in responding to this situation, before it becomes a crisis spiraling out of control. These enemy countries are fully prepared, if need be, to utilize whatever nuclear power they have at their disposal." Commander Rosenberg continued. "We have a plan designed with the intention to thwart this conspiracy before it even gets off the ground, but as I have mentioned, we have no time to waste. The Israeli military intelligence is privy to the location of chemical weapon storehouses that can be blasted without causing harm to nearby civilians, avoiding a nerve agent release, and an environmental catastrophe upon innocent citizens. Mossad has information determining exactly what chemical and/or biological agents are being stored at each one of these locations, and our scientists have determined exactly what potential harm could result from bombing the storage houses at these particular locations. In other words, we do not want the cure to be worse than the disease.

But should these countries not back down, we will be forced to focus our attention on storage sites that are just outside of major cities. As you know, our weapons can provide the kind of firepower that will induce temperatures high enough to incinerate chemical artillery. Our intention, strategically, at first, is to be as humane as possible, but if our hand is forced, we'll have to go for the jugular.

Make no mistake about it. The potential for mass destruction during this operation is more than a possibility. Nuclear weapons could be launched, and that's why we're only sending fighter jets with Star Wars Nuclear Missile Interception Defense Capability. You have been trained to effectively intercept Cruise Missiles and, even ICBMs. This is a maneuver you may very well need to carry out in the course of this operation. Because the prospect of nuclear war does not mean that just one missile will be fired. Many missiles will go up.

When a certain number of chemical storehouses have been bombed, and those attacks have been detected by our enemies, you are ordered to remain in that particular area, prepared to attack sites that will be even more dangerous to the enemy and monitor for any counteracting nuclear launches. Our intention is to convey that we are on to them, and we mean business. It will be at this point, Israeli and American officials, along with other allies, will be contacting political, military, and diplomatic leaders of these countries warning them to stand back or prepare for an all-out offensive assault. We're going to make it quite clear that we are holding them at bay. And if they don't cooperate, we're going to blow them off the face of the Earth. We have no intention of making any apologizes for turning their countries into parking lots. They, certainly, are not planning on offering Israel the luxury of leniency.

Considering that we are the ones initiating this surprise, preemptive offensive, we do not anticipate considerable confrontation from enemy bandits. Should there be a reaction to our brazen aggression, it will be more likely that the leaders of these hostile countries will decide on a nuclear attack. Once we have successfully hit our targets, it's going to be their call to either react in a dogfight with you, launch nuclear weapons, or back down.

Knowing your training, speed, and agility, you should have no difficulty whizzing directly to your designated targets to make your immediate respective strikes. But no matter how the operation plays out, we are risking the chance of nuclear missiles being launched. Based on the intelligence reports that we have received, we have no other prerogative but to strategically move forward. Since we are the aggressors on an ambush maneuver, there will be as little communication as possible between yourselves and Joshua, as well as among the pilots. Even communication between the Flight Leaders and their Wingmen should be held to a bare minimum. After you have made strikes on your targets, standby for orders to either make other strikes closer to major cities, intercept a nuclear missile utilizing Star Wars Tech, or return to base.

This basic strategy we are employing is comparable to the Six-Day War of 1967 which began with a preemptive Israeli air attack. As a result, Israel captured and secured a number of territories. Our objective in this operation is to turn the tables on those plotting against us. Their desire is to take over the nation of Israel. Therefore, we have no reservation in acquiring new regions. We aim to get the jump on their intended ambush and seize the advantage. Our objective is to snuff out this threat before it gets off the ground. I realize that we have Americans present with us, but they know better than anyone, as our friends, that when it comes to war, Israelis move in, we do our business, and then, we move out.

You will be embarking on this mission at two in the morning, so get as much rest as you can between now and then. It goes without saying that this mission is top secret, so you are all under strict orders not to discuss this operation with anyone, not even family. Prepare to man your stations early tomorrow. You're dismissed."

BATHSHEBA'S APARTMENT

David had a key to Bathsheba's apartment, but he went ahead and just rang the doorbell this time. Bathsheba answered the door in anticipation that it may be David.

"Surprise!" David shouted out, as he presented Bathsheba with a special gift.

"Look at you!" Bathsheba exclaimed, as she carefully took the German Shepherd puppy in her arms that David brought her. Bathsheba cuddled her new pet with a glowing expression on her face.

"Where did you find him, David? He's the most beautiful puppy I've ever seen." Bathsheba declared with sheer delight.

"I found him at a kennel that breeds German Shepherds. I got him just for you. There's food and toys for him out in my car too. He can keep you company when I'm away at times." David replied.

"Oh, David! How sweet of you. I just love him! And I know just what to name him." Bathsheba said with such joy.

"Well, don't keep me guessing, Bathsheba. I'm sure it will be a perfect name." David responded.

"Shalom, David! I'm going to name him Shalom, because he is going to bring us peace, safety, and protection." Bathsheba said.

"You are priceless, Bathsheba." David said with relief, realizing he had made the right decision in getting Bathsheba the ideal gift.

"Come in, David. I have a nice dinner cooked for you." Bathsheba said as she held Shalom.

David felt bad that he was not allowed to even tell Bathsheba about the dangerous mission he'd be embarking on the next morning. He did mention to her that he had to report to duty at two A.M. And he was tempted to disobey the order, and swear her to secrecy. But he didn't. David rationalized that it was better not telling Bathsheba as long as he was under orders, so she wouldn't worry. And Bathsheba, certainly, would worry where David is concerned. She worried about him in general, much less involving such a dangerous operation as he would be up against the next morning.

They had a nice candlelit dinner with casual conversation, as they watched Shalom playing with his new toys. Afterwards, David sat on the sofa, and noticed Bathsheba's Bible, containing both the Hebrew Scriptures and the New Testament. David, being the versatile, opened minded literary man he was, had read the entire

Bible through a number of times, as well as other secular literature, especially during and after sitting under his favorite Professor, Dr. Samuel Goldstein. David loved to read and recite Shakespeare.

Ever since David was a boy, he had developed a game he played that he called Bible Roulette, where he'd arbitrarily open up the Bible and see about randomly landing on a passage of biblical scripture that may be pertinent to his particular situation. Of course, the circumstances he was currently facing were more than paramount. He did it three times that evening, and "happened" to land on some very relevant verses. The first verses came from the Book of Isaiah, David's favorite book in the Hebrew Bible:

1) "'Incline to me, and come unto me.' says the God of Israel. 'Hear, and your soul shall live. And I will make an everlasting Covenant with you, even the sure mercies of David. Behold, I have given him to be a witness to the people, a leader, and commander to the people.'" Isaiah 55:3, 4

The second verse he opened up to came from the Book of First Samuel:

2) "'The Lord God of Israel has sought him a man after his own heart, and he has commanded him to be Captain over his people." I Samuel 13:14

David wondered to himself if that was too much of a coincidence considering that he was a Captain in the Israeli military as well.

Then, David happened across a portion of scripture in the thirty-seventh chapter of Ezekiel, the very chapter prophesying the breath of God reviving the Remnant of Israel, after being in a state of dry bones, causing the nation to stand upon their feet as an exceeding great army:

3) "Then, the God of Israel said unto me, 'Prophesy unto the wind, prophesy, Son of man, and say unto the wind, Thus says the Lord God. Come from the four winds, O Breath, and

breathe upon these slain. So, I prophesied as the God of Israel commanded me, and they lived, and stood upon their feet, an exceeding great army." Ezekiel 37:9, 10

David whispered under his voice, "The Bible Roulette has been just a little too incredible tonight!"
Then David recalled the conversation that he, Jonathan, and Bathsheba had with Dr. Goldstein at the Harvest restaurant near Harvard University in Cambridge, Massachusetts, when the English Professor shared with David, Bathsheba and Jonathan. David remembered that evening like it was yesterday, how Dr. Goldstein posed that the prophets of the Hebrew Bible rendered predictions revealing the future, without providing the exact details of just how these prophesies would come to pass. Surely the prophets had a limited conception of all the modern-day factors that the Israelis would be up against in the days of reckoning, and the manner in which the victory would be secured. On the surface, it appeared that all the prophets had to go by is a mesh of symbols. But perhaps, their visions were so articulate (such as Ezekiel), they were able to foresee the technology of the last days and envision exactly how it would be. In some ways, it was impossible to determine. Yet in many ways, the metaphors of the Bible (like the "wheel in the middle of the wheel" in Ezekiel 1:16, for example) appear descriptive of modern technology. But David was fully aware from the First Book of Chronicles that "The war is of God." Therefore, in David's mind, since it was God's war, everything had to, ultimately, go in Israel's favor. Of course, proponents of other religions than Judaism may insist that another God, other than Yahweh (The Eternal One), will bring them the victory. But from David's point of view, there was no other God than Yahweh.

Bathsheba came over to David after getting the dishes washed and sat next to him on the sofa. Then, David smoothly put his arm around Bathsheba.
David: "Do you love me, Bathsheba?"
Bathsheba: "Yes. I do love you very much, David."
David: "Then, I have everything I need."

Bathsheba: "To whom much is given, much is required, David. Now, let me ask you a question: Do you know the definition of unconditional love?"
David: "Yes. It's affection without any limitations. It's pure love without any conditions. Unconditional love relies on altruism, rather than egotism. Therefore, it is a complete love."
Bathsheba: "My goodness. Very good, David. And that's the kind of love that we share. You're the only love of my life. And I'm the only love of your life. It's always been that way with us. Our unconditional love brings aesthetic value, so that we always see beauty in one another."
David: "Would you be my girl forever, Bathsheba?"
Bathsheba: "I thought you'd never ask, David."

David, eventually, went to sleep on the couch with his head on Bathsheba's lap, as Bathsheba stroked his hair. David had a long day. Before dozing off, David mentioned to Bathsheba that he needed to be up by one o'clock. Bathsheba stayed up until that time, daydreaming about the day when David would outrightly propose marriage to her.

The next morning, David stood at the front door looking sharply dressed in his military uniform, holding Bathsheba as if he never wanted to let her go. He kissed her as Shalom was standing right beside them, wagging his tail with a happy expression of his face.

They released from their embrace.

Bathsheba, instinctively, knew that David was keeping a secret from her. She could sense that he was not totally revealing what was on his mind. She knew David was embarking on something that he was not allowed to talk about, but she didn't press it. David also knew that what he and his comrades were facing that day could be easily labelled a suicide mission.

"Take care of our little Buddy while I'm gone. He'll be good company for you. And I'm counting on him to guard you in my stead."
Bathsheba: "Look at him. He's already protecting me! David. Thank you so much again for Shalom. You look so handsome in your uniform. I love you, David. Be safe up there, Captain Hartman."

David: "I love you too, Bathsheba. It really is unconditional."
Bathsheba: "You left me standing here a long, long time ago, David."

David clinched his lips tightly together at a loss for words, reluctantly did an about-face and walked away, with mixed emotions about whether he should have given Bathsheba some details about the mission. Bathsheba always cried over David, and her tears flowed as she watched the love of her life depart.

GOG AND MAGOG
Ezekiel 38-39

HATZERIM AIR BASE
RUNWAY THIRTY-SEVEN

Rhetorically speaking, there was a transitory Pre-Flight Briefing awaiting the TOP GUN Fighter Pilots reporting in at 0200 hours. The Israelis kept uniform military time with the Americans. The chief directives that were made in the short briefing were to fly unnoticed by taking advantage of the stealth capabilities of the jets being flown on the mission, the pilots not identifying themselves as

they approached friendly or hostile nations, making their strikes as quickly as possible in the small and large countries assigned, staying in the region for a reasonable amount of time after the strikes had been made to determine any extreme reaction from the enemy, and, then, returning to base as promptly as possible.
David: "Zechariah Ground, at Romeo eight, requesting taxi for northbound departure with information, Soaring Eagle 017."
Zechariah Ground: "Soaring Eagle 017, taxi Bravo to hold short runway three seven, northbound departure, Zechariah Ground."

David did as he was instructed by Ground Control, getting into the movement area piloting his F-22 Raptor Fighter Jet, with Jonathan nearby in his F-35 Lightning IV.

At this point, David switched to the radio frequency of the Tower to request clearance for take-off.
David: "Jericho Tower, Soaring Eagle 017, holding short of runway three seven, northbound departure."
Jericho Tower: "Soaring Eagle 017, continue on Bravo to hold short of runway three seven, northbound departure, Jericho Tower."
David: "Jericho Tower, continuing on Bravo, holding short of runway three seven, northbound departure, Soaring Eagle 017."
Jericho Tower: "Soaring Eagle 017, cleared for takeoff on runway three seven, climb runway heading to circuit altitude, fly straight out, northbound, turn left one thousand feet, Jericho Tower."

Before moving unto the take-off surface, David repeats the departure procedures back to the Tower.
David: "Jericho Tower, cleared for take-off on runway three seven, flying straight out, northbound, turning left at one thousand feet, Soaring Eagle 017."

David and Jonathan, undetected by radar due to their fighter jet's superior stealth capabilities, made their missile strikes upon their respectively assigned chemical/biological weapon storehouses, without any civilian casualties, due to the armories being in isolated areas. All the other Israeli, American, and allied fighter pilots flew to their respective strike sites as well, out of radar detection. This would be an atypical Israeli mission. Moving in, making the strikes, monitoring the situation within the region, and if all is determined

The Pathway: Color Picture Photo Edition

clear, move out, and return to base. No communication with the other friendly fighter planes meant not knowing the overall end result until everyone made it back to base. And as ordered, David and Jonathan stayed in the vicinity of the region to see if there would be any nuclear repercussions.

David: "Joshua, everything went as intended. No bandits in sight at this bearing, Soaring Eagle."

On board Jonathan's Lockheed Martin F-35 Lightning IV, studded with advanced sensors and computers like no other aircraft, which includes the Distributed Aperture System, or DAS, taking data from electro-optical and infrared sensors, running it through algorithms, he began getting relevant 3-D moving images on his super-helmet's visor referred to as a Helmet Mounted Display System (HMDS), providing Jonathan with advanced, unprecedented 360-degree situational awareness. The helmet projects live video feeds from various cameras around the F-35 Lightning IV, allowing the pilot to see the world that's surrounding his jet. The F-35 Lightning IV's computers can identify the location of threatening missiles, and even detect the infrared signature of a boosting missile. The F-35 and the F-22 Raptor also have the ability to provide ground-based missile interceptors and other platforms with the targeting data they need to reliably take out an ICBM. The F-35 that was once plagued with bugs was no more. In time, the F-35 became the feasible combat aircraft of choice, technically and financially. And Jonathan was one of the fighter pilots who faithfully hung in there with the F-35, just as much as David chose to remain true to the F-22 Raptor (raptor meaning, "bird of prey," such as an eagle).

And the bottom line to what Jonathan had deduced from all the data being compiled is that two Intercontinental Ballistic Missiles (ICBMs) had just been launched and deployed from their nuclear silos in their perimeter, moving at speeds measured in miles per second after lift-off, with a trajectory in the direction of Israel. Jonathan, then conveyed the information over the Link 16 tactical data exchange, an important feature that relays a simultaneous broadcast to all allies concerned, such as NORAD. Simultaneously, David and Jonathan were getting reads from allied, friendly jets and other members of the Israeli fleet that they had spotted launches of a number of nuclear weapons as well.

Jonathan: "Joshua, my HMDS spiked two SS-27s airborne. Repeat, the decoys have been identified and distinguished, and the empirical data is detecting two Topol-Ms airborne, trajectory toward Israel, Greased Lightning."

Joshua: "Roger, Lightning. Non-explosive, decoy dud rockets confirmed. You and Eagle take respective action to intercept the two Super Dupers in their mid-course phase, enabling your ABL (Airborne Laser), targeting data has been exchanged, Command and Control System is integrating sensory information for the BMDS (Ballistic Missile Defense System) components. Missiles are going off all over the place. Israel, American, and allied forces are moving in to intercept from the air and ground, Joshua."

Jonathan: "Wilko, Joshua. Lightning and Eagle taking our respective courses to intercept, enabling ABL, understood, Greased Lightning."

After all the tracking calculations were made, both David and Jonathan had their powerful, fiber lasers pointing right on their targets at optimum range.

The laser beam has stealth-like qualities in terms of sight and sound, traveling at the speed of light. And there was more than enough integrated laser energy and power to burn a hole through the middle of an ICBM, ultimately intercepting, derailing, and destroying both of the long-range enemy nuclear weapons, respectively by David and Jonathan. And since they had received orders in the Pre-Flight Briefing to destroy the missile while traveling in space, rather than in its boost phase, no harm would come to human life. The F-35 Lightning IV's capability of focusing laser defenses against Intercontinental Ballistic Missiles was being realized for the very first time in actual combat and actualized a whole new dynamic to the table of strategic warfare. At a high altitude there would be the benefit of thinner air enabling the lasers to operate at longer ranges and carry with it the advantage of encountering less atmospheric obstructions. Laser technology proved to be a cost-effective route to take, with a low cost per shot and not having the risk of running out of ammunition. It was the Pentagon's determination many years prior that satellite fired lasers were not nearly as reliable against nuclear missiles as a laser missile offense effectively executed from a fighter jet. The Missile Defense Agency had advocated air-launched, high powered, long-range laser weapons to destroy attacking nuclear armed Intercontinental Ballistic Missiles as they travel through space, not during the launch (boost phase). And it was the United States Air Force's Self-Protect High Energy Laser Demonstrator program, or SHiELD, that had planned laser weapons systems become standard for self-defense capabilities on fighter jets. This method became employed by the Israelis and the allies as well. And David, Jonathan, and all those protecting Israel demonstrated that quite courageously for the first time.

Upon contact with the Intercontinental Ballistic Missiles, the laser shots from David's F-22 Raptor and Jonathan's F-35 Lightning IV penetrated the metal of the rockets enough to result in a couple of extremely powerful explosions, eventually fading out with intense, shimmering colors of red, blue, purple, and yellow, bringing absolutely no harm to life on Earth.

David: "Joshua, the two Super-Dupers are closed for business, all is clear, Soaring Eagle."

Joshua: "Roger that, Soaring Eagle. You and Greased Lightning RTB, Joshua."

David: "Wilko, Joshua. Soaring Eagle 017 and Greased Lighting 007 RTB."

David: "Dangerous Fireworks Show, Lightning!"

Jonathan: "Yeah. Fourth of July came early this year, at its worst!"

David and Jonathan soared back to base, flying exceedingly fast in parallel, undetected by the radar of nations they were cruising over, and, therefore, not being required to make their intentions known in that particular territory, whether the country be friend or foe. It would not be until they got back to base when they would get a totally clear picture of how successful all the other friendly fighter jets were at intercepting the ICBMs that they had been up against.

Jericho Tower: "Soaring Eagle 017, Delta 15 on your recovery time, Jerico Tower."

David: "Jericho Tower, Delta 15 on recovery time, Soaring Eagle 017."

　　Both David and Jonathan had switched their radio frequencies from Joshua to Jericho Tower.

David: "Jericho Tower, radio frequency check, how do you read? Soaring Eagle 017."

Jericho Tower: "Soaring Eagle 017, read you loud and clear. Remain outside of Class D Airspace until traffic clears and you are further advised, orbit north to the Galilee Bridge, left turns, expecting a three-minute delay, and one orbit, ILS Approach, Jericho Tower."

David: "Jericho Tower, will remain outside of Class D Airspace until further advised, orbit north to the Galilee Bridge, left turns, expecting a three-minute delay, and one orbit, ILS Approach, Soaring Eagle 017."

Jericho Tower: "Soaring Eagle 017, altimeter three zero one four. You are cleared to land to left base on runway three two. You are number two. Follow Greased Lightning in, Jericho Tower."

David: "Jericho Tower, altimeter three zero one four, cleared to land to left base runway on three two, number two. The traffic ahead is in sight, Soaring Eagle 017."

Jericho Tower: "Soaring Eagle 017, wind one three zero at fifteen knots, cleared to land left on runway three two, Jericho Tower."

David: "Jericho Tower, wind one three zero at fifteen knots, cleared to land left on runway three two, Soaring Eagle 017."

Jericho Tower: "Soaring Eagle 017, exit on Alpha, contact Zechariah Ground at one two one decimal three, Jericho Tower."

David: "Jericho Tower, exiting on Alpha, switching to Zechariah Ground at one two one decimal three, Soaring Eagle."

David: "Zechariah Ground, this is Soaring Eagle 017, exiting on Alpha, requesting taxi to flying club."

Zechariah Ground: "Soaring Eagle 017, you are clear. Taxi Charlie, Bravo to flying club, Zechariah Ground."

David: "Zechariah Ground, taxiing Charlie, Bravo to flying club, Soaring Eagle 017."

The canopy to David's F-22 Raptor Fighter Jet was barely open before David could hear the deafening sound of all the overwhelming revelry among the men in the immediate area of the hangers. By the time David's feet hit the ground, he was surrounded by a league of his comrades, cheering to no end, with Jonathan out front, shaking David's hand as a confirmation of victory.

All the brave pilots who went on missions reported to the Debriefing Room to discover that every last fighter pilot assigned to make a strike on chemical weapon storage houses had succeeded.

It turned out that David, Jonathan, and most of the other fighter pilots had faced the danger of encountering and destroying Intercontinental Ballistic Missiles. And by the time they had gotten back to the base, everyone in Israel and around the entire globe knew about it. It turned out that every single friendly fighter pilot who went after airborne nuclear weapons successfully blew them out of the sky, without harm to anyone.

Just like that, the Battle of Gog and Magog was over. The Israelis, Americans, and other allies performed countermeasures on those adversaries who plotted against them before the enemy even knew what happened. And not only that, but the Israelis and their friends also managed to thwart the first Intercontinental Ballistic Missile attack ever launched against them or anyone else for that matter. And they did it with style and finesse on top of everything else.

The Israeli and American invasion force, in particular, had swept over the enemy territories and prevented unfriendly military forces from covering Israel like an overshadowing cloud. By the end of the mission, the hostile nation's plot to overthrow Israel was completely foiled, subdued, overthrown, and conquered. And the manner in which Israel had "nipped it in the bud" put fear in the hearts of those who dared to consider such an underhanded conspiracy again.

Israel's overpowering military strategy combined with the God of Israel's intervention and perfect timing of execution saved the day. The defiant nations proved to be no match for Israel's tactics. The God of Israel has made it perfectly clear that he is the one who ultimately protects and defends Israel at all costs. Overall, in every respect, the plot to overthrow Israel turned into a miserable failure. More than any time in human history, people all over the globe were keenly aware that extremists shouldn't take the chance of causing trouble for God's chosen people, the Israelis and their allies, without paying a dear price. And as a direct result of the Israeli army's efforts led by David, the borders of Israel had expanded tremendously. David is appreciated for his strengths. But even more than that, the Israeli people love David because he is a man who is so human: "All Israel and Judah loved David, because he went out and came in before them." I Samuel 18:16

Now that the dust has settled from the Battle of Gog and Magog, Israel has emerged as the major player on the political field and a dominant military force in the Middle East. The triumph over the adversaries of Israel, both large and small enemy nations, literally, made Israel's foes absolutely terrified to be foolish enough to ever attempt another coup d'etat again. This would serve to be the very victory that would be the ticket to open the door and take the opportunity of rebuilding the Temple of the God of Israel.

Yet what came with the end of the Battle of Gog and Magog was the harsh reminder that the Battle of Armageddon was still ahead. And the defeat of the Prince of Rosh, Gog, merely pointed to the fact that the false messiah was out there somewhere. And as horrible and horrific of an oppressor as Gog proved himself to be, the destruction and hurt that he inflicted would merely serve as a preview of the even worse catastrophe that lay ahead at the hands of the false messiah. The Prince of Rosh (Russia/Magog) would appear to be like a Boy Scout compared to the false messiah.

David went to Bathsheba's apartment after leaving the base. Bathsheba opened the door, looking like she had been crying for a week straight.

"David!!!" Bathsheba shrieked, as she lunged to hug him. "Is this your idea of maintaining a relationship, keeping secrets from me?"

"Bathsheba, I honestly wanted to tell you, but Israeli Command swore us all to secrecy." David explained.

Bathsheba looked up at David with such an understanding expression on her face, "You were meant to be a hero and a class act, David. And you're all mine!"

"Could you see your future with a guy like me, Bathsheba." David humbly asked. "I made a pitch to the angels hoping you would say, 'yes'"

"If that's a marriage proposal, David, I happily accept." Bathsheba graciously responded.

"Well, then, please allow me to seal it with this ring." David quickly responded. "You know the golden rule about proposing marriage to the woman of your dreams, don't you?"

"What's that, David," Bathsheba asked, simply dying to hear the answer from him.

"To never make the proposal without a ring." David affirmed.

"I am so happy that you complied to the golden rule, my Love." Bathsheba said. "It's the most beautiful ring I've ever seen!"

"Now, it's official. You're my fiancée. Would you like a large wedding?" David sincerely asked.

"We'd better. All of Israel is invited." Bathsheba responded with a glowing expression, as Shalom, the newly engaged couple's German Shepherd, happily wagged his tail observing David and Bathsheba's reunion.

As Bathsheba clung to David, the bride to be was uncontrollably sobbing tears of joy, because the special man in her life was safe.

The Pathway: Color Picture Photo Edition

CHAPTER THREE
THE MARRIAGE OF
DAVID AND BATHSHEBA

"It was Sunday at the beginning of August, and the auspicious day and time of David and Bathsheba's wedding had arrived. It was a beautiful day outside with a clear, blue sky. Jewish weddings are traditionally forbidden on the Sabbath and all Jewish holidays, and the married couple to be were strictly observing that standard. The joy of a Jewish wedding should not be allowed to be mixed, and, therefore, minimized by the celebration of a holiday.

But Tu B'Av is an exception to the Jewish rule. It is celebrated on Sunday as a holiday of love, and is a favorable day for weddings in Israel. In the early days of the Temple in the Hebrew Bible, Tu B'Av marked the beginning of the grape harvest, while the holiday of Yom Kippur marked the end of the grape harvest. On both occasions, the unmarried girls of Jerusalem dress in white clothing, and go out to the vineyards to dance. In modern times, Tu B'Av has become a very romantic Israeli day. It is said to be a perfect day for weddings, commitment ceremonies, renewal of vows, or proposals of marriage. It is a day for romance, explored through singing, dancing, the giving of flowers, and reading of the Hebrew Bible, especially the Book of the Song of Solomon.

And it would be on this fine Sunday in August, the very day that David and Bathsheba had planned their wedding, that the celebration of Tu B'Av would fall upon. Bathsheba told David that it was not a coincidence. The God of Israel would not have wanted it any other way. David could not have agreed with Bathsheba more. He was a man very much in love. And how appropriate it would be that their wedding would happen to fall on the traditional Israeli day of love.

The Great Synagogue of Jerusalem, Israel located at 56 King George Street in Jerusalem, is a building with architecture modeled in the style of the beloved Jewish Temple. It's inauguration poetically took place on Tu B'Av in 1982.

Dr. Samuel Goldstein, at David's personal request, is officiating the wedding, as a duly ordained officiant and acting cantor authorized to preside over the ceremony of a Jewish marriage. David and Bathsheba would not have had it any other way. Dr. Goldstein had already discussed proper protocol of the wedding and the traditions of the reception with David, Bathsheba, and the members of both sides of the family.

Head coverings are a common tradition at Jewish weddings, and David wore a white yamaka (yarmulke, kippot, kippah) with a blue Star of David on it, while Bathsheba wore a white lace veil and wedding gown with long arm sleeves. And all the men and women attending the ceremony respectively followed suit, by wearing head coverings.

With impressive flair, David, flanked by his father, Colonel Jesse Hartman, followed by Bathsheba's maid of honor and the bridesmaids, emerged through the entrance of the wedding chamber and approached an elaborately decorated chuppah (canopy), which represents the creation of a Jewish home and hospitality to the assembled guests. David positioned himself under the chuppah, next to Jonathan, his best man, with the groomsmen, TOP GUN Fighter Pilot buddies, standing in a formation.

The fathers and mothers of both David and Bathsheba also took their place under the chuppah, as well as certain other family members.

It was then that Bathsheba gloriously appeared and walked down the aisle as the processional music played to the lyrics of the most romantic, poetic Jewish wedding song of all, Erev Shel Shoshanim, translated in Hebrew to Evening of Roses, performed by a vocalist. It was the perfect love song to identify Bathsheba Rosenberg, soon to be Bathsheba Hartman, as the Rose of Sharon, which is depicted in Song of Solomon 2:1: "I am the Rose of Sharon."

Dr. Goldstein gave a congenial nod to both David and Bathsheba before rendering a most enthusiastic greeting to those attending and watching over satellite television:

"Shalom! Blessed are you, O, God of Israel, Ruler of the Universe. Blessed are the ones who gladden this couple, David and Bathsheba. Let there soon be heard the sound of this couple as one, that is, the sound of jubilance from the song-filled hearts of this chosen couple whom God has selected to be together for all of Israel to witness. For the God of Israel is now to be among you at the calling of your hearts. Rest assured that he is, indeed, acting on behalf of both of you. And we are blessed to witness that God has created joy and happiness for the bride and groom, Bathsheba and David. And we thank God with our deepest gratitude that we may rejoice with Bathsheba and David in their love, harmony, peace, gladness, companionship, and the mirth of their song, derived from the Song of Solomon. And so it is today, that all of Israel has been called to see the God of Israel's Spirit remain as he unites the spirits of Bathsheba and David. And these two will from this day forward take a journey together to where the two shall be as one. As it has always been from the very beginning of time, so it today, a woman derives her life from her man and in return gives it back again, resulting in the intangible, eternal fruit of everlasting love. The God of Israel, the creator of all things is the God of love, and it is his desire that we share love with one another. And Bathsheba and

David are here to attest to each other and to all those present here today that their utmost desire is share their love with one another, as they have chosen today to avail themselves to each other and face the world together for the rest of their lives. They both feel that they are not only marrying the right person, but they are also both willing to grow, more and more with each passing day, to be the right partner. Therefore, we are gathered here today to celebrate one of life's greatest moments, the joining of two hearts, lives, and spirits. In this ceremony today, we will all witness the union of David Hartman and Bathsheba Rosenberg in marriage."

THE ISRAELI WEDDING WINE BLESSING: Dr. Goldstein continued, "In this glass are the fruits of God, Humankind and Mother Earth. The years of our lives are like a cup of wine that is poured out for the sake of labor, honor, and love. Many days, David and Bathsheba, you will sit at the same table and eat and drink together. Many are the experiences you will share. As with a glass of wine, one of you may find it sweet, the other dry, or somehow different. Let the drink you share today serve as a reminder that although you may perceive things very differently, being right is never more important than being happy.

With this space that you give each other, always putting your commitment to love and honor one another first, your lives together will grow deeper, richer, and greatly satisfying, like a rare and fine wine. As the Song of Solomon states: "Blessed art thou, O, Lord God of Israel, the King of the Universe, who has created the fruit of the vine." You may now drink from this fountain of love, as a symbol of unity.

I am my beloved's, and my beloved is mine." Dr. Goldstein said to conclude the Wine Blessing.

"David, do you take Bathsheba to be your wife? Do you promise to love, cherish, protect, comfort, and keep her, whether it be in good fortune or adversity, and to seek with her a life that is hallowed by your faith in the God of Israel as long as you both shall live?" Dr. Goldstein dutifully inquired.

"I do." David sincerely responded.

"And do you, Bathsheba, take David to be you husband?" Dr. Goldstein continued. "Do you promise to love, cherish, support, and keep him, whether it be in good fortune or adversity, and to seek with him a life that is hallowed by your faith in the God of Israel as long as you both shall live?"

"I do." Bathsheba graciously responded.

At this point in the ceremony, Jonathan gave David a wedding ring. After David slipped the solid gold ring on Bathsheba's finger, with an inscription on the inside of the ring, saying, "Everlasting Peace Between Us, Bathsheba. Love, David" in Hebrew, he looked directly into her eyes, and said:

"I, David, take thee, Bathsheba, to be my wife, my partner in life and my one true love before the God of Israel and all of these witnesses as long as we both shall live. I promise to cherish you today, tomorrow, and forever. I will laugh with you and cry with you. I will be devoted to you on both the difficult and the easy days. I will be there with you to share your moments of joy, and I will be there for you to comfort you in your times of sorrow. Whatever life may bring our way, I will always be there for you. As I have given you my hand to hold, so too now do I give you my life to keep. Ever since our youth, you've been my voice of reason. All the memories we've shared together were meant to be. Behold, you are consecrated to me with this ring according to the law of Moses and Israel. Bathsheba, God knows my heart. It doesn't matter where I may have met you, or what period in history I may have known you, I would have fallen in love with you, and I would have pursued you to the ends of the Earth to see if there was any chance that you would be mine. Thou art all fair, my Love, there is no spot on thee. You are, indeed, the coveted Rose of Sharon. You and I were always meant to be together."

As Bathsheba slid a gold ring that she had for David on his finger, with an inscription which read: "We are one in the God of Israel" in Hebrew, she proceeded to say:

"I, Bathsheba, take thee, David, to be my husband. And before the God of Israel and all these witnesses who are present today, I promise to be true to thee as long as we both shall live and to share my life with you. I will honor you as my husband all my life. And I promise to raise our children according to the law of the God of Israel. I will not hesitate to stand beside you when all is well or in times of extreme adversity. And with the love that we have for each other and the intervention of God's love, I will care for you and honor you all the days of my life. I will devote my life to you, in support of our mutual purpose, to watch our children grow together, and in our allegiance to the nation of Israel. Just as much as the God of Israel is the Eternal One, you and I are one with each other in all respects. I am a hopeless romantic where you are concerned, David. My love for you is eternal. Behold, you are consecrated to me with this ring by the law of Moses and Israel. I am my beloved's, and my beloved is mine."

Both the ladies in the congregation and the ladies also viewing the wedding over television really got choked up over David and Bathsheba's exchange of wedding vows. There wasn't a dry eye in the synagogue.

"And now, David and Bathsheba will collectively rejoice in the Sheva Brachot, that is, the Seven Jewish Blessings." Dr. Goldstein indicated.

And David and Bathsheba proceeded to recite the Seven Blessings together:

"We praise you, our God of Israel, Ruler of the Universe, Creator of the fruit of the vine.

We praise you, our God of Israel, Ruler of the Universe, Creator of all things for your glory.

We praise you our God of Israel, Ruler of the Universe, Creator of man and woman.

We praise you, our God of Israel, Ruler of the Universe, who creates us to share with you in life's everlasting renewal.

We praise you, our God of Israel, who causes Zion to rejoice in her children's happy return.

We praise you, our God of Israel, who causes loving companions to rejoice. May these loving companions rejoice as your people have since the days of creation.

We praise you, Elohim, our God of Israel, Ruler of the Universe, Creator of joy and gladness, friends and lovers, love and kinship, peace and friendship. O, God, may there always be heard in the cities of Israel and in the streets of Jerusalem the songs of joy and happiness, the voice of loving couples, the shouts of young people celebrating, and the sounds of children at play. We praise you, Adonai our God, who causes lovers to rejoice together."

David and Bathsheba had concluded reciting the Seven Jewish Blessings.

"Now, David and Bathsheba," Dr. Goldstein interjected. "I ask that you both bow your heads in prayer. And I also ask that your guests here with us in the synagogue and all those who are viewing by satellite television bow your heads in reverence and silently pray that God will bless the home of David and Bathsheba. And also pray that together they will achieve their highest hopes."

There is a Short Pause

Closing Comments of Dr. Samuel Goldstein:

"To make their relationship work will take love. This is the core of your marriage vows and why you are here today. It will require trust, and to know in your hearts that you truly desire what is best for one another. It will take dedication, to remain open to each other --- and to learn and grow together. We, collectively, pray, David and Bathsheba, that you will both rise above every adversity and obstacle together and grasp all the goodness in life that is yours for the taking. You'll need faith to go forward together, without knowing exactly what the future holds. And it will take commitment to hold true to the journey you both have pledged to each other here today." Dr. Goldstein remarked.

Bathsheba: "For better or worse, right, David?"

David: "For better or worse, Bathsheba."

THE SHATTERING OF THE GLASS

"Now, ladies and gentlemen, we have arrived to the final episode of this ceremony, which, as you may know, is referred to as the shattering of the glass." Dr. Goldstein pointed out. "This old Israeli custom has many traditions, with many interpretations. At one time, it was meant to scare off demons that frequent celebrations. Today, the fragility of the glass reflects the many shattered hopes of having the Israeli Temple restored on the Temple Mount in Jerusalem. And of course, the restoration of the Temple is the greatest hope of both David and Bathsheba. And both the groom and the bride consider their vows to be an irrevocable act, just as permanent and final as the breaking of this glass is unchangeable. The glass is broken to protect this marriage with the implied prayer: "May your bond of love be as difficult to break, as it would be to put back together these pieces of glass."

Then, Dr. Goldstein gave David a confident, directive nod, indicating to go ahead and crush the glass.

It was at this moment that David, as traditionally done at Jewish weddings, took a wine glass, wrapped in a cloth napkin, placed it on the floor, brought his right foot down hard, and shattered the glass to smithereens, signifying a reference to the Israeli disappointment of the destruction of the 1st and 2nd Temples, with both incidents having occurred on the 9th day of the month of Av.

"Well done, David! And now, by the authority that has been invested in me by the God of Israel, the State of Israel, the Great Synagogue of Jerusalem, the Chief Rabbinate, the Rabbinical Courts, and all the people joined with me today in Israel and around the world, being confident that you both will make tenderness, gentleness, and kindness the highest of priorities to your marriage, always focusing on what is right between you, taking responsibility for the quality of your life together being marked with abundance and delight forever. The Lord bless you, and keep you. The Lord make his face shine upon you, and be gracious unto you. The Lord lift his countenance upon you, and give you peace. And now, David and Bathsheba Hartman, it is with great personal and collective joy that I now pronounce you man and wife. What God hath joined together let no man put asunder." Dr. Goldstein said to conclude the ceremony, with watered eyes and a cheerful countenance.

David, you may now officially kiss your bride." Dr. Goldstein gladly directed.

David tenderly took Bathsheba in his arms to the sheer exultation of all the onlookers and kissed her in a manner that brought down the house, with everyone in attendance continually yelling out, "Mazel Tov!!!" Many of the ladies present could not help but express their joy with tears.

"Ladies and gentlemen, may I joyfully present to you our newly married groom and bride. Hear, O, Israel, David and Bathsheba Hartman are one." Dr. Goldstein announced to Israel and the entire world.

The marriage of David and Bathsheba was the marriage of two Stars, two Hollywood Stars.

It was at this point when David and Bathsheba in a graceful manner, slipped away to be in seclusion. This is a Jewish wedding tradition known as yichud in Hebrew. They retreated to a designated room for a period of time after the ceremony to enjoy a quiet moment with each other, talk, partake of some food together, and enjoy each other's company alone before greeting everyone at the reception.

When the couple emerged from the room after some quality time, Jonathan and his girlfriend, Tamara Schreiber, were right there at the door of the room to greet them.

"That was the most beautiful wedding ceremony I have ever witnessed!" Tamara exclaimed.

Jonathan: "A Toast: To David and Bathsheba --- May your path together lead you to everlasting peace."

It was absolutely breathtaking to observe the newlyweds, David and Bathsheba, silhouetted on the dancefloor, suspended in time to Lionel Ritchie's romantic #1 hit song, "Truly," slow dancing in a soft embrace.

Soon, David and Bathsheba would emerge out the front doors of the synagogue, smiling, wearing much more casual, sporty attire, only to be enthusiastically bombarded by handfuls of rice as they made their way to a limousine. David and Bathsheba were to be whisked away to Ben Gurion International Airport in Jerusalem, in route to their Honeymoon destination for a romantic getaway.

The limousine was waiting for them with the back door open. The couple attempted to make their way, cowering beneath the rice thrown by the well-wishing crowd. David's jolly Uncle Joel yelled out, "And so it begins," followed by laughter from the multitude.

David and Bathsheba finally made it to the limousine, only to realize their chauffeur was none other than Jonathan, accompanied by Tamara.

"Well, the newlyweds did it quite gracefully, I'd say." Tamara exclaimed with delight. "You two sure managed to get the ladies crying."

"Congratulations, Mr. and Mrs. Hartman! I'll be your chauffer and personal escort to the airport. I'm sure you're well aware that you both are in good hands. I'm happy to report that your luggage is secure." Jonathan said as he pulled off. "And you will have security guards assigned closely to you, on the way to the plane, in the plane, to the hotel, and when you're out on the town in Paris. They will be keeping a close watch on you, considering David may not be too popular with certain rivals after the Battle of Gog and Magog. Of course, you couldn't have done it without a little help from myself."

"Jonathan, you are so arrogant." Tamara said, half-way serious and half-way teasing.

"Tamara, I can't wait for tomorrow, because I get more handsome every day." Jonathan replied, confirming Tamara's comment. "Besides, there are a lot of people out there now saying: 'Hey, maybe there is something to this biblical prophecy stuff.'"

"Oh! Do you see how he is?" Tamera exclaimed.

"Tamera, I've known how Jonathan is for a long time now. I couldn't change him. Perhaps, you'll have better luck." David remarked.

"I'll get some of that recklessness out of him. Other than that, he does have some redeeming qualities." Tamara replied.

They arrived at the Ben Gurion International Airport located near Tel Aviv, which also serves Jerusalem. Jonathan and Tamara escorted them inside, still in close view of the bodyguards assigned to David and Bathsheba. Finally, they made it to the boarding gate.

"I'll also be your chauffeur when you two get back, David." Jonathan said. "Nothing but first class, jiffy service for you and the blushing bride. You married the love of your life, and Tamera and I are very happy for you two, Buddy."

"Yes." Tamera reacted, with a glowing smile. "I'll never forget your wedding ceremony in my life!"

David firmly took Jonathan by his right hand and put his left hand on his best friend's upper arm.

"Thank you for everything, Jonathan and Tamera. You both have made this day very special. I am more than confident that it'll come back to you. Hold down the fort while I'm gone." David said with a smile. David epitomized the composure of newly married man half-dazed from being caught up in the moment.

Bathsheba and Tamara hugged.

"Nothing but the best for you and David, Bathsheba." Tamara said with envy of the day she would one day be married. "You two should see yourselves right now. You both look so beautiful together."

THE SHANGRI-LA HOTEL PARIS
PARIS, FRANCE

The Shangri-La, Paris Luxury Hotel has excellent amenities, and the characteristics of its interior are similar to that of a palace with a spiral staircase. It was the perfect honeymoon getaway. All the suites and rooms were colored in shades blue, white, and ecru, in keeping with European Empire aesthetics. All the suites had a separate living room, marble bathrooms, custom-made furniture, with crystal finishing. A flat-screen TV with in-house movie channels, an iPod dock, and the best computer money can buy, complete with the Internet and email were provided in every room. The wellness and leisure services included an indoor swimming pool, spa, and a fitness room bathed with plenty of natural daylight streaming in. The billiard room was accentuated by a prominent fireplace. And many of the most popular sights and the sounds of Paris, the City of Lights, were very close by.

The Pathway: Color Picture Photo Edition

THE SHANGRI-LA PARIS LUXURY HOTEL
THE HONEYMOON OF DAVID AND BATHSHEBA

THE SHANGRI-LA PARIS RESTAURANT

So, David and Bathsheba had arrived to a place where they could spend their Honeymoon in style. And they wasted little time kicking off the festivities in celebrating their union together once they arrived in Paris, France. They decided to dine at the magnificent Shangri-La Hotel Paris Restaurant because of its elaborate interior and unsurpassed service. The entire hotel was loaded with class, and that did not stop at the Shangri-La Paris Restaurant's doors.

The decoration of the porcelain-ceiling of the restaurant was super modern. A large cluster of crystal chandeliers hanging from the ceiling is the very first thing David and Bathsheba couldn't help but notice as they entered. Candelabrums were positioned on the walls in between the windows which were graced with fancy Grand Palace drapes. The uniquely patterned wooden floor was quite an impressive novelty to match all the décor. And the tables were perfectly dressed with tablecloths, napkins, and silverware.

The Pathway: Color Picture Photo Edition

While David and Bathsheba did absorb their surroundings while dining and chatting, they were eager to commence to a night on the town in Paris, and they were dressed quite formally for the occasion.

It was a glorious night in Paris, with a magic array of stars portrayed against a moonlit sky. David was escorting Bathsheba around the City of Lights with an old-fashioned gallantry that she found attractive. Bathsheba continually embraced all the memories between herself and David. And as new memories were being made on her Honeymoon night, Bathsheba thought how particularly handsome David looked that evening. There was an inner excitement about David that matched and complimented Bathsheba's dynamic.

David was dressed in a tuxedo, and Bathsheba looked dazzling in a black, chiffon evening gown. A professional photographer who captured weddings performed at the Shangti-La Paris Hotel was asked to follow David and Bathsheba around Paris, so they would be able to savor the cherished memories of their Honeymoon in the years to come via the photographs. And of course, David and Bathsheba had Israeli Security Police chaperoning them very close by, never letting the couple out of their sight.

"I feel like a Princess in a fairy tale." Bathsheba exclaimed. "I never knew it was possible for someone to be so happy. I have butterflies being with you right now, David. I'm a blushing bride."

"You are a princess, Bathsheba!" The happy groom responded.

It took all Bathsheba could do to keep from singing out loud, and she adored David for being her prince.

The Pathway: Color Picture Photo Edition

DAVID AND BATHSHEBA OUT ON THE TOWN IN PARIS

The Trocadero, the site of the Palais de Chaillot, is in an area of Paris found 1,650 feet away away from the Shangri-La Paris Hotel, and right across from the Eiffel Tower. It was first arranged for the 1867 World's Fair. Adolf Hitler, with the Eiffel Tower in the background, was photographed there during his tour of Paris in 1940. It was in the Palais de Chaillot that the United Nations General Assembly adopted the Universal Declaration of Human Rights in 1948. In April of 1952, it became the headquarters of NATO, but later moved to Porte Dauphine in Paris early in 1960, and then to Brussels, Belgium to stay in 1967. Today, the Trocadero houses a number of Museums. It is a popular tourist destination where people take pictures of the Eiffel Tower.

David and Bathsheba strolled along, hand in hand, viewing the sidewalk cafes near to the Eiffel Tower.

"It's rather Renaissance here in Paris, Bathsheba." David said, attempting to maintain clever conversation.

"Rather!" Bathsheba replied. "We ought to check out a nice museum."

"Your wish is my command, Bathsheba. I'll serve as your duly appointed tour guide. I just happen to know that the Paris Museum of Modern Art has many masterpieces that you would enjoy." David replied, having done his homework on the sites of Paris in an effort to keep the ball rolling to impress Bathsheba. "You're somewhat of a masterpiece yourself, Bathsheba."

"Somewhat?" Bathsheba responded, giving David a playful glare.

"Allow me to rephrase myself. You are, indeed, a masterpiece yourself, Bathsheba." David corrected himself quickly and humbly.

"Thank you, David. Going to a museum sounds romantic to me." Bathsheba responded.

"Perfect place for a couple of hopeless romantics like us to visit." David concurred.

"You'll never be any different than the man who I've always loved, David. I know that." Bathsheba confidently said.

"What higher praise!" David quipped.

"Who's your girl, David?" Bathsheba asked.

"You are, Bathsheba." David confirmed.

"I'll always be your girl." Bathsheba replied.

They visited the Paris Museum of Modern Art with great delight, commenting on the works of art, until it came time to return to the hotel.

David and Bathsheba made it back to their hotel room at the Shangri-La Paris Luxury Hotel.

They relaxed on the balcony of their hotel room, sipping French Bordeaux wine and taking in the stunning, unique view they had of the Eiffel Tower.

VIEW FROM DAVID AND BATHSHEBA'S
HOTEL SUITE BALCONY

David: "A toast to Bathsheba, my beautiful, glamorous wife. I am the man who accompanied you to Paris, and I've thoroughly enjoyed it."
Bathsheba: "Oh, David. You always manage to find all the most romantic lines."

They continued to enjoy the evening, until they went to sleep in their luxurious bedroom. Every aspect of the bedroom was in various shades of blue that were so soft and soothing that the long, eventful day simply lulled Bathsheba and David to sleep in each other's arms.

The meant-to-be couple were enjoying some well-deserved time with each other. And Paris, France was rapidly becoming a city that was just as special to them as Jerusalem, Israel. They would never forget any of the Honeymoon memories accumulated in Paris.

DAVID AND BATHSHEBA'S HONEYMOON BED-CHAMBER

The next morning, as David and Bathsheba were sitting at the table in the living room sharing a room service breakfast, the telephone rang.

"I can't imagine who that would be." David curiously said.

"Perhaps the President of France to wish us well." Bathsheba joked, getting a laugh from David.

"That would be most appropriate." David responded, as he slowly picked up the hotel phone receiver. "May I help you."

"David!" Jonathan loudly said in an excited tone of voice, practically coming though the phone. "I hate to disturb you and Bathsheba on your honeymoon, but I have an incredible newsflash for both of you that just couldn't wait!"

"Okay. It must be something big." David responded, wondering what in the world it could be.

"David, you recall in the First Book of Samuel how the people of Israel clamored for a king to look up to and fight their battles. The people wanted a king that they could see with their eyes."

"Sure." David confirmed.

"Well, the people in Israel right now in this modern day are desiring the exact same thing, and after everyone observed you become a hero and champion warrior during the Battle of Gog and Magog, and witnessed you and Bathsheba's wedding, they overwhelmingly want you and Bathsheba to be the king and queen of Israel. You and Bathsheba would become the first King and Queen of Israel since our nation split into the Kingdom of Judah and the Kingdom of Israel in 931 B.C., when King Solomon of the Hebrew Bible passed away. The entire nation has lit up with electrifying energy at the prospect of you two accepting the roles!" Jonathan explained. "All of Israel wants a monarchy. In our case, a monarchy of democracy."

"Whaaat?" David exclaimed. "Don't they think Bathsheba and I are somewhat young?"

"David, the people of Israel wouldn't care if you and Bathsheba were teenagers. Everyone is crazy about you two." Jonathan responded. "The people of Israel are convinced that you two are the perfect fit to be Israel's royal couple. They even want to build a palace near the Temple Mount for both of you to live and work in."

David finished his conversation with Jonathan, and set the receiver carefully on the phone, even slower than he had picked it up.

"Who was that, David?" Bathsheba enquired with a puzzled look on her face. "And why did you ask if we might be too young? Too young for what?"

"It was Jonathan." David informed. "He had some fascinating news for us."

"I hope it's good news." Bathsheba said, still having a perplexed expression.

"I'm glad you're sitting down, Bathsheba. Jonathan called to tell us that the people of Israel feel strongly about us becoming their king and queen." David said, like he was breaking it to her gently.

"Whaaat?" Bathsheba responded, exactly as David had.

COMMERCIAL FLIGHT 626 APPROACHING LOD, ISRAEL

The Israeli EL AL 737-900 Boeing Airliner from Paris to Ben Gurion International, twelve miles from Tel Aviv, carrying David and Bathsheba flew in gracefully, arriving right on time.

It absolutely appeared as though the Earth was shaking in Jerusalem, due to the collective throngs of people lined up at the airport and out in the streets on a parade route. David and Bathsheba were holding hands as they emerged from the cabin of the 737, only to be met by a tremendous outpouring of love from an enormous crowd who must have literally forced themselves close to where David and Bathsheba's plane had taxied in. If it had not been for all the positive energy that was being conveyed, one could have easily described the scene to be pandemonium. But the cheerfulness and well-wishing of the mob dispelled any hint of disorder, confusion, or negative uproar. The collective cheers of the Israelis was deafening. It was quite clear that the people were there to catch a glimpse of their brand-new king and queen. It was almost as if their presence there would provide insurance that David and Bathsheba would not decline the offer of becoming the chosen leaders of Israel's new monarchy of democracy.

No one in Israel, America, or any nation representing democracy in the world questioned anything about this spontaneous development. Even David and Bathsheba were so overcome with the affection being shown to them upon their return to Israel that they became very open to the idea themselves. In fact, it didn't look like they really had a chose in the matter. The people of Israel had emphatically decided, and they weren't going to have it any other way. They simply were not going to take "no" for an answer.

Jonathan and Tamara greeted David and Bathsheba at the bottom of the stairs of the airliner and escorted them to a limousine that was part of a motorcade outside the airport, with Jonathan once again as the designated driver. Their limousine was flanked by police motorcycles on all sides. And other limousines were lined up in front and way behind David and Bathsheba's limo, full of dignitaries representing Israel and other countries.

There was so much exhilaration in the air that David and Bathsheba had barely enough time to look at each other in astonishment of everything that was going on. But the two had quickly determined that there was some kind of divine intervention backing up the Israeli people's emphatic desire for a king and queen.

"Then all Israel gathered themselves to David unto Hebron, saying, 'Behold, we are thy bone and thy flesh. And moreover, in time past, even when Saul (The first king of Israel) was king, you were the one who led out and brought in Israel. And the Lord God of Israel said unto thee, Thou shalt feed my people, Israel, and thou shalt be ruler over my people, Israel.' Therefore, came all the Elders of Israel to the king to Hebron: And David made a Covenant with them in Hebron, according to the word of the Lord by Samuel, the Prophet. And David and all Israel went to Jerusalem."
I Chronicles 11:1-4

"Then, all the Elders of Israel gathered themselves together and came to Samuel. And they said unto him, 'Make us a king to judge us like all the nations. And Samuel prayed unto the Lord God of Israel. And the Lord said unto Samuel, 'Hearken unto the voice of the people in all that they say unto you, and show them the manner of king that shall reign over them. And Samuel told all the words of the Lord unto the people that asked of him a king. And the people of Israel said, 'We will have a king over us. That we also may be like all the nations. And that our king may judge us, and go out before us, and fight our battles. And the Lord said unto Samuel, 'Hearken unto their voice and make them a king." I Samuel 8:4-7, 9, 10, 19, 20, 22

THE KNESSET --- ISRAELI PARLIAMENT
KING DAVID'S INAUGURATION
TELEVISED SPEECH DELIVERED BY DAVID HARTMAN
IN FRONT OF THE KNESSET, THE ISRAELI PARLIAMENT,
IN JERUSALEM, ISRAEL ON THE SABBATH

AN ISRAELI MONARCHY OF DEMOCRACY ESTABLISHED

"Shabbat Shalom!" David Hartman opened to address the Israeli people and the world. "Bathsheba and I would both like to take this opportunity to express how honored we are that the wonderful people of Israel have desired to bestow upon us the celebrated roles of being the King and Queen of our great nation of Israel. This very moment in time is most reflective of the days in the Hebrew Bible, that is, in the eight chapter of the Book of First Samuel, when the Israeli people first expressed a desire to have a king to establish a Throne in Israel. The people of Israel wanted justice in the land. And they wanted the God of Israel to inaugurate a man who would be committed to fighting the battles for our nation's cause. And I would, at this time, like to acknowledge that I fully understand and appreciate the significance of establishing the Throne in Israel, because that is a direct reference to the necessity of the Temple being rebuilt in our modern day. I do fully realize the importance of maintaining fair justice in our community, and I just so happen to be the kind of man who is more than willing to fight any and all battles necessary to keeping peace sacred and preserved throughout the land of Israel. I will do everything in my power to secure and preserve lasting peace in Israel.

Due to the newly acquired oil fields that recently became Israel's property as spoils of the Gog and Magog War, I am happy to announce that we have the ability to enrich our country with two new air bases to reinforce Israel's protection. One air base will be named Golda Maier Israeli Air Force Base, to be built on the other side of the Temple Mount, from where Jerusalem Israeli Air Force Base is located, and the other military air base will be named Yitzhak Rabin Israeli Air Force Base, to be built in Tel Aviv. These new bases, of course, will operate in conjunction with Jerusalem Israeli Air Force Base.

Also, plans are in the making right now, with a priority emphasis, for construction of underground bomb shelters in Israel with the capacity to provide protection for all our citizens, and the ability to care for all of our people in need, in the midst of any wartime emergency and/or medical crisis.

While Israel does, indeed, possess the most advanced world-renowned missile defense system, made up of the Iron Dome, David's Sling and Arrow 3 technology, it must still be acknowledged that no defense system is 100% full proof. Therefore, further measures will be taken to keep our people safe, especially in regard to defensive capabilities of our fighter jets.

In 1951, according to Israeli civil defense law, all residential homes, commercial buildings, and industrial structures in Israel were required to have bomb shelters. However, there are people in Israel today who cannot afford a bomb shelter or keep it up to civil defense standards. We have a plan that will be implemented immediately to provide access to bomb shelters and upgrading of existing bomb shelters to every single citizen in Israel for protection of all of our families. We do not want anyone to not be safe in the event of an attack of war, especially of a chemical or nuclear nature. At the very least, people may make use of jointly shared shelters. And I am personally appointing inspectors who will ensure that all Israelis have enough provisions in their shelters. If necessary, we will reenforce currently existing bomb shelters with concrete and steel, in order to seal-proof buildings for protection against nuclear and biological weapons. And we will make sure that there is quick access to all of these shelters. All of this will be at no cost to any Israeli citizen. This will provide additional fortification for our public buildings, schools, and businesses as well. We're going to issue specialized masks to every single citizen in the nation of Israel. We are also providing more money to the Jewish National Fund, with the purpose of providing more rocket-proof places for children to play, including playgrounds with protective, concrete tunnels.

Israel's international, commercial airline, EL AL, is widely regarded as the safest airline in the world, especially in regard to flights departing from Israel's Ben Gurion Airport. Nevertheless, hijackings and subversive terrorist activities have taken place at our airports and other Ports of Call, and we fully intend on taking measures to keep any further hijackings from ever happening again. The number one priority is to keep the people of Israel safe!

Out of great consideration for my wife and myself, a palace is already under construction where the king and queen of Israel may reside and be productive for our country. This palace will be conveniently located directly across from the Temple Mount. I've seen the blueprints, the plans, and the pictures projecting the finished work, and I think we can all agree that this will be a palace that we will collectively, as a nation, be proud of, right down to the landscaping. This will, indeed, be Israel's White House. And there is great significance in the palace being directly adjacent to the prospective site of the third Israeli Temple.

We are all aware, as the people of the God of Israel, of the struggle there has been to not have a Temple in Jerusalem on the Temple Mount for so long. It has had a correlating impact upon our sovereignty as a State. Notwithstanding, the most glorious report that I can possibly make to my beloved country of Israel is that the rebuilding of the Temple is within reach. We no longer have false hope. All those who have opposed the idea of the Israeli Temple being rebuilt are now open to negotiate with us. There is nothing wrong with Israel that cannot be corrected by what is right with Israel. Being an Israeli is not what you do. It's what you are. It will be the Israelis who write the story of the next generation. On behalf of Bathsheba and myself, thank you. And may the God of Israel always bless you and keep you."

Needless to say, David's speech was met with great, enthusiastic applause. The content of the speech served as a confirmation that David and Bathsheba had accepted their invitation to become the king and queen of Israel. David delivered the speech in the protective, professional manner of a devoted leader.

The people of Israel were most enthusiastic and pleased to see their new king and queen settled in the new palace that was projected to be their residence. Many people had already seen the pictures of the palace and how it would look after being completely built. The excitement of having such a dynamic, charismatic couple in what would be referred to as "The Israeli White House" was absolutely electrifying to the entire nation of Israel and the entire world. And certainly, the cherry on top would be the promising prospect that the Temple, it appeared, would actually be rebuilt after all these years. Israel was being perceived by the outside world as a country that was living out its dream.

THE PALACE OF KING DAVID AND QUEEN BATHSHEBA, ALSO REFERRED TO AS "THE ISRAELI WHITE HOUSE"

King David and Queen Bathsheba were involved in the latter stage of the Israeli Palace's architectural plan. They decided upon a very modern exterior for the building, rather than one characterized by the antiquity of palaces in so many countries. Yet the inside of the palatial palace would be just as lavish, luxurious, and extravagant as any other palace. Queen Bathsheba dazzled everyone with her expert, natural flair as an Interior Decorator after the palace was built. David and Bathsheba were in a race to build a Jerusalem that was just as modern-looking as Tel Aviv, Israel. And the perfect place to start would be with the Palace of Israel. A palace had not been occupied by a King or Queen of Israel since the nation of Israel split into the Kingdom of Judah (the House of Judah to the South) and the Kingdom of Israel (the House of Israel to the North), after King Solomon's death in 931 B.C. Yet the God of Israel, in Jeremiah 33:17, promised that David would never fail to have a man sit on the Throne of Israel.

"And the men of Judah came, and they there anointed David king over the House of Judah." II Samuel 2:4

"Then came all the Tribes of Israel to David unto Hebron, and spoke, saying, 'The Lord said unto thee, Thou shalt feed my people, Israel, and thou shalt be a Captain over Israel.' So, all the Elders of Israel made a league with King David in Hebron before the Lord. "And they anointed David king over all Israel." II Samuel 5:1-3

"All these men of war came with a perfect heart to Hebron, to make David king over all Israel. And all the rest also of Israel were of one heart to make David king." I Chronicles 12:38

"And the Lord preserved David and Bathsheba whithersoever they went." II Samuel 8:14

"And all of Judah and Israel loved David, because he went out and came in before them." I Samuel 18:16

The new palace of King David and Queen Bathsheba would be located within very short distance from the Temple Mount, where the new Temple was hoped to be built. Its architecture was an exact duplicate of the palace built in the Hebrew Bible, with some very impressive, up-to-date embellishments.

At its worst, as exemplified by numerous autocratic regimes of the past, a monarchy can be synonymous with tyranny. Yet at its best, however, monarchy can, indeed, be seen as a repository of meaning. Kingship itself is a monarchy. Royalty, by its very nature, is the stuff of fairy tales, and fairy tales are a manifestation of myth, and myth is a creative attempt to account for reality. Underlying the concept of royalty is the principle of a dynasty. A royal marriage of a couple (a king and queen) along with the continuation of a family line romanticizes the concept of a monarchy and perpetuates the values that embody a dynasty as well. A monarchy, highlighted by a romantic king and queen couple (The King and Queen of Israel, David and Bathsheba), is the substance that dreams are made of.

Monarchies have functioned as a principle of duration and continuity. Both perseverance and perpetuality are important aspects of meaning. To the extent that it reflects endurance and unity, a monarchy can serve as a repository of meaning. And in order to maintain its status in the contemporary world, a monarchy must keep up with the times. The Kennedy Clan of the 20th century, which ushered John F. Kennedy into the White House as President of the United States, may certainly be regarded as a modern-day dynasty of its time.

David and Bathsheba gave the impression of two people destined to remain together for eternity. Their relationship with each other was meant to be, and they were both suspended in time. The electric, emotional connection they shared lightened up every room they entered, and no one in Israel could take their fixation and focus off the charismatic couple.

The Restored David had now become a warrior-king in the eyes of Israel. And once again, the nation of Israel had a king and queen that they could see with their eyes.

Yet even more than the Jews in the Hebrew Bible of the First Book of Samuel, the extremely adamant, current-day people of Israel, especially after the Battle of Gog and Magog, were considerably more demanding to have a king and queen. They insisted on having a monarchy of democracy, and they were willing to fight for it. They wanted a royal couple to unite them. They greatly desired a king and queen who would rule them in a manner that they trusted, and to fight their battles as effective leaders. And no other candidates presented any competition or came even close to carrying the qualifications of David and Bathsheba Hartman.

One of David's top priorities and first order of business as king would to build enough bomb shelters in Israel to accommodate the entire population of the country. David promised that these fortified shelters would be able to withstand the force of any nuclear attack. And David, with tenacious determination for his people, would, eventually, be successful in this endeavor.

The Israelis were ready to rebuild Solomon's Temple of the last days (the third Israeli Temple).

Upon David's arrival for the very first time to his office at the palace, he knew what his priority order of business would be. As he walked past his secretary's desk to get to his office, he said, "Naomi, please get in touch with Dr. Samuel Goldstein in the English Department at Harvard University. I need to speak with him as soon as possible."

"Right away, David." Naomi replied, having no problem addressing the king by his first name, knowing that David found it refreshing to keep things as casual as possible.

David dawdled around his new office, determining what books would be the most appropriate in his bookshelves. He looked over his calendar showing his agenda for the day. But most of all, glared out of his office window at the spectacular view of the Temple Mount, picturing how the new Temple would appear once it was built.

David's intercom buzzed.

"Yes, Naomi." David said.

"Dr. Goldstein on Line 1 for you, David." Naomi informed.

"Thank you very much, Naomi." David replied. "Dr. Goldstein, I'm very glad Naomi was able reach you so quickly after I requested it of her. You may have heard about some new developments that have taken place in Israel since the wedding."

"Oh, yes, indeed, I have, David." Dr. Goldstein joyfully responded. "You and Bathsheba have most appropriately, I must say, been duly designated as the King and Queen of Israel. I can't think of anything more glorious. And you and Bathsheba have just had a son, as predicted, named Solomon in the course of the palace being built. I've seen photographs of your handsome, curly-haired son. He looks like a wonderful lad. And not only that, but it appears that the path is clearing for the Temple to be rebuilt."

"Yes, that's right. I'm looking out of my office window right now from the palace envisioning how incredible the Temple will look from here after its construction. What a view it's going to be! And incredibly, Dr. Goldstein, Solomon already possesses a demeanor of royalty! Bathsheba and I have been greatly blessed." David exclaimed.

"It's all, obviously, part of a divine plan for many people, David. I couldn't be happier for you and Bathsheba." Dr. Goldstein replied.

The Restored David and Bathsheba, along with all of Israel, were overcome with joy over the birth of the Restored Solomon. And people adored Solomon as they watched him grow. It was quite reminiscent of the verse, I Chronicles 22:9, being revived in a new age: "Behold, a son shall be born unto you, who shall be a man of rest. And I will give him rest from all his enemies round about. For his name shall be Solomon, and I will give peace and quietness unto Israel in his days."

In the midst of Israel's confusion, uncertainty, and despair, an eternal ray of hope had shined into the world by the name of Solomon, a name that means "peace" in Hebrew. Solomon's presence would serve to counteract any and all of the world's hopelessness.

"Dr. Goldstein, the main reason for contacting you is that I was hoping that you would be part of this divine plan by considering to be my Chief Advisor here in Israel. I am well aware of how much you love your current position at Harvard, but your country is in great need of you right now. That's a given."

"You're too kind, David." Dr. Goldstein said. "I will do it for you, Bathsheba, Solomon, and all of Israel. I would, indeed, be proud to be one of your appointees."

"It means everything to me, Dr. Goldstein! If you only knew. It's meant to be." David responded in utter joy. "It's really meant to be."

CHAPTER FOUR
THE HYPNOTIC MOON

"The Sun shall be turned into darkness, and the Moon into blood, before the Great and Terrible Day of the Lord shall come."
Joel 2:31, Matthew 24: 29, 30, Revelation 6:12-17

While the Israeli triumph of the Battle of Gog and Magog was a decisive victory, initially bringing celebration in the streets of many parts of the world, at the same time, a diabolical dichotomy was taking place as well. A sinister entity of untold proportion, who had been lurking in the shadows, was sensing his cue. The unmistakable, unprecedented events taking place were making it loud and clear that it was just the right time to appear on the world stage. To the false messiah, these unfolding occurrences were an abundantly loud and clear signal that this was the very moment he was waiting for.

And as this instance was creeping ever, ever closer, a distinct aura of evil could be sensed in the air by just a few astute people. Yet these very few couldn't quite put their finger on exactly what was happening. This sinister force was more than determined to steal away Israel's joy of winning the Battle of Gog and Magog. This culprit wanted to impede the power entrusted by the people who crowned David and Bathsheba to become King and Queen of Israel. And this evil entity desired to stop the wheels of progress that were turning for Israel's monarchy of democracy. And the false messiah had a devious plot up his sleeve, of course, to corrupt the third Israeli Temple once it was built.

All that seemed to be going well was being overwhelmed by something horrible. Whatever this horrible force was, most everyone could not detect it outright. And it was completely permeating the atmosphere. You could cut it with a knife. For most people, it was quite unnoticeable and elusive. And nothing could be done to reverse the overall influence of this sensation of eerieness.

In the midst of what should have been a great time of happiness and celebration in the wake of David and Bathsheba becoming man and wife as well as the King and Queen of Israel, the Moon became a source of hypnosis, affecting people's emotions, thoughts, actions, and judgment, resulting with many lives around the world being helplessly manipulated like puppets being pulled by controlling strings. It was almost as if the usual slate of thought processes of a great deal of people were wiped clean, and replaced by a train of thought that derailed them from their normal walk of life. People wrestled in their sleep, tossing and turning, in a futile attempt to fight a battle of maintaining control of their personal fortitude and dignity. This subconscious resistance was absolutely in vain for most poor souls. But some were strong enough mentally to maintain at least some resemblance of their own life, with its normal routine and regular drill. While people's outward appearance did not seem altered, inside they were steadily becoming a collective population of the mindless living dead. And terrifying enough, even high ranking officials of every government, including that of Israel and the United States, were succumbing to this mesmerism. Politicians,

Heads of State, members of the United Nations, those in Parliament, leaders in the Israeli Knesset, the United States Joint Chiefs of Staff, the United States Congress, respectable military personel of every allegiance, leaders of various regimes including terrorist groups, all civilians of good and bad character, you name it, were all unsuspectedly affected by a bewitching Moon. What people were experiencing was no less than being in a trace, waking up with exaggerated, bloodshot eyes, and appearing to be in a drunken stupor in their waking hours. All of this came in the perfect timing of the false messiah's arrival, in that eager moment he had been so anxiously awaiting. Only a mere handful of people somehow managed to even partially keep their wits about them, but no one on the planet, other than Prince Solomon, could keep the scales from their eyes more than Dr. Samuel Goldstein, despite the fact that he had been horribly affected himself.

THE WAILING WALL IN JERUSALEM

In Israel, the feeling of helplessness to stop what was described as impending evil caused the Jews to flock in droves to seek answers in pray at the Western Wall, better known as the Wailing Wall. The people of Israel could sense that something was terribly amiss and horribly wrong. Many perceived the situation to be so hopeless that they came to the wall out of sheer terror. Desperate prayers to God seemed to either go unnoticed, or they were being intercepted and hindered by a harmful entity. The Hebrew verse, Jeremiah 33:3: "Call unto me, and I, the God of Israel, will answer thee and show thee great and mighty things," had lost all credibility in the face of whatever was happening. The mixed emotions created by the situation drove the Jews in abject fear to the Wailing Wall.

The Jews are aware and do believe that Satan does have the power to mesmerize even those of strong mental fortitude. They concede that the devil has the power to dazzle people through the magnetism of his deception. The Jews know all too well that Satan is capable of creating a craving for knowledge, delighting the ear with music and the eye with entrancing beauty. The devil knows how to exalt people to dizzy heights of worldly greatness and fame, yet tragically, with a high price to be paid. He knows how to even control people to the extent that they become suspecting and unsuspecting proponents of his dirty work.

Satan has battled Israel at every turn throughout her history, just waiting for the right moment to indwell the false messiah, who would be the devil's final masterpiece. And considering the world climate that more than adequately managed to create significant circumstances, Satan was well aware that his opportune moment had finally arrived. A new supremely evil world order was his first order of business, but certain pertinent phenomenons would need to take place first, namely, as priority, the building of the Tribulation Temple, otherwise known as Solomon's Temple rebuilt. The false messiah had his own personal motives to see the Temple rebuilt. The Jews intense desire for the construction of the new Israeli Temple was the false messish's ace in the hole.

It is not difficult, given the current international structure and the need for a persuasive authority figure to superficially guarantee a peaceful coexistence for the entire world. And this powerful, charismatic, contemporary world leader coming on the scene had a "gift" for tickling people's ears. The greatest seducers of all have one thing in common: They can use the natural needs and instincts of other people for their own desired ends. Seduction is the most callous form of exploitation, because it tricks the victim into becoming an unwitting accomplice. The false messiah would seemingly be the most incredible leader the world has ever known. The false messiah is only interested in controlling and destroying the lives of many, many innocent people. The false messiah's chief ambition is to track down anything and everything that's good and decent in our world to totally annihilate it. That is what the false messiah is all about.

THE FALSE MESSIAH
THE GREAT IMAGE/DANIEL 2:25-45
THE IMAGE OF THE BEAST/REVELATION 13:15

Things were becoming so precarious in the world, that certain world leaders were making statements like: "We do not want another committee. We have too many already. What we want is a man of sufficient stature to hold the allegiance of all the people, and to lift us out of the economic morass in which we are sinking. Send us such a man, and be he God or be he the devil, we will receive him."

It was Daniel, in the Book of Daniel in the Hebrew Bible (the Old Testament), who described the false messiah as being a stern-faced king, and a master of intrigue. He went on to state that the false messiah would be a contemptible person, who would invade the kingdom of Israel, when its people felt secure. Then, Daniel predicted that the false messiah, from the Temple (The Holy of Holies), would exalt himself above every god, and say unheard of things against the God of Israel. It is written that the false messiah will be successful until the time of his wrath is complete, for what has been determined must take place. Revelation 12:12-17

The false messiah will take advantage of the world's desperate search for meaning. He will quickly arise on the international scene promising to bring peace and prosperity to the entire globe. He will receive the support of the European community, equivalent to the new Roman Empire or the modern-day Babylon, and eventually control the planet. He will be like an oversized, gigantic octopus with an endless number of tentacles extending throughout the world, with people not even realizing the insurmountable danger they're in until it's too late.

The false messiah will rise to the occasion as he pleases, offering peace and prosperity. And yet while the person of the false messiah is going to make himself visible in human form, the spirit of the false messiah has already been in the world all along, that is, long enough to even know the Hebrew Bible (Old Testament) and the New Testament backward and forward.

"Beloved, believe not every spirit, but try the spirits to determine whether they are of God, because many false prophets are gone out into the world. And every sprit that does not confess Jesus Christ as

Lord is that of the Antichrist (The false messiah), whereof you have heard that it should come, and even now is it already in the world." I John 4:1, 3

"Shall we much rather be in subjection unto the Father of spirits and live?" Hebrews 12:9

"He that dwelleth in the secret place of the Most High (God) shall abide under the shadow of the Almighty." Psalm 91:1

The false messiah's desire is to finally arrive to the place of comfortably persecuting the Jews along with all proponents and advocates of Jesus Christ openly without fear of retaliation. Coming with it will be the nagging difficulty of fathoming that any single individual could possibly be as evil as the false messiah. The advent of his appearance will mark the very beginning of a world that is spiraling out of control like never before. His chief objective, once again to emphasize, will be to track down anything good in this world and utterly destroy it, kill it, and annihilate it. The false messiah's allies will perpetrate many, many atrocities without batting an eye of guilt or shame.

The trademark of the false messiah's cold regime will be to trample upon innocent people with calloused indifference. He will set the example of blasphemy against the God of Israel in every possible way imaginable. And he will leave a staggering amount of human carnage, physically, emotionally, spiritually, and otherwise in his wake. He will misconstrue, misalign, and manipulate innocent people's lives at every turn, intentionally, to make life unbearable, totally strangling and choking any and all joy out of human existence.

The false messiah, as "Big Brother on Earth," will create such harsh conditions in the world that people will be maliciously killing each other over the almighty dollar. The love of money will be the root of all evil like never before. I Timothy 6:10 Just as much as Pharaoh was a cruel taskmaster in Egypt to the children of Israel in the Hebrew Bible in the Book of Exodus, so too will the false messiah prove himself to be an ambitious, overbearing tyrant to the entire world in the last days.

The God of Israel has laid the ax to the root. Matthew 3:10 - In other words, that is extremely strong language to indicate that people will either have the Mark of the God of Israel upon them or be branded with the Mark of the Devil. It will be either one or the other. There is no in between. The official day has come when everyone must ultimately choose whom they will serve.
Joshua 24:15

A parable from the 2nd Book of Samuel is most applicable and descriptive of this situation:

"There were two men in one city. One was rich and the other was poor. The rich man had exceedingly many flocks of sheep and herds of cattle, while the poor man had nothing but one little ewe lamb, which he had bought and nourished up. The little lamb did eat the poor man's own food, drank from the poor man's cup, lay in the poor man's lap, and the grew up in the poor man's home with his children. One day, a traveler arrived at the rich man's home. The rich man did not want to take one of his own flock or herd to prepare a meal for his guest. Instead, the rich man took the poor man's only lamb to cook a meal for his visitor." II Samuel 12:2-4

From the parable of II Samuel 12:2-4, we may derive the rich man, in this analogy, to be the false messiah, who seeks to deprive all of God's people, depicted by the poor man. The false messiah will prove himself to be an expert at developing complex problems for the world that didn't exist in the first place. To sum it up, the false messiah will prove to be a genuine monster and a supreme creep. The false messiah is the epitome of deviance.

The fact that people will so easily follow someone like the false messiah is a statement that confirms that people will blindly follow anyone, like sheep without a shepherd. John 10:11-18. But Jesus said, "I am the good Shepherd. I know my sheep, and my sheep know me. My sheep hear my voice." But many people in the last days will not be attuned to the voice of Christ. They will be confused and oblivious, stubbornly and recklessly determined to adhere to their own inclinations.

Today, Israelis recite three times daily the words: "May it be thy will, O, Lord, that the Temple be speedily rebuilt in our own time." Many of these prayers are expressed by the Jews at the Western Wall (The Wailing Wall), which is all that remains of the second Jewish Temple.

"Be merciful, O, Lord our God, in thy great mercy, towards Israel, thy people, and towards Jerusalem, thy city, and towards Zion the abiding place of thy glory, and towards the Temple and thy Habitation, and towards the kingdom of the House of David, and your righteous Anointed One (Jesus Christ, the Israeli Messiah). Blessed art thou, O, Lord God of David, the builder of Jerusalem." (Jewish Prayer of Daily Ritual; Shemoneh Esrei, Benediction 14)

"The Lord God of Israel bless thee and keep thee. The Lord make his face shine upon thee and be gracious unto thee. The Lord lift up his countenance upon thee and give thee peace. And they shall put my name upon the children of Israel. And I will bless them." (Numbers 6:24-27; The Lord God of Israel; Yahweh, the Eternal One; A Hebrew Prayer)

But just as John, the Apostle, had prophesied in the Book of Revelation in the New Testament of the Holy Bible (Revelation 12:1, 2, 13), the Blessed Mary and Jesus Christ, Mary's son, will be the devil's (Red Dragon's) primary targets. And so the war to end all wars will begin, escalate, and furiously rage. David and Jonathan are to be anointed as the designated Witnesses of Jesus Christ in the last days. Revelation 11:3 the assistance of the other designated Witness of the last days, Jonathan (Revelation 11:3). Michael, the Archangel, and all the angels of God will collaborate with Jesus Christ and his saints in white robes to rise to the occasion. The strategic military and social conflicts on Earth are a direct reflection of the invisible war taking place in heaven.

"And there was a war in heaven. Michael and his angels fought against the dragon. And the dragon fought and his angels."
Revelation 12:7

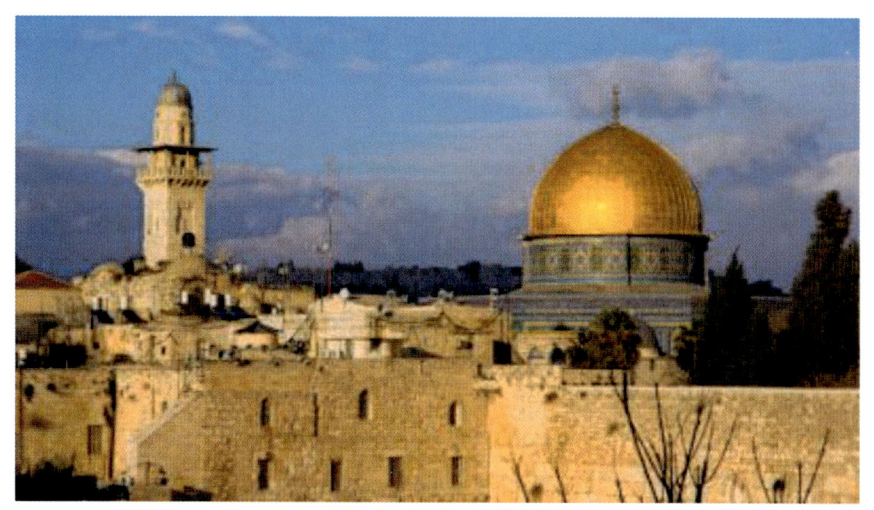

GROUND ZERO
THE TEMPLE MOUNT

"And the Lord said to David and to Solomon, his son, 'In this House, and in Jerusalem, which I have chosen, will I put my name forever.'" II Kings 21:7

The Israelis, who either live right in Israel or who come to visit Israel on pilgrimages, gather on the Temple Mount once a year, on the Ninth of Av, which is the day that the Jews commemorate the destruction of the First and Second Temples. The 9th of Av, "Tisha B'Av" in Hebrew, will fall on a day either in July or August on the Western (Gregorian) Calendar. It is a day of fasting and national mourning for the Jews, both in Israel and around the world.

To this day, since the Jewish Temple was destroyed by the Romans in 70 A.D., Israelis pray three times a day for the restoration of Solomon's Temple, that is, the third Israeli Temple, expected to be built by the Restored Solomon in the last days. To witness the building of Solomon's Temple in modern times would, certainly, be an incredible miracle.

"PRAY FOR THE PEACE OF JERUSALEM. THEY SHALL PROSPER WHO LOVE THEE." PSALM 122:6

Israel, a country which can be flown over by a jet in a matter of minutes and driven across by automobile lengthwise (north to south) in a mere five hours, should not be blamed for protecting herself from her surrounding enemies, whose only ambition by means of holy jihad is to drive the Israelis into the Mediterranean Sea. Many military strategists are convinced that Israel's forceful retaliations have spared the Jewish nation from potentially more devastating attacks.

One major understanding between Israel and the false messiah would be that the priesthood of the Tribe of Levi is to be reinstated. This will not be an option to the Jews, and the false messiah will be well aware of that fact. As an integral part of his overall plot, the false messiah will know that it's imperative to make this short-lived promise that the priesthood be restored once the third Israeli Temple has been built. The particular types of animal offerings and their significance, details of the priests' sacrificial performance of their duties and so forth are listed in the Book of Leviticus 1:1 through 7:38 (i.e., the burnt offerings). Aaron, Moses' brother, and his descendants were chosen to be God's priesthood. The vital function of the priests (especially the High Priest) in Temple (or Tabernacle) is central to Judaism. Participation on behalf of people in a Temple service includes the playing of music and singing. It is a joyous time. The Tribe of Levi is considered to be the most important Tribe among the Twelve Tribes of Israel, responsible for the spiritual leadership of the Jews. Some may say that animal sacrificing became obsolete when the Israeli Messiah (the Lamb of God and the Great High Priest – John 1:29 – Hebrews 4:14, 15) was "cut off" (Daniel 9:26), but that is simply incorrect. If anything, the reinstatement of the Israeli priesthood, with sacrificing of animals, points directly to Christ and honors him. The restoration of the Temple to the Israelis means that the performances of the priests of the Tribe of Levi are FULLY reinstated. So, for the false messiah to blaspheme, desecrate, and defile anything so sacred to Jews as the priesthood of the Tribe of Levi, the Temple, the Holy of Holies, the Ark of the Covenant, and anything to do with the performance of offering sacrifices to God is a mockery beyond belief. In the last days, it is predicted quite clearly in the Hebrew Bible (the Old Testament) that the false messiah will perpetrate such an atrocity (Daniel 7:25). This ultimate wrongdoing is labeled by Daniel, the Hebrew Prophet, and the Israeli Messiah, Jesus (Matthew 24:15, 16), as the Abomination of Desolation (Daniel 9:24-27). It will take place in the Great Tribulation, which is the last half of the Seven Year Tribulation. Jesus Christ is the Great High Priest after the order of Melchisedec. And Jesus abides as the Great High Priest forever. There is no disputing this eternal fact. Genesis 14:18-20, Hebrews 6:21, Hebrews 7:1-3, 14-17, 21-27, Hebrews 9:2-8, 11-15, 22-28

While it is predicted and expected that the false messiah will appear to bring about successful negotiations between the Israelis and the Muslims (through his empty promises), to make it possible for the Temple to become rebuilt on the Temple Mount, the truth of the matter is that it is the presence of David's son, Solomon, in the world alone that ensures that Solomon's Temple will be rebuilt. Should Solomon have never been born, there would never be a Temple rebuilt no matter what. So, while the false messiah may think he is duping the Israelis, in direct proportion, he is unwittingly being duped by the God of Israel. So it is written. So shall it be done.

FALSE MESSIAH'S HYPNOTIC EFFECT UPON THE WORLD

THE CONFERENCE ROOM
OF DAVID AND BATHSHEBA'S PALACE

David had chosen to hold an emergency conference meeting, with his top military men and trusted advisors, including Dr. Goldstein, surrounding the table. Many vital issues had to be covered in discussion of making it possible for the Temple to stand once again. David saved the most important topic toward the end before concluding the meeting: Someone to serve as the Chief Diplomat in working with the Muslim nations surrounding Israel. The Arabs were vulnerable after the Battle of Gog and Magog, and this would be a golden opportunity to seize the moment and persuade them to allow the Israeli Temple to be rebuilt. Colonel Ichabod Cohen, highly esteemed, retired, and known by all to be a Jewish Israeli Air Force war hero, was the quickest to respond.

David relinquished the floor to Colonel Cohen.

"Thank you, Your Royal Highness, Commander Hartman," Colonel Cohen said in a respectful tone of voice. "I do feel that I would qualify most appropriately for this position, due to the fact I have a good deal of experience in diplomat relations, and I am quite certain that I would be especially effective in this capacity while our overwhelming victory of the Battle of Gog and Magog is fresh in the minds of our neighboring adversaries."

"There's not a man or woman at this table who is not familiar with Colonel Cohen's record." General Aaron Becher promptly responded. "I make a motion that we have a vote for Colonel Cohen to serve in this diplomatic position of standing in the gap for Israel."

"I second that motion," Colonel Jacob Bergen concurred.

"We have a second motion," David said. "Therefore, we shall put it to a vote. All those in favor of Colonel Cohen working on behalf of Israel in this all-important diplomatic position, say, 'Aye.'"

Everyone at the table with the exception of Dr. Goldstein raised their hand.

"The Ayes have it, for the most part." David said. "But it appears, Dr. Goldstein, that you have an objection or a reservation, keeping this vote from being totally unanimous. I would like to think everyone's in agreement on this important matter."

Dr. Goldstein had a mysteriously blank expression on his face. After about five to seven seconds, he finally mumbled in a voice that was mostly inaudible, "There's something just not right about this."

"I couldn't quite hear you, Dr. Goldstein." David said. "Would you like to express an objection?"

Colonel Cohen firmly stared at Dr. Goldstein with intense focus, as the two men looked directly at each other from across the conference table.

Then, Dr. Goldstein reversed his disposition, sat up higher in his chair, raised his hand, looked at David, and slowly said in an unsteady manner: "No, no. I do not have an objection. I would like to make the vote unanimous," almost sounding as if he was forcing himself to say the words with a gun to his head.

"Therefore, the vote is unanimous." David confirmed. "Colonel Cohen. We would all like to congratulate you on being selected as our Diplomatic Ambassador in this pivotal situation."

"Your Highness, if you please. There is a request that I would like to make of you." Colonel Cohen interjected. "As you may know, my lineage as an Israeli is of the Tribe of Levi, our priestly tribe. While I am aware that a computer data base list exists to provide a complete compilation of many Jews around the world, whose heritage indicates that they are descendants of our Israeli priestly tribe, I would like to request, should I be successful in my efforts to persuade the Muslims not to allow any hindrance in the rebuilding of the Temple, that you would allow me to serve as High Priest in the Temple afterwards. I know you're aware that Cohen is a very common last name for someone from the priestly Tribe of Levi. And I can assure you, based on my knowledge and background, that I would serve the people of Israel well in this function. Of course, it would be a tremendous honor for any descendant of the Tribe of Levi to be delegated as High Priest in Israel, after service in the Temple has not been rendered since the destruction of our second Temple in 70 A.D. I feel confident that I would excel in an exemplary manner in this capacity."

"Colonel Cohen," David said, "I have the authority to appoint the new High Priest on my own, and I can assure you that if you are instrumental in successfully getting the Temple rebuilt, I will, indeed, appoint you to the position of High Priest."

"Should that be the case, your Highness, then, I will be more honored than Aaron, the brother of Moses, to be our High Priest. Israel's first High Priest, Aaron, could not possibly have felt more flattered than I would be."

No other statement could have possibly given Ichabod Cohen more credibility in King David's Conference Room with all the dignitaries present than the affirmation he had just rendered about being more honored than Aaron, the first designated High Priest of Israel.

Yet it had all occurred just a little too fast, to virtually no one's detection.

And Colonel Cohen, a veritable silver-tongued devil, was successful and masterful in his diplomacy with the hostile nations, and a pact of peace was made. The rebuilding of the Israeli Temple on the Temple Mount was actually in close reach. On the surface, it appeared that Ichabod Cohen was the one who skillfully manipulated the Muslims like an entertainer on stage controlling the audience. But in total actuality, it was Solomon's presence in the world that had struck once again.

"Colonel Cohen received rave reviews in the media, repeating the statement that the colonel had made to King David in the king's conference room top priority meeting, "I am more honored than Aaron, the brother of Moses, to be the High Priest of Israel."

Yet in all actuality, it was Solomon, perhaps the only one on Earth totally unaffected by the hypnotic Moon, who was used by Almighty God to see the 3rd Israeli Temple constructed. Young Solomon, based on his complete confidence in the Lord, was wise keeping many secrets to himself. Solomon, like his father, had great fortitude, and he was able to handle keeping all these valuable secrets in his heart.

And so, Solomon's Temple was rebuilt. No expense was spared in the construction of this glorious tribute to Israel's independence and sovereignty. David saw to it that the Temple was designed in a fashion much like the original Solomon's Temple of the Hebrew

Bible, yet larger and including modern specifications. The vast majority of people who were once aware that the rebuilding of Israeli Temple would mark the beginning of the Seven Year Tribulation, according to the ninth chapter of the Book of Daniel, were now oblivious to the fact, by the influence of the hypnotic Moon. The memory of an upcoming Seven Year Tribulation had been wiped blank like a clean slate.

So far as the Temple being built, the false messiah was just as thrilled as anyone else, because he was counting on the Temple one day serving as his headquarters where he intended to carry out his agenda. The Israeli Temple would be the very place where he would blaspheme the God of Israel, also according to the Book of Daniel.

Prince Solomon was well aware that the Hebrew meaning of his name was "Peace/Shalom." And he keenly understood and executed the gifts that God had imparted to him for the benefit of Israel.

The Restored Solomon is an extremely clever, young man, who never questions his calling, especially after all that he had learned from his mother and father. Whether or not people were cognizant of the fact that Solomon had a special purpose, the impact of this young man's power, comfort, and encouragement were having its way.

"Also, Solomon sat on the Throne of the kingdom."
(I Kings 1:46)

"And behold, I purposed to build a House unto the name of the Lord my God, as the Lord spoke unto David, my father, saying, 'Your son, whom I will set upon thy Throne, he shall build a House unto my name." King Solomon - I Kings 5:5

"So, Solomon and all the children of Israel dedicated the House of the Lord God of Israel." I Kings 8:63

The toning down of the enemy threat to Israel, after the Battle of Gog and Magog, just prior to the Seven Year Tribulation, provided enough daylight to rebuild the Jewish Temple, Solomon's Temple, on the site of the Temple Mount in Jerusalem. The Temple Mount underwent a thorough sanctification process, that is, cleansing ritual, performed by priests of the Israeli Tribe of Levi. And then and only then, the long-awaited 3rd Israeli Temple was built. Solomon's

Temple rebuilt was the 3rd earthly Israeli Temple. The display of power that the God of Israel has shown to destroy Israel's foes in the Battle of Gog and Magog allowed for the Temple to be built in its rightful place, on the sacred Temple Mount. The only one rebellious enough now to stand up to the Israelis would be the prophesied false messiah.

The outcome of the Battle of Gog and Magog, to all outward appearances, contributed to the resulting, manifested peace, as the opposing nations are forced to reckon with the divine protection uniquely afforded to Israel (and her allies) by the God of Israel. At this point, Israel's enemies were aware that there are serious consequences of annihilation for any nation that goes against Israel. Israel's military and civilian disposition after this particular war is one of confidence. All of Israel's enemies (the defiant nations) had been subdued and brought to honor the God of Israel (Yahweh, the Eternal One). Yahweh has demonstrated himself in an overwhelming, supernatural display of power on behalf of the Israelis. But when the false messiah appears on the scene, posing as the true Israeli Messiah, many Israelis, unfortunately, will fall into a snare. The restoration of the State of Israel in 1948, secured through military strength, was confused by a number of Israelis to be the Restoration of the Throne of David (Isaiah 9:6, 7), which can only be brought about by the power of God's Spirit (Zechariah 4:6). Genuine everlasting and irreversible peace will be the distinguishing characteristic of the Millennial Kingdom. (Isaiah 2:4; Isaiah 9:7; Isaiah 11:6-9; Micah 5:4, 5) The everlasting Covenant that God has promised for Israel in the Millennial Kingdom is a Covenant of abiding peace. The symbol for the peace that God has promised will be his presence (The Shekinah Glory of God), established in the Millennial Temple on an eternal basis. Through the false messiah's deception, since these conditions would appear to be fulfilling and meeting the requirements of the restoration expectations of the Hebrew Prophets of the Hebrew Bible, many Jews will be duped into believing that the Era of Redemption has finally arrived. The timing of the appearance of the false messiah at the end of the Battle of Gog and Magog (the beginning of the Seven Year Tribulation) will be no coincidence. Yet before Israel receives the Restoration Temple (The Millennial Temple), which is promised in Ezekiel Chapter 37:1-7, 9-14, 21, 22, 24-28 (under the command of the Israeli Messiah, with the Restored David, having Yahweh's hand upon him, blazing the way) and revealed in blueprint form in Ezekiel chapters 40-48, the world must inevitably witness the Seven Year Tribulation first.

And just prior to the third Temple being rebuilt, another child was welcomed into the royal family. David and Bathsheba became the proud parents of a bouncing, baby girl, who they chose to name Charity. The name Charity is synonymous with Love. And that's exactly what this little girl embodied and represented to all of the people of Israel: Love.

CHAPTER FIVE
SOLOMON'S TEMPLE REBUILT

PRINCE SOLOMON

"Behold, a son shall be born to thee (David and Bathsheba), who shall be a man of rest. And I will give him rest from all his enemies round about. For his name shall be Solomon, and I will give peace and quietness unto Israel in his days. He shall build a house for my name. And I will establish the Throne of his kingdom over Israel forever." I Chronicles 22:9, 10

"Then, Solomon began to build the House of the Lord God of Israel I Jerusalem at Mount Moriah where the Lord appeared unto David, his father, in the place that David had prepared in the threshingfloor of Ornan, the Jebusite." II Chronicles 3:3

"Thus, all the work that Solomon made for the House of the Lord was finished." II Chronicles 5;1-14, II Chronicles 6:1-21, II Chronicles 7:1-18, I Kings 7:48-51, I Kings 8:1-27, Acts 7:47

The hypnotic Moon was undeniably instrumental in causing much deception among the human beings of Earth. But the God of Israel somehow overruled that deception, leaving the false messiah in an eclipse of that hypnotic Moon.

All of God's people were given his personal, indelible, permanent mark of ownership, and it was secure upon them. Revelation 22:3, 4 - And it had always been in the heart of the Israeli Messiah that David's son, Solomon, was intended to be the moving force in the world to make it possible for Solomon's Temple to be rebuilt.

The Hebrew name for Solomon's Temple is "Beit HaMikdash" which means: The Holy House. The Temple is also referred to, in the Hebrew Bible, as "Beit Adonai" which means: The House of God.

"So, Solomon built the House of the Lord God of Israel, and he finished it." I Kings 6:14 ------ SOLOMON'S TEMPLE REBUILT

The rebuilding of the Israeli Temple in Jerusalem, Israel on the very site of the Temple Mount (Mount Moriah) stirred up more adulation and wonder in Israel than any and all momentous events put together that had ever taken place in the nation's history.

And yet, in the midst of all the pomp, pageantry, ceremonial splendor, and rapture of the moment, the distraction of the hypnotic Moon intensified and was still much in control of the entire world.

After the Battle of Gog and Magog, which commanded utmost respect for Israel's military from their enemies and everyone worldwide, Colonel Ichabod Cohen had appeared to play a critical role in negotiating with the Arabs and others to pave the way for the Temple to be rebuilt. And for this, Colonel Cohen was esteemed greatly as a hero, with his strong, faithful supporters giving him all the credit. In return, as promised by King David, Cohen was entrusted to the office of High Priest of Israel.

With the Tribe of Levi and the priesthood being reinstated, this gave Cohen tremendous power over the people of Israel. The majority of Israel considered the Tribe of Levi to be the most important of the Twelve Tribes, directing the spiritual leadership of the nation, especially after being dormant in the Temple since 70 A.D. Ichabod Cohen and the priests performed all the ritual service that was required on them in the Temple. And the expected manifestation of results from the spiritual service rendered in the new Temple would be the absolute, unprecedented focus of every Jew in Israel and around the world from here on out. The Israelis would never allow themselves to be deprived of this luxury again. Too many painful lessons in history had been learned by the Jewish people, especially the Holocaust. So, people, at the very least, were going to be quite curious how the first High Priest, after so many years, would be handling his position. Cohen's every move would be followed, not only by those he served with, but also by the media. And the way he conducted himself would be conveyed over international television. This elevated Colonel Ichabod Cohen to celebrity status. People were dazzled by the reinstated Israeli priesthood.

So, the nation of Israel now had a new king and queen, a rebuilt Temple, a priesthood, and a euphoric people. One could possibly say, "All is well." II Kings 5:22, II Samuel 18:28

It was a perfectly beautiful, clear-sky day, with a mixture of a cool breeze and chirping birds. There wasn't a cloud in the blue yonder. It was an outstanding day to dedicate the third earthly Israeli Temple, and by the Queen of Israel no less. And as queens go, Queen Bathsheba was a classy, sophisticated, glamourous queen, and all of Israel loved her.

The very name of "Solomon," by definition, does mean, "Peace." And while it may have seemed to evade everyone that the presence of this young boy in the world contributed mostly to the Temple being rebuilt, the fact was not elusive to Solomon himself. He was a gifted, highly intelligent young man, and he loved the God of Israel with all his heart, as well as his parents. Solomon was quite capable of being introspective. For his age, he thought in very realistic terms. His mother reenforced to Solomon that his prevalent influence would affect all the world. Solomon's essential nature was very gentle. He is pure as the driven snow. Solomon had a way of making his presence known throughout all of Israel. Many world events would pivot upon Solomon's influence. And just as much as Solomon's presence in the Hebrew Bible brought rest to Israel from all her enemies, the very same super phenomenon would take place thanks to the Restored Solomon of the last days, yet on a much more paramount, high-drama scale.

The inevitable rebuilding of Solomon's Temple is based upon the prophecies in the Hebrew Bible(Old Testament) and the New Testament and patterned after the Temple of God in Heaven. Within the Temple is a room referred to as the Holy of Holies, also known as the Most Holy Place and Kodesh Hakodashim in Hebrew. This is where the Ark of the Covenant has been designated to rest. The Holy of Holies is also where the High Priest is allowed to enter once a year on Yom Kippur, the Day of Atonement, to atone for the sins of the people of Israel. But King David had chosen for now to not allow the Ark to be brought into the Temple, to the great disappointment of the new High Priest, Colonel Ichabod Cohen. David justified this action by stating that the priests who served in the second Temple did manage to function without the Ark in place. Nevertheless, Ichabod Cohen felt deprived not having the Ark at his disposal.

And now it was the moment that the Jews had been waiting for so long, since the 2nd Israeli Temple on Earth had been destroyed by the Romans in 70 A.D., with the exception of the Western Wall. A powerful spirit of elation and exhilaration possessed all the Jews, along with every, single last person who loved Israel and what she stood for. The glorious time had finally arrived to dedicate the third Temple to the God of Israel.

Everyone assumed that King David would be the obvious person to render the dedication speech. But David had other plans. He felt that the speech would require a very sensitive expression, that is, a woman's touch. And who would be better qualified to successfully carry out that particular assignment than his lovable, caring wife, Queen Bathsheba?

It was standing room only all around the Temple of the living God that day. All of Israel's leading dignitaries stood on the platform, waving to the massive crowd present and those watching by television around the world. There were many who could not believe their eyes, as they observed the Jews reveling in so much joy. The celebration delivered all the pomp and pageantry that one would expect from a climatic, unprecedented royal event. Certainly, the God of Israel was looking down upon the city of Jerusalem on this glorious day.

King David, Queen Bathsheba, young Prince Solomon, and Princess Charity were, of course, positioned on the platform close to the podium, alongside all the other dignitaries. As David approached the microphone to speak, there were people in the assembled multitude literally yelling out, "Long live King David!"

"It's impossible to not be overwhelmed with the momentum of this grand, unprecedented occasion." David said to open his introduction of Bathsheba's Dedication Speech. "We, as a people, have, at this glorious moment, reached a crossroads of immeasurable proportion, the dedication of our 3rd Israeli Temple.

We are collectively witnessing an event that will inevitably lead us all to everlasting peace."

The reaction of the mass of people to David's words was absolutely electrifying. David had no chose but to pause for a moment until the exuberance subsided somewhat.

"Today, we, the nation of Israel, stand united with our ancestors to include Abraham, Isaac, and Jacob at this juncture to lead Israel to victory. It is on this very day that there is the total assurance that we as a people will advance to the Eternal Promised Land that the God of Israel has prepared for us. And now, with the building of the Temple in our time, we have undeniable evidence today that God's promise has come to pass. Ladies and gentlemen, the third Israeli Temple has officially been built in dramatic fashion, and we are all here together with the stark realization of the significance of what is nothing less than a glorious miracle. Israel's sovereignty has been secured. We are all assembled as one here today to collectively dedicate this masterpiece to the God of Israel. The light of this beacon will shine throughout the entire world indicating that the Millennial Temple is soon to become a reality.

It was King Solomon in 959 B.C. who appropriately dedicated the first Jewish Temple on Earth. Today, the honor has been bestowed upon my wife, Bathsheba, your devoted queen, and the doting mother of Prince Solomon and Princess Charity. She is my better half, and she is the person who brings radiance to the Palace of Israel. To know her is to love her. So, without any further ado, may I present Israel's First Lady in our hearts, Queen Bathsheba Hartman."

The crowd burst out with exuberant joy as Bathsheba approached the podium. It took longer for the people to simmer down from welcoming Bathsheba than it took when they were reacting to David. The Queen of Israel was the Star of the show. At long last, the accolades from the crowd toned down enough to make it possible for Bathsheba to speak.

"Thank you." Bathsheba responded to the jubilant crowd. "Thank you so much, and God bless you. Words are limited to express just how happy we are in Israel today. Our hearts and hands are joined together as one, and we have every reason now to be optimistic concerning our future. Our Temple has been rebuilt, and our national sovereignty has been restored. Once again, our God has a dwelling place on Earth. It was Israel's fourth Prime Minister, Golda Meir, who said: 'I never did anything alone. Whatever was accomplished in our country has been accomplished collectively.'

We can all take credit today for the presence of this wonderful monument before us which represents our strong, abiding heritage. In 1948, under horrible duress, Israel was formed as a nation, and now, the realization of the Temple being present in our midst, to fill the void that existed far too long, signifies loud and clear that nothing will prevent the complete restoration of our people in the land. For far too many years, right here at the Wailing Walling, with countless tears shed, the earnest Hebrew Prayer of the Israeli people has been: "May the Lord establish his kingdom in our lifetime, in our days." And today, by way of the Temple that we see before us, the Lord has honored our prayers and lamentations, and confirmed that he will bring this actuality to pass, as he promised that he would. This supreme hope of the Israeli people is finally being realized today."

Everyone spontaneously broke out with revelry in response to Bathsheba's dynamic oration. It was all too apparent that the people of Israel loved their queen. All of Israel was delirious about Queen Bathsheba, the First Lady of the Jewish nation. Bathsheba epitomized all the charm and elegance of Jacqueline Bouvier Kennedy, America's First Lady. And Bathsheba always managed to steal the spotlight away from David, just as much as Jackie commanded the spotlight from John F. Kennedy.

"In our travels, David and I have been allowed to visit many places around the world. And my main observation has been that the happiest children I have ever witnessed in my life are living in the land of Israel. Now, the adults as well as the children have cause to rejoice in Israel and many nations on Earth.

And the fact that the God of Israel is capable of constructing this wonderous work of art serves as a powerful statement that our God is capable of accomplishing anything. He is, as he always has been, worthy to be trusted. God has not forgotten his people. Therefore, it is safe to say that the Messiah of Israel has not forgotten us. And there is soon coming a day when our Messiah, as prophesied by the Israeli Prophet Malachi, will prepare a way for us all, and suddenly come into his Millennial Temple."

Once again, the crowd was out of control with joy. It was more than obvious that Bathsheba had an anointing upon her just as much as David.

"We, as a people, will never forget where we've come from. While our father, Abraham, endured hardship over four thousand years ago, our difficult plight continued through the days when Moses was used by the God of Israel to part the Red Sea and deliver the Israelites from bondage in Egypt, who then journeyed through the wilderness led by a pillar of cloud by day and a pillar of fire by night. Then, Joshua was used in 1250 B.C. to conquer our enemies in the Promised Land, the land of milk and honey. This progressed to the time when David of the Hebrew Bible conquered Jerusalem. This inherently led to the period when Solomon, David's son, built and dedicated the first Jewish Temple on Earth. Tragically, the Babylonians destroyed the first Temple and carried the Jews into captivity in 586 B.C. Our second Temple was destroyed by the Romans in 70 A.D. Both the first and second Temples were demolished on 9th of Av. And many atrocities were perpetrated upon the Jews up to and through World War II, when the Holocaust took place. Then, the vicious attack from Israel's neighbors came in 1948, when our country struggled and succeeded to become a nation. We endured the Six Day War in 1967 and the Yom Kippur War in 1973. During the 1980's and 1990's, thousands of Jews were brought to safety in their homeland from Iran, Iraq, and the Soviet Union, highlighted when Israel rescued 8,000 Jews who were held hostage in Ethiopia, in an effort that was referred to as "Operation Moses." Then, horrifically, came September 11th, 2001, known as 9/11, when the United States was savagely attacked for their love and devotion of Israel, democracy, and free enterprise. This long journey has led the Israelis to our present day. And we will never forget. The reason that we can never fail to forget is because of the fortitude that has been instilled in us as a result of the hardship that we have incurred and endured. And through all these years, the Jews have passed that same fortitude on to their children and their children's children.

Ladies and gentlemen, Israel has survived. We have endured, and we have persevered. Being a Harvard graduate, I feel led to quote a former student of the same university, the 35th President of the United States, John F. Kennedy, as he stated: 'Israel has become a triumphant and enduring reality. Even while fighting for its own survival, Israel has given new hope to the persecuted and new dignity to the pattern of Jewish life. For Israel was not created in order to disappear. Israel will endure and flourish. Israel is the child of hope and the home of the brave. Israel can neither be broken by adversity nor demoralized by success. Israel carries the shield of democracy and honors the sword of freedom. Peace be within your walls and plenteousness within your palaces.'

Today, because of our endurance, we have hope as we never have before. Today, we may concur with the Prophet, Isaiah, when he confidently wrote our current king's favorite verse, Isaiah 40:31, in the Hebrew Bible: 'But they that wait upon the Lord shall renew their strength. They shall mount up with wings as eagles. They shall run, and not be weary. And they shall walk, and not faint.' Today, there is no doubt that our God will fulfill the remainder of his promises in regard to Israel, because of the prophecy that has been manifested before our eyes today, the Israeli Temple now on Earth again, patterned after our Lord's radiant Temple in heaven. And today is the glorious day that we are allowed to reinstate the service of the Tribe of Levi in the Temple.

The future may not come without adversity, but now, with Solomon's Rebuilt Temple as our beacon to the world, we have the resolve to face any difficulty, after everything that we have all observed today. We have fervently prayed for our coveted Temple to be built. Now, we most sincerely pray for the coming of our Messiah, Mashiach ben David, who will fulfill all the remaining prophecies of the Bible. And the end result of his appearance will be the laying down of all weapons, in order to make way for permanent, everlasting peace. As the Hebrew Prophets, Isaiah and Micah declared: 'It shall come to pass that the mountain of the House of the Lord shall be established, and the people shall flow into it. And many nations shall come, and say, Let us go up to the mountain of the Lord, and to the House of the God of Jacob, and he will teach us his ways, and the word of the Lord from Jerusalem. And they shall beat their swords into plowshares, and their spears into pruninghooks. Nation shall not lift up sword against nation, neither shall they learn war anymore.' This is what will occur when our Messiah comes. May he come quickly in our time.

When President Kennedy spoke in Berlin in June of 1963 of a peaceful and hopeful globe that is to come, little did he realize that he was referring to the great day of the coming of our Messiah. Therefore, it is with abundance of love in my heart for you all that I recite our cherished Hebrew Prayer from the sixth chapter of the Book of Numbers: 'The Lord bless you and keep you. The Lord make his face to shine upon you. And be gracious to you. The Lord lift up his countenance upon you, and give you peace. And the Lord shall put his name upon the children of Israel. And he will bless them.'

As we unite together as one, we will embrace the world with our love, and our friends all over the world will support us. We are, indeed, one in the Spirit, and we are one in the Lord. And just as Zechariah, the Prophet, once said in his immortal words: 'Not by might, not by power, but by my Spirit, says the Lord.' That's exactly how this magnificent Temple was built. And that's exactly what it will take for our ancestors and ourselves to witness the victorious coming of our Messiah. On behalf of David, myself, Solomon, Charity and even our palace dog, Shalom, God bless you all. And may God bless the nation of Israel forever and ever with everlasting peace. Thank you and Shabbat Shalom!"

The house absolutely came down after Bathsheba had concluded her address to the people of Israel. Even the modestly dressed, bearded Jews in their holy garb and hats, who usually observed strict standards of conduct, could not contain themselves in the ocean of excitement that they were treading in. Bathsheba loved the people of Israel, and the people of Israel were crazy about her. Bathsheba portrayed royalty as a lady of grace and virtue, just as much as Audrey Hepburn in the movie, "Roman Holiday." You could not help but get the strong sensation that it was meant to be for Bathsheba to be the perfect person to deliver the dedicatory speech for the 3rd Israeli Temple. The multitude was proud to have David and Bathsheba as their king and queen. The Israelis, honestly, believed that the hand of Almighty God was upon their king and queen, in a designated period of time.

Queen Bathsheba had won the hearts of the Jewish people with her Dedication of the Temple speech in leaps and bounds. She was the Sweetheart of Israel.

Yet it could be said that an acute crisis of meaning and uncertainty about the exact direction required to attain Israel's goals was still taking place. There was, in the back of people's minds, a subliminal awareness that something was disastrously wrong. And it was all due to this trance that everyone was sensing, but they just didn't have the wherewithal to explain or rationalize it in totality.

On the surface, the future seemed to be unequivocally rosy. It seemed to be a time of ebullient optimism. Every new endeavor seemed to be within reach and obtainable. Nothing but progression was offered to be the ongoing norm, without the hang-up of unforeseen difficulties, bitter disillusionment, and paralyzing trauma. The long period of contingency came across as being over, and the new state of awakening implied that everything was full speed ahead.

But a man capable of any sort of evil had been predicted to bring a severe, lingering storm when all looked calm. This man was said to be capable of inducing hysterical fanaticism, demonic energy, ferocity, and utter chaos. People would appear to be in a drunken stupor via his intoxicating chants and venomous charisma, working everyone into a twisted frenzy.

This evil character, emerging on the world scene, is prophesied to bring about a new world order, that is, a one world government, a one world church, and a one world economy.

And in the midst of all this outward, novelty elation, there was sinister activity lurking in the background, hidden by a formidable, impenetrable mask of deception. And this cloaked man behind the scenes operated with the motive and laser beam focus of building the most dastardly empire ever established, conceived in the notion of having absolute power over mankind. This man would be referred to as the false messiah, and this impostor would manage to create a monster out of himself. In other words, the false messiah would make Adolf Hitler look like an altar boy.

KING DAVID AND QUEEN BATHSHEBA'S PALACE

It was Friday morning. David arrived to his office a little after nine. Naomi, his secretary, rushed in with an urgent message: "Dr. Goldstein called, David, and said you need to call him as soon as you come in. He also wants Jonathan to be present when he meets with you. He asked that you and Jonathan meet with him in the conference room at eleven o'clock.

David squinted his eyes, as if somewhat puzzled, and said, "I wonder what's going on?"

"I could tell by the tone of his voice that it was something quite urgent." Naomi replied.

THE ROYAL PALACE CONFERENCE ROOM

When David and Jonathan entered the conference room, Dr. Goldstein was already there, seated in his usual chair close to the head of the table. David sat down at the head of the table, with Jonathan on his immediate left side, and stated, "I understand there's a very serious matter you need to discuss."

"Yes, David," Dr. Goldstein said. "It's a matter that's quite extraordinary. I've had a very vivid vision."

"A vision? What kind of a vision?" David responded, not really understanding what Dr. Goldstein was talking about.

"Even modern-day prophets have visions, David." Jonathan remarked with a grin, at the risk of sounding like a smart aleck. "That's confirmed in the Books of Joel and Acts."

"Yes. Especially modern-day prophets. And be that as it may, this vision is doozy, a real humdinger." Dr. Goldstein said emphatically.

"When did you have this vision, Dr. Goldstein?" David asked.

"Last night, actually, at my home. It was quite vivid. You, Jonathan, and I need to go to Mount Tabor as soon as possible." Dr. Goldstein insisted.

"Better known as the Mount of Transfiguration." David said with an element of premonition in his voice, that something good may lie directly ahead.

"Exactly, David." Dr. Goldstein responded, once again astounded by another perfect response from David. "I would suggest that we go this evening. It will be quite poetic to go on the eve of the Sabbath. All three of us are being beckoned to go. And I can assure you with confidence that any and all questions you have right now will be clarified when we get there. It's approximately a two-hour drive from Jerusalem to Galilee and the eastern end of the Jezreel Valley. Then, we'll take the winding road to the top of Mount Tabor. On the way there, I'll provide you with some explanation, but nothing I say will adequately prepare any one of us of what we are about to experience. There will be no chauffeur driving us, David. There will be no security or bodyguards. We are doing this on our own, incognito as much as possible. It would be best to go in my car. We'll even trust Greased Lightning here at the wheel."

"Boy, you really are throwing caution to the wind, allowing Jonathan to be at the helm of your car." David quipped yet being half-way serious.

"You're in charge of this mission, Dr. Goldstein!" Jonathan insisted, in all seriousness.

Dr. Goldstein, David, and Jonathan made it to the top of Mount Tabor all in one piece at about 11:00 PM that Friday night, despite the fact that Greased Lightning had been at the wheel. But Jonathan had to be given some credit for being on good behavior, as he did manage to keep the reckless driving during the trip down to a minimum, because he realized the gravity of the situation, and he was hanging on every word Dr. Goldstein had to say concerning his vision. As promised, on the way to the destination, Dr. Goldstein did render some rationalization for this impromptu visit to Mount Tabor. Dr. Goldstein had brought a Bible with him and flipped to the pages of the seventeenth chapter of Matthew. The first eight verses of the chapter depicted Jesus bringing three of his disciples, Peter, James, and John, to Mount Tabor, also known as the Mount of Transfiguration, where Moses and Elijah appeared and spoke with Jesus. At a very critical point, a bright cloud overshadowed all of them, and a voice spoke out of the cloud. Dr. Goldstein read Matthew 17:5 "This is my beloved Son, in whom I am well pleased. Hear ye him." Obviously, this transformation reflected a pinnacle point in the life of Jesus Christ. Peter, James, and Jesus' beloved disciple, John, were not ever the same again afterwards either.

**MOUNT TABOR/THE MOUNT OF TRANSFIGURATION
MATTHEW 17:1-8**

When Dr. Goldstein, David, and Jonathan reached the top of the mountain, Jonathan asked Dr. Goldstein where he should park.

"Go to the Catholic Church, the Church of the Transfiguration." Dr. Goldstein instructed.

"That's the site traditionally believed to be where the Transfiguration of Jesus took place." David remarked. "The transfiguration is a sign that Jesus would fulfill the law and the prophecies of the prophets. It also assured his believers that he's the Messiah."

THE CATHOLIC CHURCH OF THE TRANSFIGURATION
MOUNT TABOR (GALILEE), ISRAEL
MATTHEW 17:1-8
REVELATION 11:1-19

"You are correct, David. You're becoming as open minded as myself." Dr. Goldstein said, as Jonathan pulled into the parking lot of the Church of Transfiguration. "And should the vision I received play out as I believe it will, history is going to be made tonight."

After Dr. Goldstein, David, and Jonathan got out of the car, Jonathan asked, "Are we going inside the church, Dr. Goldstein?"

"No, that won't be necessary." Dr. Goldstein instructed. "We will remain outside. All three of us will know when we are positioned at our appointed bearing. Let's head toward that cluster of trees."

There was no shortage of beautiful green trees surrounding the Catholic Church of the Transfiguration. The church building that stands today was built by the Franciscans in 1924. It is the largest church in the Holy Land. The view from the church at the top of Mount Tabor is magnificent and breathtaking. As Dr. Goldstein, David, and Jonathan made their way to the cloak and cover of the trees resembling a forest, they could not help but sense that the entire area was engulfed with incredible peace. They didn't have to venture out terribly far until they suddenly found themselves encircled by a funnel of wind that, obviously, resembled that of a tornado. The phenomenon could be easily described as a whirlwind. Dr. Goldstein, David, and Jonathan looked around in all directions, realizing that whatever was taking place was backed by a tremendous source of power. They hardly had any time to know how to react. They were simply left to quickly attempt to calculate, as best they possibly could, what was taking place.

Then, their attention was directed to an open area among the trees, and three glowing figures appeared out of nowhere. The three appeared to be conversing with each other, until they looked up, simultaneously, at Dr. Goldstein, David, and Jonathan to acknowledge their presence.

"Boy, Bathsheba is going to have trouble believing me when I tell her about this!" David said as he slightly nudged Jonathan with his elbow, without any intention of trying to be humorous.

"Dr. Goldstein," Jonathan opened, with a dazzled look on his face, "After what you just read to us, the three people we're looking at are apparently Jesus, Moses, and Elijah."

"That's right, Jonathan." Dr. Goldstein confirmed. "And if I'm not mistaken, I believe they are indicating that they want us to come closer."

Dr. Goldstein, David, and Jonathan did just that. But there was no fear on their part, just anticipation. The peacefulness of their surroundings completely negated any tendency of fear.

MOSES, JESUS CHRIST, THE SON OF GOD, AND ELIJAH
ZECHARIAH 4:2, 3, 6, 11-14
MATTHEW 17:1-8
REVELATION 11:3-13

And as they approached the three luminous figures, Dr. Goldstein, David, and Jonathan were in absolute awe.

They were drawn, that is, summoned toward the three historic Israeli giants, who at one point or another were regarded by many as dead and gone. Actually, of the three, only Moses was known to have had a gravesite where he was buried, having passed away close to where the children of Israel had entered into the Promised Land of Canaan, at Joshua's command. But based on the New Testament, Jesus had resurrected from the dead and ascended into heaven from the Mount of Olives. And according to the Second Book of Kings, Elijah "went up by a whirlwind into heaven in a chariot of fire, and horses of fire." Nevertheless, the shining trio had just made a supernatural manifestation that could safely be considered miraculous. And the Mount of Transfiguration was a place where Jesus was once transformed in a meeting with Moses and Elijah, and, apparently, the same intention was divinely meant for David and Jonathan, as reflected in the eleventh chapter of the Book of Revelation.

Once Dr. Goldstein, David, and Jonathan came close and closer to the aura that surrounded Jesus, Moses, and Elijah, the intensity of the spiritual power being emitted was much more than what could be described as overwhelming. Words were very limited to adequately explain exactly what was taking place. Initially, nothing verbal or audible was spoken. But the three visitors found themselves bombarded with various thoughts. It was as if the swirls of light encompassing Dr. Goldstein, David, and Jonathan were piercing their hearts, minds, souls, and spirits with particular concepts of understanding and clarification. They perceived that they were receiving specific enlightenment that would equip them for the designated purpose in their lives. For David and Jonathan, it meant a very special purpose that would propel them both on a mission of rescuing the world from a devastating fate. This new work designed and custom-made for David and Jonathan would be entirely based on the work that Jesus had accomplished on Earth over two thousand years ago, and the foundation that Christ had built. I Corinthians 3:11 - Hence, the words of Jesus Christ: "Greater works shall you do." John 14:12 – It was the God of Israel's intention to use the Restored David and the Restored Jonathan to restore the worldwide, universal Church of Jesus Christ.

First and foremost of the thoughts being conveyed came directly from the fourth chapter of Zechariah and eleventh chapter of Revelation. And without warning, Jesus spoke out loud, in a tone of voice that reverberated with an echo: "Behold, I will give power unto my Two Witnesses, and they shall prophesy for three-and-a-half years. These are the Two Olive Trees, and the Two Candlesticks, and the Two Anointed Ones standing by the God of the Earth. And if any man shall hurt my Two Prophets, fire will proceed out of your mouths, and devour your enemies. Just like Elijah, you will have the power to shut heaven so that it will not rain. And as Moses, you both will have power over the waters to turn them into blood. And the Impostor, who has deceived many, including yourselves, has ascended out of the Bottomless Pit to make war with you. And you both shall know the great sorrow of being killed in the street of Jerusalem before many witnesses in the world. And people from all nations of the world will share the sorrow of your suffering. But my Spirit will quicken you, and you both will ascend to the great heights of heaven to bring glory to Israel and my name. Revelation 11:3-13 - You are my Two Anointed Ones foretold by the Prophet, Zechariah. And I empower you on your mission of restoring my Church. You will have have great victory not by might, not by power, but by my Spirit." Zechariah 4:6

**THE TWO ANOINTED ONES OF THE GOD OF ISRAEL
ZECHARIAH 4:1-14**

And when Jesus said these words, there were many great voices echoing in heaven, collectively saying: "The kingdoms of this world are become the kingdoms of our Lord, and of his Christ. And he shall reign forever and ever. We give you thanks, O, Lord God Almighty, who is, and was, and is to come. Because you have ruled with great power and have reigned." Revelation 11:15, 17

And at that very moment, Dr. Goldstein, David, and Jonathan miraculously and unexplainably witnessed the Temple in heaven open, the very Temple that served as the architype and blueprint for all the Israeli Temples built on Earth, and they saw the Ark of the Covenant in the heavenly Temple. And it began to thunder, and lightning struck, and there were voices, and the ground beneath them shook, exactly as it is mentioned in Revelation 11:19.

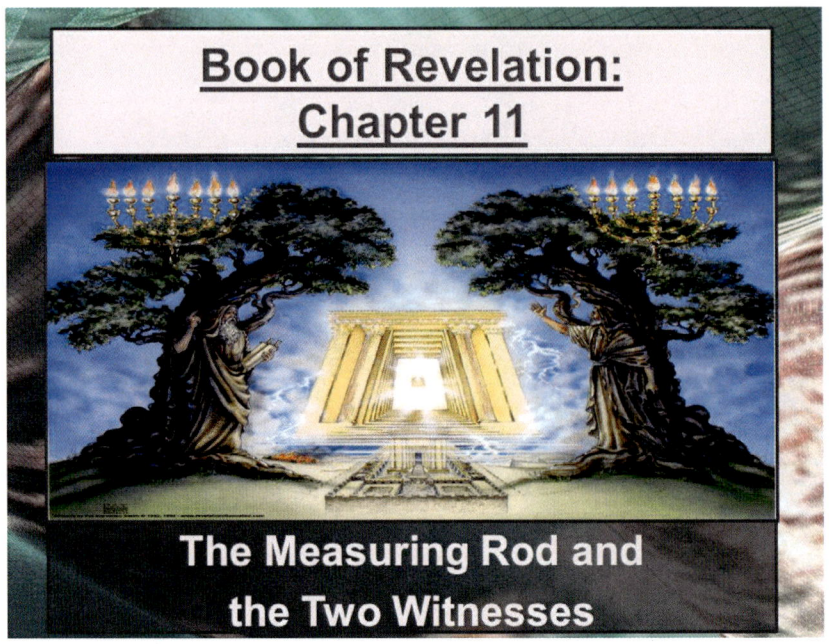

THE RESTORED DAVID AND RESTORED JONATHAN
THE TWO CHOSEN WITNESSES
REVELATION 11:1-19

Dr. Goldstein, David, and Jonathan were able to look upon the face of Jesus - Matthew 17:8, when Christ began to speak again: "The measuring rod that I gave to my beloved disciple, John, in the Book of Revelation to measure the Temple of God, the altar, and those who worship in it – Revelation 11:1-3 – reveals my purpose you, David and Jonathan, my two chosen Witnesses. My two Olive Trees, my two Candlesticks, and my two Prophets. I have all knowledge of my people, and I will use you both to protect the people of my Church amidst tribulation and persecution. And I will carefully watch over my faithful flock as their Good Shepherd. Protect your Queen, Bathsheba, David. The Red Dragon will persecute her and your children. Have faith that I am with you always. Surely, I will come quickly. I am the Light of the World. Vengeance is mine. I will repay."

Then, immediately after Jesus had rendered these words, a most powerful voice spoke like thunder from above as sudden lightning struck the Earth from clouds directly over where they were standing, saying, "This is my beloved Son, in whom I am well pleased. Hear ye him," just exactly as it occurred on the Mount of Transfiguration in Matthew 17:5 in the New Testament of the Bible. When the words from above had been said by the heavenly Father, Jesus commandingly said, "In my Father's house are many mansions. I go to prepare a place for you. And if I go to prepare a place for you, I will come again, and receive you unto myself. That where I am, there you may be also."

With that, Jesus turned slightly turned toward Moses, and then, toward Elijah, rendering acknowledgement to them both. Then, Christ, nonchalantly, lifted his right arm in the air with his index finger pointed upward and ascended toward heaven with his encourage of two until all three of them were no longer in sight, leaving Dr. Goldstein, David, and Jonathan going back and forth from staring up at the sky to looking around at each other, as the tornado of swirling, flickering light of various colors surrounding them began to dissipate.

MATTHEW 17:1-8   REVELATION 11:3-6
MOUNT TABOR/THE MOUNT OF TRANSFIGURATION

Neither David, Jonathan, nor Dr. Goldstein felt that they had just witnessed a bizarre event. They all thought it had been quite extraordinary, positive, and pertinent. And they would never be the same again!

THE ISRAELI ROYAL PALACE IN JERUSALEM

Dr. Goldstein, David, and Jonathan arrived back in Jerusalem in the early hours of that Saturday Sabbath morning, following their overnight encounter. There was little conversation on the drive back from Mount Tabor, as all three were absorbed in a plethora of dazed contemplation. Dr. Goldstein's vision had come to pass just as quickly as it had been given to him, once again solidifying and confirming his position as a modern-day prophet. No one ever needed to persuade Dr. Goldstein of that fact, and if David and Jonathan ever doubted it before, at this point, they required no further convincing that Dr. Goldstein was, indeed, the Restored Israeli Prophet, Samuel. Therefore, it followed suit, after such an extraordinary vision being realized, that David and Jonathan were actually the Restored David and Jonathan who had, in all reality, originated in the history of the Hebrew Bible. I Samuel 20:42

Once Dr. Goldstein, David, and Jonathan arrived back to the palace in Jerusalem, just after the Sun had come up at dawn, all three decided, being unable to sleep, to meet in the conference room to gather, capture, and interpret the collective thoughts of their eventful evening of the night before.

"What was the one single issue foremost to you that came out of our enlightening meeting last night? The one single issue?" Dr. Goldstein asked David and Jonathan.

"That we've all been unsuspectedly deceived, the three of us and the entire world." David answered immediately.

"Exactly." Dr. Goldstein responded, as he snapped his fingers with his right hand. "And I get the feeling that, just like me on the drive back to Jerusalem, you and Jonathan have been putting the pieces together on exactly how we've all been deceived, connecting all the dots. It is quite apparent that the transformation we experienced last night has imparted a great deal of wisdom to us through the process. Let me ask you this. Does any particular person come to mind as someone you suspect who's spreading this deception that's affecting our world?"

"Colonel Ichabod Cohen!" Jonathan said emphatically, with perfect clarity.

"The very guy who's been nagging me to give him the Ark of the Covenant!" David pointed out, experiencing a eureka effect. "But it should have been so obvious to us all that something is wrong with him."

"That's right." Dr. Goldstein said. "And I recall that I fought the urge very strongly in that meeting when we had to cast our votes for him to become Israel's High Priest. But the hypnotic suggestion was just too powerful, and I relinquished, not even thinking any more of it."

"That means Colonel Cohen is not who we think he is." David said.

"Or what we think he is, David! Someone that possesses this kind of power couldn't possibly be human! It means that he is something that we don't even understand, that is, he is, obviously, not of this world, since he commands this sort of broad deception. He has the entire planet under some kind of a spell. And it's most apparent now that he isn't really a Jew. He's an enemy of the Jews. He's an impostor in every sense of the word, just as Jesus stated, rendering the term, 'Impostor.'" Dr. Goldstein stressed. "Look at it this way. Most Israelis are familiar with the prophecies of the Bible. They know about the predictions of the 3rd Temple being rebuilt. They know about the Seven Year Tribulation. And they know about the Millennium. They know about the expectation of the Israeli Messiah in the end time. The Israelis also know that in the middle of the Seven Year Tribulation they are going to realize that they have been duped, because the false messiah is going to show his true colors (or "fruits," as Jesus puts it; Matthew 7:15, 16). So, if the Israelis know ahead of time that they are going to be deceived, they will just simply assume that being adequately informed enough will prevent them from being vulnerable. Which, on the surface, makes perfect sense. BUT should the entire world succumb to a trance so powerful and overwhelming that we become oblivious to anything other than what the hypnotist convinces us to believe…"

"…Then, we are all in grave danger." Jonathan deduced, interrupting Dr. Goldstein.

"We are all, indeed, in grave danger." Dr. Goldstein stated repeating Jonathan's comment. "Every last one of us are in danger, not only because we are being controlled on an overt basis, but also in a very subtle, covert manner as well. Our normal patterns of thinking are continually under attack! Alien invaders could not have contrived a scheme so intricate. All of us are subject to every little whim of this dictator, because we haven't been in control of ourselves. And none of us even know what hit us. And if it isn't stopped, it's going to lead to an absolute melee of unprecedented proportion, a veritable cornucopia of ongoing, confusing struggle. Mankind won't even need nuclear weapons to make himself extinct. It will provoke a hand-to-hand fight among every man, woman, and child in the entire world. And considering the fiendishness of the situation, that very well may be the result that Colonel Cohen is after, a nice, slow torture of the human race at the hands of ourselves. We'll all be at each other's throats."

"I see." David said. "It's all becoming quite clear. And we were beckoned to the Mount of Transfiguration so that our thinking would get straightened out. This is a part of the transformation process that is taking shape. And this process is ongoing."

"Yes." Dr. Goldstein affirmed. "And it also served the purpose of imparting the power that you and Jonathan are going to require at each and every turn of your decision-making process as all future events unfold. I venture to say that both of you have been endowed with lightning-fast agility in your thinking to take the appropriate course of action in even unexpected scenarios…"

"…And the determination to back up those actions." Jonathan said, finishing Dr. Goldstein's sentence.

"That's exactly right, Jonathan." Dr. Goldstein agreed. "And at the very least, Christ, Moses, and Elijah are the source of that determination supporting you two young men. And I'd say you're in exceptionally capable company with Jesus, Moses, and Elijah, I would add."

"That means, at this point, other than any allies of Colonel Cohen, we're the only three on the planet of Earth who know about all this." David said. "And it also means, for the sake of international security, Ichabod Cohen is our chief focus."

"Yes. And it also means that any and all records that we have on file for Colonel Cohen are doctored and completely bogus." Dr. Goldstein elaborated. "And he's been misleading all of us by operating over worldwide satellite television acting as High Priest from the Temple for almost three-and-a-half years now. Between his broadcasts on the Sabbath, the viewings of the daily animal sacrifices, Cohen's feigned demonstrations of healing people, mocking Christ's genuine ability to heal, and all the rest, he has developed quite a following. We have to get more of an idea of what we're dealing with here. We know something is seriously amiss with Colonel Cohen, but what makes this guy tick. And I have a plan that will serve as a very effective first place to start."

"What do you have in mind, Dr. Goldstein?" David asked.

"To get a sample of his DNA, and then, on the basis of scientific findings, see what we can determine from there." Dr. Goldstein responded. "While Colonel Cohen may be something we don't understand, there is one thing we can safely surmise about him."

"What's that?" David asked.

"Cohen may be paranormal," Dr. Goldstein remarked, "but he still has limitations. He doesn't know everything. While you, for a certainty, David, do know where the Ark of the Covenant may be, the Colonel, with all of his hypnotic abilities, doesn't have a clue. There's some element keeping him in the dark and tripping him up. We can only safely assume that it's the God of Israel who's responsible for it. That, of course, is the only possible explanation."

"Right. I can't think of a better rationale than that." David said. "Makes perfect sense to me."

"It makes you wonder who's duping who." Dr. Goldstein remarked, almost jokingly. "The Colonel likes to think that he's the only one who's not being duped. Oddly enough, that arrogant attitude of his could work to our advantage."

David and Jonathan knew exactly what Dr. Goldstein meant.

MONDAY MORNING
DAVID AND BATHSHEBA'S ROYAL PALACE
DR. SAMUEL GOLDSTEIN'S OFFICE

"Dr. Goldstein." The Israeli Advisor's secretary said, through the intercom system.

"Yes, Avivit ("Avivit" means innocent or springtime in Hebrew)." Dr. Goldstein said, expecting to know the nature of her topic.

"I have Colonel Cohen for you on Line 3, as requested." Avivit informed.

"Thank you, Avivit." Dr. Goldstein said, as he picked up the receiver on his desk.

"You're welcome, Dr. Goldstein." Avivit replied, with a hint of curiosity in her voice, as she was wondering why in the world the Chief Advisor to King David couldn't help contacting the High Priest of Israel. Dr. Goldstein made sure that his office door was shut, ensuring that his conversation with the Colonel would not be overheard.

"Colonel Cohen! Good morning!" Dr. Goldstein said chipperly. "Thank you for returning my call so quickly."

"Well, receiving your message was quite an unexpected pleasure, Dr. Goldstein." Colonel Cohen responded, with an impressive air of diplomacy. "This is quite an honor hearing from the king's right-hand man. How may I be of service to you?"

Ichabod Cohen was acting in such an amiable fashion. But Dr. Goldstein knew that he could never, of course, possibly be friends with the Colonel under any circumstances. The Israeli Chief Advisor to the King of Israel was not disarmed one bit by Cohen's charm. Other than being forced into a position of putting on an act, Dr. Goldstein knew in his heart that he would be required to endure the hypocrisy of pretending to be platonic friends with the fallacious High Priest and suspected false messiah, who was attempting to create a world of chess pawns under his command.

"It's concerning a subject of mutual interest, Colonel Cohen." Dr. Goldstein mentioned, having no intention of making a recommendation of getting on a first name basis.

"Sounds intriguing, Dr. Goldstein. And what might that topic be?" The Colonel asked, with a very sincere degree of curiosity.

"The Ark of the Covenant." Dr. Goldstein responded, knowing full well that the Ark was his ace in the hole topic to get the High Priest's attention enough to meet with him.

There was a long enough pause over the phone to provide Dr. Goldstein with complete confidence that he had grabbed the Israeli High Priest's 100% total, undivided attention.

"Yes. The Ark of the Covenant. Of course, that is the one essential item that would make the new Temple complete, as I have posed a number of times to the king. Has King David had a change of heart?" The High Priest enquired.

"There is no doubt that this is a delicate topic, and I would like to discuss the matter with you in depth over lunch sometime, on a day that's convenient for both of us. Of course, I'm well aware that you have a hectic schedule." Dr. Goldstein replied, intentionally dodging Colonel Cohen's question. "I'll be happy to answer any and all your questions in detail at that time."

Although Dr. Goldstein had mentioned to David in the early going that the Ark of the Covenant, by no means, should be brought into the Tribulation Temple, he still had to lead the Colonel on to think that he was open to the idea of assisting the High Priest in getting the Ark into the Holy of Holies. Yet even without the Ark in the Temple, it would still be possible for the false messiah to be able to perpetrate the travesty of the Abomination of Desolation. With or without the Ark of the Covenant in Cohen's possession, either way, he could still desecrate the Holy of Holies in Solomon's Temple Rebuilt through his outrageous, profane deeds. But it was imperative that the Ark of the Covenant remain out of the Temple. The false messiah was fully expected to openly blaspheme the Most High God day and night from the Temple, then, of course, by all means, keeping the Ark out of the Most Holy Place had to be avoided. Yet Dr. Goldstein was in a position where he had to give the impression that, as the king's closest advisor, he was understanding of the best interests of the High Priest of Israel.

"Allow me to say this, Colonel Cohen," Dr. Goldstein continued, hoping to seal the deal for a solid lunch appointment, "I have a vested interest, as an Israeli, to see that Levitical Priesthood be functioning at its full capacity."

Once again, there was a noticeable pause over the phone. There had been many more times than one that Colonel Cohen had noted to himself, if not said out loud, that "Goldstein is a sly, old fox." And Cohen had not forgotten how Dr. Goldstein was the only one who even came close to hesitating and resist voting him in as the

High Priest of Israel, before Dr. Goldstein eventually regressed, and became totally overtaken like everyone else by the hypnotic spell. Dr. Goldstein (other than Prince Solomon), more than anyone else on Earth, appeared to have the lowest natural threshold of susceptibility to this trance of deception. And now, after having been a part of the recent transformation at the Mount of Transfiguration, not a whole lot was getting past Dr. Goldstein. His powers of perception had never been greater. And the very same thing could be said of David and Jonathan.

"Well, we both have the best interests of Israel at heart, Dr. Goldstein. How does Wednesday at eleven o'clock at the restaurant of your choice sound to you?" Colonel Cohen asked, not wanting to delay any longer on making the lunch appointment official. He was sold on Dr. Goldstein's pitch to meet with him.

"I'm sure you're familiar with the restaurant at the top of the Herbert Samuel Hotel." Dr. Goldstein said.

"Splendid choice, Dr. Goldstein." Cohen said. "I've dined there on a number of occasions."

THE HERBERT SAMUEL HOTEL ROOFTOP RESTURANT
JERUSALEM, ISRAEL

The Herbert Samuel Hotel Restaurant in Jerusalem is a Five Star Hotel, located in the heart of Jerusalem at Zion Square, showcasing such exceptional luxury and style that it is considered to be a beautiful oasis to escape the hustling, bustling streets of Jerusalem. The Herbert Samuel Rooftop Gourmet Restaurant is the crown jewel of the hotel, located on the top floor, that is, the eleventh floor. The restaurant offers a spectacular view of the entire center of the city of Jerusalem. The restaurant's modern design, including a gold-plated ceiling manufactured in India, creates a charm and atmosphere like no other restaurant in the world, incorporating a sense of décor that is private and cozy. From the very first day that the rooftop restaurant opened, it was destined to become one of Israel's all time top-ranking places to go for a sumptuous dining experience. One thing you can count on at the Herbert Samuel Restaurant is to experience Kosher Cuisine to be taken to a whole new level.

Dr. Goldstein and Colonel Cohen both eagerly kept their lunch engagement with each other for their Wednesday morning at eleven o'clock appointment. They were seated at a table that provided them with a breathtaking view of Jerusalem. Ichabod Cohen had ordered the Norwegian Salmon with the sliced mini cucumbers, while Dr. Goldstein chose the Meagre fillet a la plancha, with ratta potatoes and seared baby zucchini, the lunch special of the day.

"You and the king have known each other since his college days at Harvard, I understand, Dr. Goldstein." Cohen said.

"Yes. David and I developed a rather fast rapport with each other, both of us being natives of Israel. I was his English Professor at the time. Among the king's assorted gifts, he does, indeed, possess the heart of a poet."

"I can see that about him." Ichabod Cohen noted, desiring to appear complimentary toward King David. "Our king is an extremely multi-faceted man. He does, certainly, have a Shakespearean side about him. I'm curious, Dr. Goldstein. Is the king aware that you have an appointment with me today?"

"As a matter of fact, Colonel Cohen, the king does know that I'm meeting with you today. And he also knows the main topic that you and I have in mind." Dr. Goldstein said, predicting that the conversation would be getting off the ground at this point, and predicting to himself that the High Priest would not waste any time getting to the issue at hand. Dr. Goldstein had to carefully choose every word he employed in the conversation. Obviously, Ichabod Cohen didn't just fall off the turnip truck. The High Priest's powers of perception were just as keen as his ability to deceive.

"I see. Well, I must admit. That does baffle me somewhat, considering that the king has seemed quite adamant about not allowing the Ark to come into the Temple up to this point. He doesn't appear to see my point of view, as Israel's High Priest, after the order of Melchizedek (Melchisedec, New Testament spelling), I might add. Can you explain the king's hesitation in this matter? Israel has a glorious new Temple once again after all these years, but alas, with the absence of the Ark of the Covenant." Cohen said in a remorseful tone.

"Well, that's exactly why I wanted to meet with you today, Colonel Cohen." Dr. Goldstein interjected. "I've discussed this with David and mentioned to him that you and I are on common ground where the Ark of the Covenant is concerned. The king does not want you to take it personally that he doesn't feel comfortable allowing the Ark of the Covenant into the Temple right now. Of course, he will decide to make that move at the proper time, and, of course, when that special moment comes, you will be an integral part of that celebration with all of Israel. The king, myself, and many others don't need any convincing of your qualifications as our High Priest in Israel. It's an inherent part of your family history, and you have carried out the task quite admirably. That goes without saying. And it's reflected by your popularity with the people of Israel as well. And I do concur with you that the Ark is a vital necessity to the function of the rebuilt Temple. I would like to see this event expedited myself. Granted, we have all been carrying out our separate duties, and some effective communication has been slipping through the cracks. But to make up for lost time, the king does want me to let you know that he is getting close to making a move in that direction." Dr. Goldstein said, hoping that wasn't laying the flattery on a little too thick, and praying that Cohen could not see through the fact that he was lying through his teeth. He was aware that Cohen was quite adept to reading between the lines. He, even more than David, if possible, had absolutely no intention of relinquishing the Ark to Ichabod Cohen. Even Colonel Cohen's overwhelming power of hypnosis could not bend David's fortified will to instinctively keep the Ark of the Covenant out of Solomon's Temple. Dr. Goldstein's ulterior motive of acquiring a DNA sample from the High Priest came with the cost of mandating that he would not be totally honest with his luncheon guest. Dr. Goldstein rationalized his falsehoods by utilizing the old Israeli axiom for military combat that he learned as a serviceman in the Israeli Defense Forces (IDF): "By way of deception, thou shalt do war." Using this Israeli military axiom as his justification, Dr. Goldstein was hoping he could match deceptive wits with the expert himself, Colonel Ichabod Cohen. And in a high-stakes, face-to-face meeting with the Ark of the Covenant going to the winner, you can be certain that the Colonel would be utilizing his bag of tricks to reinforce his expertise at cunningness.

"Yes, well, it is most encouraging to know that you and the king have been pleased with my work. Do you feel that the king has a timetable on when he may implement this plan?" The High Priest cautiously enquired, considering carefully the timetable of his own personal agenda.

Dr. Goldstein could not help but notice that Colonel Cohen had actually psyched himself into thinking that it was his power of influence that brought the two men together for lunch that Wednesday. Dr. Goldstein figured there's no harm/no foul in playing on the devil's ego, which is as big as all outdoors.

"He is working out the details, and when the proper time comes, he will include you in on those details, and seek out your advice and recommendations." Dr. Goldstein assured, bluffing in order to close the deal of gaining the High Priest's confidence.

Cohen leaned back in his chair, with a pleased look on his face, and said, "Well, I, personally, consider this to be great progress for Israel, and as a loyal patriot, I would like to acknowledge that I feel this is heading in a momentous direction. I will be honored to work with the king in any way I can to ensure the great success of this endeavor."

The High Priest picked up the check that the waiter had left on the table. "Allow me to take care of this, Dr. Goldstein." Colonel Cohen emphatically said.

"No, no, no. I must insist. This one is on me." Dr. Goldstein said, being strongly assertive and practically demanding.

"Well, if you insist." Colonel Cohen eventually relented.

Both Dr. Goldstein and Cohen stepped out of the restaurant after the bill was paid and stood at the 11th floor elevator, when Dr. Goldstein turned to the Colonel, and said, "Oh, my goodness! How silly of me. When I dine out, I usually pay the tip in cash. I neglected to do so. The waiter did such a fine job of serving us. I want to let him know it was appreciated. Allow me just a second to take care of it. I'll be right back."

Dr. Goldstein made a quick dash back to the table, hoping that no one had time to clear it yet, walked directly up to where Colonel Cohen had been sitting, and carefully inserted the cloth napkin Cohen had used during his meal into an adequately sized plastic bag, which Dr. Goldstein gently put into his left, inside coat pocket.

"Is everything all right?" Ichabod Cohen asked Dr. Goldstein upon his return from the table, as the good doctor had emerged from the restaurant back to the 11th floor elevator.

"Everything is just fine." Dr. Goldstein responded, confident that his ploy had been successful.

THE JERUSALEM DNA TESTING CLINIC
JERUSALEM, ISRAEL

Dr. Goldstein had become a man on a mission. He was determined to get to the bottom of Colonel Ichabod Cohen's true identity. The first step of his mission was cleverly accomplished by obtaining the cloth napkin that Cohen had used during lunch at Herbert Samuel Rooftop Restaurant, using the Ark of the Covenant for bait. Now, the second phase would be set in motion by paying a visit to Dr. Goldstein dear friend at the Jerusalem DNA Testing Clinic. And Dr. Goldstein wasted no time going to see her.

As a leading scientist in the field of DNA Analysis, Dr. Esther Schindler was, certainly, no stranger to the research laboratory, analyzing genetic origins of tissue samples and their properties. Highly esteemed by her colleagues and world renowned by other scientists through her award-winning work and recognized publications in regard to groundbreaking research, Dr. Schindler was a genius, and she had extensive knowledge of the different branches of tissue sample analysis, worked with law enforcement as a forensics expert, conducted research activities to decipher the unique genetic code of the human body to provide immunity against diseases, inspected crime scenes, collected evidence, and testified in Courts of Law disclosing the results of DNA testing. She also had access to the largest DNA Database in the world. Dr. Schindler was a genius, with an astronomical I.Q. to prove it.

"How's my favorite DNA Analyst doing today?" Dr. Goldstein asked in a rather cavalier manner, standing in the office doorway of the mature, single, quite attractive, blonde haired Biomolecular Chemist, Dr. Esther Schindler.

"Samuel!" Dr. Schindler responded with great enthusiasm, as she looked up from reading what appeared to be some important paperwork.

"I hope you don't mind me just popping in like this, Esther?" Dr. Goldstein politely asked.

"No. Of course not." Esther said, as she got up from her desk, and hurried to give him a hug. "I was so happy to hear from you when you called me yesterday."

Dr. Goldstein may have been on a vital continuance of a mission to get some DNA analyzed, but it was becoming rather apparent that a little hanky-panky was included with the caper. The joy of seeing each other again after quite some time was rapidly developing into something more than just two casual friends being brought back together. They had met at the Hebrew University in Jerusalem when they were both doing their undergraduate work. They were very involved with each other at that time in their youth, and it didn't take long for the sparks to naturally fly just as intensely as they once did before. The many memories that they shared together were all spontaneously coming back to both of them. You could immediately sense the rekindling and chemistry of the relationship. Nature, once again, was taking its course and having its way. They were simply picking up very quickly where they had left off years ago. For Esther Schindler, Dr. Goldstein's returned air of savoir-faire was a welcomed sight, and it showed.

"Well, I had to have a valid reason to be an imposition to you, Esther." Dr. Goldstein stated modestly.

"Samuel, you and I have been through enough together so that you know my door is always open to you. Coming by to visit me is all the excuse you need." Esther replied.

"Well, since you're putting it that way, I'll make a point, then, to come see you more often. You let me know if I'm wearing out my welcome." Dr. Goldstein responded, prompting a look of joy on Esther's face.

"I'd like seeing you more often, Samuel!" Esther replied most sincerely. "And you could never wear out your welcome."

"Esther, here is that DNA sample I had mentioned to you." Dr. Goldstein abruptly segued, pulling out the plastic bag containing Cohen's cloth napkin from his inner jacket pocket on the left side. "I know you're quite a busy lady, but I can confidently assure you that this case justifies the priority of your immediate attention. In fact, it may very well develop into the most outstanding case of your career. I handled that napkin as carefully as possible in an attempt to not contaminate it with my DNA."

"My goodness, Samuel." Esther exclaimed. "What is the origin of the DNA?"

Dr. Goldstein hesitated a couple of seconds, and then, said, "It's regarding our High Priest. I obtained the napkin from a luncheon engagement he and I had yesterday. Once you do the testing and evaluate the results, I will tell you the entire story. But of course, the details of your findings must remain confidential between yourself and those colleagues that you completely trust. It's imperative that the analysis you're conducting on this DNA be kept utterly top secret."

"Colonel Ichabod Cohen." Esther responded inquisitively. "He's a suspect or a person of interest in some respect? I'm surprised. As popular as he is, I sort of gathered that he's a real man of the people, completely above board and beyond reproach. I suppose this would definitely fall into the category of being classified, as you say."

"Yes, well, let's just say for now that he's, certainly, a person of interest, Esther." Dr. Goldstein said, not wanting to divulge too many details until he had received Dr. Schindler's results. "Trust me. I wouldn't indulge upon you unless it was completely warranted."

"Oh, Samuel. You don't need to convince me about your credibility. I can sense your urgency of the situation." Esther said in total agreement, and then, with a deep breath continued. "All right. I will set aside my entire workload and analyze it this afternoon or tomorrow morning at the latest." She knew Dr. Goldstein well enough to know that he wasn't exaggerating. "And with your permission, I'll look up your DNA in the Jewish Ancestry DNA Database to insure there's no confusion, Samuel. I'll search Colonel Cohen from the Jewish Ancestry DNA Database and the International DNA Database."

"You have my consent, Esther. You're a lady and a scholar, and you, unsurprisingly, remain a Sweetheart as well." Dr. Goldstein said, brightening up Esther's day, considering the source of the compliment. "Now, I don't mean to be impolite, but I do have some pressing matters to tend to today."

"And I see you're still the man of mystery, Samuel." Esther kidded. "I'll call as soon as possible with the outcome."

"Au revoir." Dr. Goldstein said with glee from the office doorway. And then, King David's Senior Advisor was out of sight, hoping that he managed to make a debonair exit.

And he succeeded, leaving Esther with a cheery grin and a spinning head, knowing full well that Dr. Goldstein had a little scoundrel in him.

KING DAVID AND QUEEN BATHSHEBA'S ROYAL PALACE
SAMUEL GOLDSTEIN'S OFFICE
SENIOR ADVISOR TO DAVID HARTMAN

"Esther Schindler on line three, Dr. Goldstein." Avivit informed over the intercom.

"Thank you, Avivit." Dr. Goldstein replied chipperly. "Esther! I didn't expect to hear from you so soon. Good morning."

"Samuel! I must see you immediately! We have an emergency on our hands!" Esther exclaimed, with distinct terror in her voice.

"What in the world has happened, Esther?" Dr. Goldstein said, sounding quite alarmed in reaction to Esther's intense tone.

"I am hesitant to say anything over the phone, Samuel. I know you told me where you got this sample from, but I will say this for now. We've observed some terrifying results." Esther informed. "All indications are showing it's a sample from hell. There are valid reasons to be most fearful!"

"I'm leaving right now for the laboratory, Esther." Dr. Goldstein said.

"No, Samuel! Don't come. I'm going to have to come to the royal palace and bring a few of my colleagues with me. Right away, Samuel. Top Secret. And the king is going to need to be present as well. It's safe to say that there is potential here for a national crisis, probably international." Esther insisted. "Just please use the utmost discretion in who is allowed to join us in this meeting. Make certain that they may be trusted! And whatever you do, stay away from Ichabod Cohen!"

"Esther, I'm sending a limousine out to you this moment. You and your colleagues stand by. The chauffer will be there very soon to pick you up and bring you to the palace. You and your colleagues will be escorted directly to the king's conference room." Dr. Goldstein instructed.

"We'll have all our findings with us, Samuel." Esther mentioned.

"You'll have clearance at the door of the palace, Esther." Dr. Goldstein confirmed. "The king and I will be waiting for you in the conference room. I will also be mandating security personnel to accompany the limousine."

"Thank you, Samuel." Esther gratefully acknowledged.

KING DAVID AND QUEEN BATHSHEBA'S ROYAL PALACE THE ISRAELI PALACE CONFERENCE ROOM

"Based on what you've told me, Dr. Goldstein, there's no telling what to expect when Dr. Schindler arrives." David said, sitting at the head of the table in the conference room.

"I believe it's safe to assume that we can fully expect an international crisis, David!" Dr. Goldstein retorted.

Jonathan was seated at the table on David's left. Other trusted advisors, in dress military uniforms and civilian apparel, were present in the meeting as well. Jonathan was clad in his military dress uniform, while David and Dr. Goldstein were wearing casual attire. Everyone present at the conference table were people who David trusted explicitly, and that would, of course, include Israel's current and youngest Prime Minister ever, Sharon Spielberg.

"One thing I can predict with certainty, David. From the way, Esther sounded over the phone, it's going to be something quite earthshaking. She was absolutely frantic. I know Esther. She is not one to panic or overreact. She's the most poised person I've ever known." Dr. Goldstein indicated.

"It's safe to say that this is not going to be boring." Jonathan added, hoping to contribute a hint of levity to break the tension.

Two Israeli military palace police officers in standard issue uniforms, packing high caliber pistols drawn from their holsters entered the conference room first, with Dr. Schindler and her entourage following, and then, two more security officers followed behind them.

The initial thing that was most noticeable, especially to Dr. Goldstein, is how Esther was making every effort to maintain her composure.

All of the men and women seated with David at the conference table stood up, practically out of deference and definitely out of concern. Based on what Dr. Goldstein had told him, David instructed the Israeli police officer in charge to post two guards at the door of the conference room, and that security be doubled at each entrance to the Israeli palace. David had no choice but to convey to Israeli palace security that Colonel Ichabod Cohen was not, under any circumstances, allowed to enter the conference room during the priority meeting.

"Good afternoon, ladies and gentlemen. I am Dr. Steven Spitzer. I am Chairman of the Department of Molecular and Human Genetics at the Jerusalem DNA Testing Center." Dr. Spitzer said, by way of introduction. "Of course, I know at least a few of you present today are familiar with Dr. Esther Schindler, our head Biomolecular Chemist and DNA Analysist at the Testing Center. And to her right, we have Dr. Barnabas Abelman, our Professor of Bioengineering, Genetics and Genome Sciences, and to my left, Dr. Rachel Morningstar, Professor of Physiological Psychology and Neuroscience. We are all most honored to meet with you and your highly esteemed cohorts in this very critical meeting, Your Highness."

"Thank you, Dr. Spitzer. You, Dr. Schindler, Dr. Abelman and Dr. Morningstar please be seated." David politely responded. "The honor is all ours, having you four distinguished scientists with us today. We, certainly, realize that you have dropped everything to focus all of your energy on this matter we've brought to your attention. And that is very much appreciated."

The four scientists sat at the conference table in their respective chairs, after placing down their attaché cases.

"Of course, our Prime Minister, Sharon Spielberg, needs no introduction." David continued. "I believe all the professors are probably, at least, somewhat acquainted with Dr. Samuel Goldstein, my Senior Advisor. Seated to my left is one of my top security chiefs and military leaders, Jonathan Diamond. To my left, we have our Minister of Defense, Samson Manasseh. And then, our Commander-in-Chief of our Israeli Defense Forces (IDF), General Sarah Majesky. We have a few of the General Officers under her command with us: Major General Alon Zuckerman, Brigadier General Aaron

Felderman, and Brigade Commander, Colonel Benson Jacob. Also, our Chief Warrant Officer and Senior NATO Liaison, Dinah Jupiter. Jordan Weiner, the Director of Mossad, our national intelligence agency. Samantha Newfield, member of the Knesset as Minister of Intelligence. And then, our Chief of Israeli Security Forces, Judith Vered. I'd like to, personally, assure each of the four scientists that everyone present in this room can be fully trusted with any information that you have to relay to us today. I am confident, based on the serious nature of this meeting, that we all will concur that everything said here today will be received with utmost confidentiality."

All of the officials around the conference table had nodded to the professors, as they were being introduced. They also nodded their heads in an affirmative manner to confirm that they were all sworn to secrecy.

"Dr. Goldstein, would you care to take the floor, and get us started?" David directed.

"Yes. Thank you, Your Highness." Dr. Goldstein formally responded to David, under the circumstances. "Dr. Spitzer, we would like to very sincerely thank you and all the scientists for coming today. Your timely appearance is an indication to us all that we have made the correct decision in bringing this matter to your attention, because, obviously, you have made discoveries that need to be brought to our immediate consideration."

"Thank you, Dr. Goldstein." Dr. Spitzer broke in. "Now, I would like to make just one statement first to preface everything we are about to share with you. But I must make sure that everyone in this room knows about the person who is in question here."

"Everyone in this room has been officially cleared and briefed, Dr. Spitzer." Dr. Goldstein assured. "We appreciate you extending that courtesy of caution. All of us here today are fully aware that Colonel Ichabod Cohen, Israel's acting High Priest, is the person who's in question today."

"Dr. Goldstein, the very first thing that needs to be mentioned before we render any explanation is say up front that there is no such person as Colonel Ichabod Cohen!" Dr. Spitzer exclaimed, with an undoubtedly contorted look of adject terror on his face.

There was a distinct grasp in the conference room among the dignitaries.

"Colonel Ichabod Cohen does not exist. The person of Ichabod Cohen is a figment that he himself has created in all of our imaginations. He has that capability, and he has that kind of power." Dr. Spitzer elaborated. "He is not who or what we have been led to believe he is. Ichabod Cohen is an extremely dangerous individual. He is much more than just a foreigner, pretending to be a Jew. He is an alien, posing as a human being. We have been sorting through the inconsistencies concerning Colonel Cohen in the Jewish DNA Ancestry Database and the International DNA Database and determined that he was not born in Israel as his falsified background records show. We'll even go so far as to say that his records may have been doctored supernaturally, for lack of a better term."

With that, everyone transitioned from a gasp to an uproar. All of the members at the conference table were looking at each other and reacting with one big collective: "Whaaaaaat?"

"Dr. Spitzer, you mean to tell us, that despite the fact that most of us in this conference room today have distinct memories of a professional relationship with Colonel Cohen, in reality, none of us really know this man at all?" Dr. Goldstein enquired, not quite as totally shocked as everyone else who was listening to Dr. Spitzer's testimony.

"Please allow me to interject on that question, Dr. Spitzer." Responded Dr. Rachel Morningstar, Professor of Physiological Psychology and Neuroscience at the Jerusalem DNA Analysis Center. "That's exactly what we're saying, Dr. Goldstein. The memories that we have of Colonel Cohen are all lies, deceptive implants in our minds, all part of a carefully designed, most elaborate scheme, creating a web of dream state entanglement. Some of us are not quite as susceptible to the dream, but most are totally unaware we're dreaming. A good analogy was posed by the French philosopher, Rene Descartes, when he asked the question: If we use the same senses while awake and dreaming, how do we definitely know if we are awake or dreaming? Our senses can deceive us in a dream or wakened state, making it impossible to distinguish between the two experiences while actively experiencing them and virtually impossible to determine our state of consciousness. Ichabod Cohen is sadistically playing on this premise. Everyone on Earth right now is in the midst of an extremely terrifying nightmare. If you hadn't have had the wherewithal to bring that napkin to Dr. Schindler, Dr. Goldstein, I venture to say that the vast majority, if not all of us, would be clueless that Colonel Cohen is even capable perpetrating such a travesty. It is the harshest of realities, and we have yet to determine all the worst-case scenarios that may occur. Potentially, Ichabod Cohen may very well be the source of everything that is evil."

"Yes. When I last spoke with Dr. Schindler over the phone, it was more than apparent that she was quite shaken." Dr. Goldstein responded. "Now, I'm totally understanding why!"

"Dr. Goldstein, the way all this initially came to my attention is when I heard the most blood curdling scream that I have ever heard in my life coming from Dr. Schindler, who at the time was making observations in the laboratory of that napkin you left her." Dr. Spitzer broke back in and stated. "And please allow me to say this as well: Our scientific team can provide extensive findings, even in graphs and charts, to this committee today to illustrate our findings. But with each and every fact we convey to you, the bottom-line, nagging question will continue to remain: 'What are we going to do about Colonel Ichabod Cohen?' We cannot allow him to remain in the capacity of being our High Priest. But to remove him from office will not be an easy endeavor. Obviously, obtaining the position of High Priest was part of his masterplan, and he succeeded."

"Dr. Spitzer, you're making it sound like we're dealing with some sort of an alien creature here." Dr. Goldstein said, trying to get right to the point.

"That's exactly what we're saying, Dr. Goldstein!" Dr. Spitzer blurted out. "Something that goes back, without exaggeration, to the beginning of time. And this creature only has a propensity for that which is evil. That's the reason for its existence. And that's reflected in its very molecular structure. There's little wonder why Dr. Schindler responded the way she did looking into that electron microscope while utilizing X-ray diffraction. I, literally, would have responded exactly the same way, if I had not had any forewarning."

"And based on the conclusions you've come to, Dr. Spitzer, you and your colleagues are emphasizing that it is in the best interest of the people of Israel to remove Ichabod Cohen from the office of High Priest." Dr. Goldstein asked.

"Yes, Dr. Goldstein." Dr. Spitzer said. "We are highly recommending to this most esteemed committee that Colonel Cohen be withdrawn as Israel's High Priest. But even if he is no longer serving in that position, it will, by no means, stop the impending danger that is imminent. It will merely prevent him from carrying out his intentions from that particular place of power, which is significant, because he has access to the Temple. He is covered by the media literally more than the Pope, and people trust him. It is imperative that Colonel Cohen be isolated. I may even go so far as to use the term, "quarantined.""

"And allow me to add, Dr. Goldstein," Dr. Barnabas Abelman, Professor of Bioengineering, Genetics, and Genome Sciences, interrupted, "Colonel Cohen is trusted because he appears to be doing a good job, and people think that he has been appointed by his worthy peers. But Ichabod Cohen is an actor as well as a charlatan, and he has, incredibly enough to believe, substantial hypnotic power to put the entire world into a binding, never-ending spell. And this is occurring right now in history according to his own agenda. We're not totally certain what this anomaly is, at this point, but we have managed to come to some very concrete deductions. But just as much as we can analyze the DNA of an animal of any species and say with 100% accuracy that it's not a human being, so we may, therefore, conclude with 100% confidence that Colonel Ichabod Cohen is not human. But in his case, there is much more to the story than just merely determining that he is not human. Colonel Cohen intends to abolish anyone who does not conform to the organized plan that he has already set in motion. And he has supporters, whether they be overt or covert. But one thing is certain: Colonel

Ichabod Cohen is a subversive enemy of Israel. And the Petri Laboratory Dish containing Colonel Cohen as a specimen, so to say, by way of analysis, reveals quite clearly that he is a microscopic and macroscopic threat to the entire world."

"We've been successful in determining many of Colonel Cohen's characteristics from his chromosomes, and not one of those traits of his genes can be described as pleasant." Esther finally spoke up, as head of Biomolecular Chemist and DNA Analyst for the Jerusalem DNA Analysis Center. "And it needs to be mentioned that none of his traits follow the pattern of that of a normal human being, or a human being at all. Ichabod Cohen is a chameleon, and he can change color or take on any form that he chooses at will. He could be described as a very counteractive missing link, because he is the complete antithesis of continuity or acquisition of complete knowledge. Whatever Colonel Cohen may be, his purpose is not to fill in the gaps between the species to provide more understanding. His total ambition leads to nothing but utter annihilation of anything that's good and decent in the world, to track down everything wholesome in life and stamp it out forever. Placing Colonel Cohen in a Petri Dish shows us that every last colony of microorganisms present in the dish within the reach of the colonel will be completely destroyed, and he is a hideous pathogen to witness as the last one standing. So, decisions need to be made as to how this situation should be approached and confronted, whether it be scientific and/or spiritual. We are up against an ordeal of unparalleled, epic proportion. Colonel Cohen does not have Israel's best interests at heart. Neither does he have the world's best interest at heart. Colonel Ichabod Cohen does not have a heart. That's what needs to be the focus in this meeting more than anything else."

Dr. Goldstein recognized the duress that Esther had been under, and feeling mostly responsible, out of sheer empathy turned to David, and said (addressing the king formally), "Your Highness, all four of these scientists have chosen, out of a great sense of urgency, to get right to crux of the matter, rather than going through the usual procedure of explaining the in-depth scientific details that led them to their conclusions. The discoveries these scientists have made led them to determinations that are, without a doubt, no less than momentous. I believe that I speak for all of us when I say that I fully embrace the impact of their deductions. Also, I would say that some consideration needs to be shown on our part that these scientists could use some rest and further protection from our security forces. We have been provided with enough information so that we have the idea, and I would suggest we schedule another time to let these scientists inform us of all the essential particulars."

David concurred and rescheduled a day and time for the four scientists to return, so they may get some well-deserved rest.

Dr. Goldstein made a special point to catch Esther just as she exited the conference room door, saying, "Esther!" As he took her gently by her arm. "I had no idea it would be something of quite this magnitude and proportion. I'm truly sorry."

"No one could have possibly foretold it, Samuel. I was only glad to be of assistance to you --- and to Israel." Esther responded, taking both of her arms and pulling Dr. Goldstein in closer to her, not at all concerned that anyone may notice. "Now, Samuel. I know you all too well. You approach this very carefully, Dear. You're right on the front lines."

"I'll act accordingly, Esther." Samuel confidently said, gazing Esther directly in her eyes as they embraced. "You know, the biggest mistake I ever made in my life was letting you go."

"You never lost me, Samuel" Esther said, holding his hand and keeping him within arm's reach until they both let go., but not before she kissed Dr. Goldstein passionately on his lips. Reluctantly, Esther tore herself away from him to walk toward the front Royal Palace exit, to the limousine waiting for her. But Dr. Goldstein quickly followed her out to the limousine, opened the door, and gently helped Dr. Schindler in.

"In actuality, Esther, I've never let you go, because you've always been on my heart." Dr. Goldstein confessed.

"You as well with me, Samuel." Esther replied, clinching her lips as a single tear streamed from the corner of her right eye. "You stay out of harm's way, you dear man!"

Then, the limousine pulled away.

Dr. Goldstein turned around and came back to the Royal Palace Conference Room entrance, where it was just David and Jonathan remaining.

"Something's got to be done about this guy, Dr. Goldstein." Jonathan remarked, as he stood beside David.

"I couldn't agree with you more, young man." Dr. Goldstein replied.

"Dr. Goldstein, do you remember our dinner together at Harvest Restaurant in Cambridge, when we all speculated about playing God in regard to destiny?" David asked.

"I do, indeed, David." Dr. Goldstein replied. "I remember that entire conversation as fresh as if it happened yesterday. It's quite fascinating how we've had a number of dramatic manifestations come to pass in regard to our discussion that evening."

With that, David simply looked up at the modern-day prophet, and said with a nod, "You're quite a guy, Dr. Goldstein."

"Ditto, David. You as well, Jonathan. You two boys are my heart. You and your families mean the world to me." Dr. Goldstein rendered, nodding back at David and Jonathan. And then, the Senior Advisor to the King of Israel was gone.

THE ISRAELI TEMPLE
JERUSALEM, ISRAEL

The people of Israel had not been able to offer animal sacrifices at the altar since 70 A.D., after the Romans destroyed the Temple. Now that the Temple had been rebuilt, Israelis had been coming twice a day for the regularly scheduled times in the morning and evening for the burnt offerings, or on other Jewish special occasions such as Passover, Israel's most popular holiday and David and Bathsheba's favorite Jewish holiday. Just as described in the Book of Leviticus in the Hebrew Bible (the Old Testament), when the God of Israel gave Moses the plan for the Tabernacle, the altar for the burnt offerings in the new Temple as well was made out of acacia wood, overlaid with bronze, about eight feet square, and four-and-a-half feet high. And in respect to the Temple, as one entered its

Outer Court, the altar would be at the top of the steps. And between the altar and the doorway to the Temple would be the bronze laver where the priests purified themselves. As stated in Leviticus 17:1: "Animal sacrifices are rendered in regard to the atonement of the soul." The people would come to make an offering, and the priests would take the risk for Israel of moving into God's presence.

The Tribe of Levi is the most important tribe in Israel because the priests were responsible for the spiritual leadership of the Jews. Hence, the High Priest is the center of attention, and the current High Priest, Colonel Ichabod Cohen, had an extremely high approval rating among the Israelis. But now, more light had been shed on the subject. Now, it was crystal clear to Israelis in high-ranking places that all of Israel had been deceived on a grandiose scale. And it was more than confirmed to Dr. Goldstein that his hunches had been right on target all along.

It was Friday evening, at the beginning of the Sabbath, and the High Priest, Ichabod Cohen, was burning offerings at the altar in the Outer Court of the Temple on behalf of the Israeli people, wearing his holy garments and breastplate bearing twelve various colored gems representing the Twelve Tribes of Israel. The regulations for the burning of offerings are very rigid, and violations are taken quite seriously. The way in which the offerings are sacrificed as outlined in the Book of Leviticus must precisely follow God's guidelines, and Colonel Cohen was smart enough to keep up all appearances.

The Pathway: Color Picture Photo Edition

Yet unnoticed to the High Priest as he stood alone at the altar, Dr. Goldstein had come up the steps of the Temple within a range of fifty feet of the Colonel's right side, pulled out an Advanced IWI Jericho 941 semi-automatic, 9 mm handgun from a holster on his left side covered by his jacket, aimed it in the Colonel's direction, and shouted out in a firm, authoritative voice, "Cohen!!!"

Colonel Cohen looked up from the altar to his right, and before he even had a chance to change his facial expression, Dr. Goldstein, without any hesitation, opened fire on the High Priest, making consecutive shots from a pistol possessing a sixteen-round capacity. All the bullets fired were intentionally directed dead center at the forehead of the High Priest. Cohen fell to the surface of the Outer Court, having been inflicted with multiple gunshot wounds. Dr. Goldstein's prior IDF training and continued target practice provided him with deadly accuracy.

Dr. Goldstein brought the handgun down slowly to his right side. And with the semi-automatic gun still clinched in his hand, Dr. Goldstein looked up at the sight of Ichabod Cohen's fallen body, and very solemnly uttered, "Shabbat Shalom!"

Suddenly, without warning, three Temple police guards came out of nowhere with Tavor Assault Rifles blazing a spray of machine gun fire right at Dr. Goldstein. The Chief Advisor to King David went down immediately and curled up into a fetal position. Dr. Goldstein had made no effort to defend himself against the guards. He was well aware that he had embarked on a suicide mission.

Considering it was the Sabbath, there were a number of people at the Temple. Many were running in all different directions, and women were screaming in terror in the midst of what appeared to be the crime scene of a cold-blooded murder of the High Priest of Israel, not realizing that it was a justifiable homicide. The entire incident was broadcast over satellite television in broad daylight.

Jonathan furiously came running into the den area of the King and Queen's Palace where David and Bathsheba liked to relax after the workday with Solomon, Charity, and Shalom. The highly intelligent palace German Shepherd was intentionally making everyone laugh with several of his dog stunts.

"David! Bathsheba! It's Dr. Goldstein. He shot Ichabod Cohen just now. Dr. Goldstein was gunned down by Temple guards! It's been broadcast all over Israel!" Jonathan blurted out loudly.

Everyone jumped up simultaneously.

"Bathsheba, you stay here!" David urged.

"No, David. I'm coming with you." Bathsheba insisted.

David did not have the luxury of time to disagree with Bathsheba. They all ran as fast as they could out the front door of the Israeli Palace, and sprinted across the yard, to the turmoil awaiting them in the Outer Court of the Temple. Prince Solomon and Princess Charity followed closely behind. The two royal children loved Dr. Goldstein just as much as their parents. David could see the body of Ichabod Cohen slumped behind the altar. The sound of sirens could be heard close by, and then, David came to Dr. Goldstein laying in a puddle of his own blood. David didn't need to ask why this had happened. He and others knew why it happened, including Esther Schindler, who couldn't stop the tears from streaming down her cheeks. She was crying her eyes out, as she watched the horrific scene from her television monitor. The love of her life, who she had just seen at King David and Queen Bathsheba's Palace, was the focus of a live broadcast on worldwide television, laying in a pool of his own blood at the Israeli Temple.

"Oh, my God!" Bathsheba screamed out, crying uncontrollably, as she looked upon Dr. Goldstein.

A physician, who happened to be in the vicinity, was tending to Dr. Goldstein when David knelt down.

"I'm Dr. Lazarus Zelnick, Your Highness." The elderly doctor said. "I'm a Medical Doctor. I'm familiar with Dr. Goldstein. He'll die, if he doesn't get immediate medical attention in a hospital. I've examined the High Priest. He took three bullet wounds to the head. He's dead."

"And I stood upon the sand of the sea, and I saw a Beast (the false messiah) rise up out of the sea, having seven heads and ten horns, and upon his horns ten crowns, and upon his heads the name of blasphemy. And the Beast which I saw was like unto a leopard, and his feet were as the feet of a bear, and his mouth as the mouth of a lion. And the Red Dragon (the devil) gave him his power, and his seat, and great authority. And I stood and I saw one of his heads as if it were wounded to death. And his deadly wound was healed. And all the world wondered after the Beast. And they worshipped the Red Dragon which gave power unto the Beast, and they worshipped the Beast, saying, 'Who is like unto the Beast? Who is able to make war with him?'" Revelation 13:1-4

And before David had a chance to respond, a horrific scream in unison from both men and women went out that put chills down the king's spine. When David looked up, there was as plain as day, Ichabod Cohen standing in the Outer Court in his own strength behind the altar of the Temple.

"I thought you said Cohen was dead. He's on his feet now heading in our direction!" David said to the physician, but at the same time, not doubting for a second that the doctor knew what he was talking about.

"That's impossible! He was dead, Your Highness! If I'd had enough time, I would have written out a death certificate." Dr. Zelnick exclaimed. "It doesn't even appear from here like he has any blood or wounds on his face."

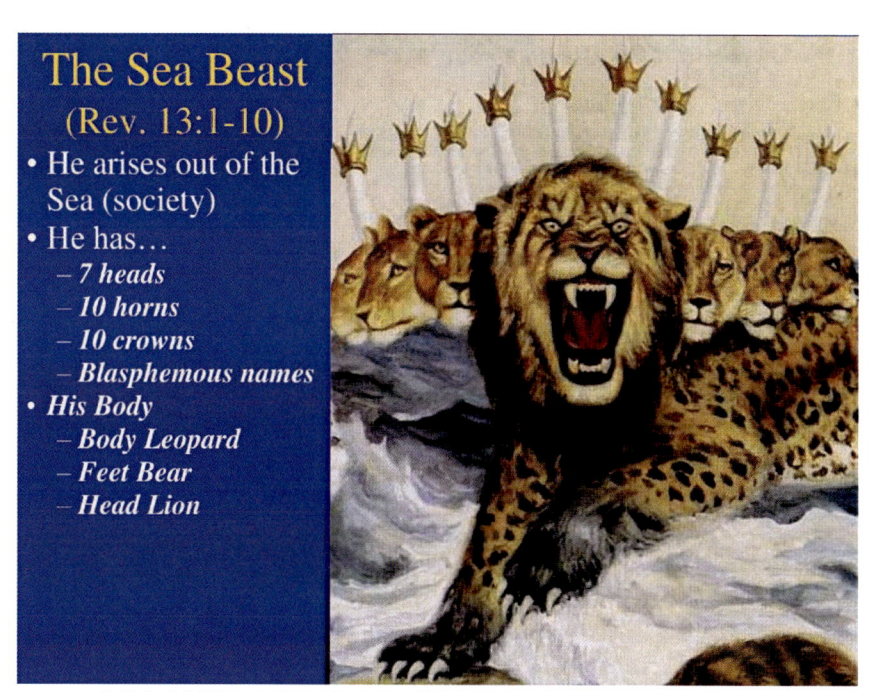

The Sea Beast
(Rev. 13:1-10)
- He arises out of the Sea (society)
- He has…
  - *7 heads*
  - *10 horns*
  - *10 crowns*
  - *Blasphemous names*
- **His Body**
  - *Body Leopard*
  - *Feet Bear*
  - *Head Lion*

COLONEL ICHABOD COHEN IS IDENTIFIED AS THE FALSE MESSIAH, THANKS TO DR. SAMUEL GOLDSTEIN

Colonel Cohen, flanked by a respectable number of Temple police guards armed with assault rifles, began walking toward David. All the people witnessing Colonel Cohen approaching the king in person at the Temple and those observing over television were absolutely paralyzed with fear and gripped with terror.

Cohen walked right up to David, without even a hint of a scar on his face, and said to his comrades, "Seize the Queen!"

And before David or anyone had a chance to react, the closest Temple guard reached out, grabbed Bathsheba, and held her at bay with his gun, quickly pulling her behind another Temple police guard, to use him as a barrier.

"I want that Ark, David! Perhaps, you'll grant my request now. You and I will talk terms in due course." Cohen said, with the look of an absolute madman on his face.

"No harm will come to the queen, Cohen!" David yelled out.

"The Ark of the Covenant will not work on your behalf, Cohen! The Ark of the Covenant is against you!" Jonathan shouted out.

"I'll take my chances, Jonathan. You bring that Ark to me, David! And just to show you that I mean business ---" Colonel Cohen began his threat, as he turned to one the Temple police guards. "--- Gun down Jonathan. We have no use for him."

Just as the Temple police guard was about to take fire on Jonathan, a distinct ferocious growl was heard, and all of a sudden, Shalom, the Palace's Royal German Shepherd, emerged from crowd. What had begun as a low, fierce barking developed into frenzied growling, as Shalom leapt into the air to attack the guard who was cocking his assault rifle, intending to take Jonathan down.

"Shalom!" Prince Solomon cried out.

"Jonathan, take cover now!" David screamed out. "Everyone, take cover!"

Shalom was in mid-air as the Temple police guard was just about to fire upon Jonathan. But the bullets tore into Shalom instead, causing the dog to hit the ground, whining and yelping in horrible pain. Prince Solomon and Princess Charity began crying over their mother being held hostage and the assault upon Shalom, knowing with certainty that their beloved, heroic dog was badly wounded.

Suddenly, the sky opened, and in plain view was the Ark of the Covenant in heaven, the architype of the Ark on Earth. And it began thundering, just as reflected in Revelation 11:19, the very chapter predicting David and Jonathan to be the Two Witnesses of the last days and making reference to the heavenly Ark of the Covenant.

After the Temple police guard was delayed by Shalom for a moment in carrying out Cohen's order to shoot Jonathan, he took aim at Jonathan again, and just as the guard was about to fire his assault rifle, a sharp, thick, jagged bolt of lightning streaked through the sky from the heavenly Ark of the Covenant, and hit the guard with such intensity that it completely disintegrated him, leaving nothing remaining but a smattering of ashes on the Outer Court of the Temple.

And so, it was demonstrated that David and Jonathan could call down fire from heaven just like Elijah, the Israeli Prophet. Yet Cohen did not appear to show the first stirring of panic.

Colonel Cohen yanked Bathsheba from the Temple police guard who was holding her and said, "I'm not impressed in the least. That parlor trick doesn't faze me one bit. These are my men, David. Not yours. They never were your men. You and all of Israel have been deceived on the largest scale imaginable. From now on, you are going to witness a dramatic shift in power. I'll have absolute power. I've had it all along, but, from this point on, it will become quite apparent to you."

"David!" Bathsheba screamed out, as Cohen yanked her inside the Temple.

"Bathsheba!" David shouted back.

"I want the Ark of the Covenant. Make no mistake about it. You will finally see it my way, or you and Israel will no longer have a queen. It's as simple as that." Cohen yelled, letting out a terrifying, reverberating, maniacal laugh that echoed in the Temple courtyard.

With that, Ichabod Cohen entered the Temple, with a host of Temple police guards posted at the door and all around the Outer Court.

The people who observed the events at the Temple, whether in person or on television, were simply in shock and utter disbelief. It had all happened so fast, a rapid series of devastating surrealistic events. The Temple in one quick, horrifying moment was transformed into a building of foreboding hopelessness. Solomon's Temple Rebuilt had, in one brief scene, been metamorphosized into the Tribulation Temple, plummeting the world into the Great Tribulation, Jacob's Trouble. Jeremiah 30:7, Daniel 9:27, Revelation 7:13-15, Revelation 11:3

David ran back to the spot where Dr. Goldstein laid. The doctor and Bathsheba had been caring for the fallen Prophet as much as possible until the ambulance's arrival.

David got on his knees and took Dr. Goldstein in his arms. Dr. Goldstein looked up at David, and said, "I saw the whole thing, David. Now, you know what you're up against. Listen to me. You're the one who's going to get Bathsheba back. You're the one who's going to make it happen. You and Jonathan are going to get the world back into proper alignment. Jesus Christ is going to use you and Jonathan to restore his Church. That's what this is all about. And rescuing your beloved Bathsheba will be the momentum to get our world back to the place it should be. I love you, my boy. You have a good heart. You are a man after God's own heart, David."

"I love you too, Dr. Goldstein." David said, as tears streamed from his eyes. And with that, Dr. Samuel Goldstein closed his eyes, tilted his head unto David's left arm, and passed away, leaving David to rock Dr. Goldstein back and forth, wailing and bellowing in pain as no human being had ever suffered before. The overall scene at Solomon's Temple Rebuilt was absolutely heartbreaking.

CHAPTER SIX
JACOB'S TROUBLE

> Alas! for that day is great, so that none is like it: it is even the time of Jacob's trouble; but he shall be saved out of it.
> —Jeremiah 30:7

"When you, therefore, shall see the Abomination of Desolation, spoken of by Daniel, the Prophet, stand in the Holy Place, then let them which be in Judah flee into the mountains." Jesus Christ – Matthew 24:15, 16

"And there was given unto the Beast a mouth speaking great things and blasphemies. And power was given unto him to continue three-and-a-half years. And he opened his mouth in blasphemy against God, to blaspheme his name, and his Temple, and them that dwell in heaven." Revelation 13:5,

"And the Beast shall speak great words against the Most High, and shall wear out the saints of the Most High." Daniel 7:25

"And one of the Elders answered, saying unto John, the Apostle, 'Who are these that are arrayed in white robes? And where did they come from?' And John said unto the Elder, 'Sir, thou knowest.' And the Elder said unto John, 'These are they who have come out of the Great Tribulation, and have washed their robes, and made them white in the blood of the Lamb. John 1:29, I John 1:7-9 – Therefore, they are before the Throne of God, and serve him day and night in his Temple. And he that sits on the Throne shall dwell among them. For the Lamb of God (Jesus Christ) who is in the midst of the Throne shall feed them, and lead them unto the living fountains of waters." Revelation 7:13-15, 17

"And in the middle of the Seven Year Tribulation (the beginning of the Great Tribulation), the evil prince shall cause the sacrifice and the oblation to cease, and for the overspreading of abominations he shall make it desolate." Daniel 9:27, The Abomination of Desolation

"And they shall pollute the Sanctuary of strength, and shall take away the daily sacrifice, and they shall place the abomination that makes desolate." Daniel 11:31, The Abomination of Desolation

"And the Beast caused all, small and great, rich and poor, free and bond, to receive a mark in their right hand, or in their foreheads. So that no man might buy or sell, unless he has the mark, or the name of the Beast, or the number of his name (666)." Revelation 13:16, 17

The official unveiling of the false messiah masquerading as the High Priest of Israel immediately ushered in a worldwide civil war. And this particular war would be spiritual in nature. It really is a new kind of war. On one side of the civil war were those with the Mark of the Beast. And on the other side were those with God's Mark. The God of Israel was most insistent of anyone who was not concerned with the best interests of his people: "Touch not my anointed!" Psalm 105:15. This became the landmark day when everyone in the

world would ultimately choose whom they would serve.
Joshua 24:15

There was not one single doubt in the mind of any Israeli around the world now as to the true identity of the false messiah. With absolutely no sense of shame, the pretensive Ichabod Cohen had openly made a loud and clear declaration of being the all time archenemy and ultimate nemesis of the Israeli people on international television. And given the devilish, demonic, and shocking manner in which the fiendish High Priest revealed himself, it was obvious now that he laughed in regard to how cleverly he had feigned to falsely have allegiance to Israel. And right in the very middle of the Seven Year Tribulation, a large segment of the world's population, without conscience, is rooting Ichabod Cohen on, while the remainder of the people on Earth are aghast beyond words. Jacob's Trouble, if there ever was trouble on the planet of Earth, was now being openly manifested as the Israeli Prophet, Jeremiah, had accurately predicted. Daniel, the Prophet, had also prophesied the ongoing three-and-a-half year event - Daniel 9:27, but it was Jeremiah who coined the term, "Jacob's Trouble." The Supreme Troublemaker's identity, Colonel Ichabod Cohen, was out of the bag.

There were now two distinct camps that comprised popular opinion in the world. One camp declaring that Cohen is the greatest thing to ever come along since sliced bread, and the other camp asking: "Who does this guy think he is?"

A tremendous shift of power became quite apparent in the world on the day Ichabod Cohen dramatically rose from the dead in false messiah form, returning to life to immediately kidnap the Queen of Israel, and hold her captive in, of all places, the Israeli Temple (now officially the Tribulation Temple), not far from the very spot where Bathsheba had ironically dedicated the third Jewish Temple three-and-a-half years earlier to the God of Israel..

And it was from the room of the Holy of Holies in the Temple that Ichabod Cohen made worldwide broadcasts, proclaiming himself to be "The Most High (God)," declaring that he alone is the long awaited Messiah.

But Cohen still does not feel that his blasphemy is complete without having the Ark of the Covenant in his possession. Having possession of the Ark is an imperative requirement of Cohen's arrogance.

The prior three-and-a-half years of pseudo-peace were now over, and that was just fine for Ichabod Cohen. He didn't like the pretense of being a patriot of Israel. He was more than happy that things were all out in the open now, and that his magic moment in time had finally arrived. And while he did not have the Ark of the Covenant, he had the next best thing to insure that the Ark would become his prize soon, and that of course, being the Queen of Israel as his hostage.

So, the Abomanation of Desolation in the Holy of Holies, the place usually reserved exclusively for Almighty God's divine presence (Shekinah glory of God – equivalent to everlasting peace – Ezekiel 37:25-28), would take place even with the absence of the Ark of the Covenant. But Ichabod Cohen's chief ambition of defiling and desecrating God's Temple would not be complete until he had procured the Ark of the Covenant. In the meantime, Cohen fully intended on giving the impression that all authority had been usurped from the God of Israel and King David, and been given to him alone. The Holy of Holies in the Tribulation Temple was oriented toward heaven. And the false messiah considered himself to have conquered both heaven and the planet of Earth.

Ichabod Cohen had not only became transparent in betraying the Jews, but also the treaty that he had arranged to appease Israel's enemies was realized to be a bogus joke from the very beginning. The reaction of the Israelis and especially King David was: "How could we have been so stupid?"

Shalom, the palace dog, was fighting for his life, and under the care of the best veterinarians in Israel. Bathsheba, the Queen of Israel, was being held hostage in the Temple. And Dr. Samuel Goldstein was shot and killed in front of the Temple. Dr. Goldstein tragically died in an effort to nip the entire situation in the bud, by eliminating Israel's most archnemesis.

For Bathsheba's sake and safety, David made limited responses to the Press, with the exception of pointing out that had it not been for Dr. Goldstein's courage, the entire world could still be under the strong hypnotic suggestion and delusion that all was well in the world. David brought this fact concerning Dr. Goldstein to everyone's attention in an effort to dispel any and all misleading rumors. As the nation mourned, King David ordered that all Israeli flags be flown at half-mast in Dr. Goldstein's honor. He encouraged the grieving people of Israel to pray earnestly for the safe return of their queen and for the full recovery of the palace German Shepherd, Shalom.

No factor of deception prevailed now. Everything was plainly out in the open. Not even a hypnotic Moon could cloak the harsh reality of recent events. The shock value of what had recently taken place caused everyone with any shred of decency and awareness to permanently be snapped out of their trance. People were waking up for good, and smelling the coffee. But they weren't waking up from a nightmare. They were waking up to a nightmare of the stark, bitter, real world that had to be faced. And those who were never affected by the hypnotic Moon were the ones who were conspiring with the false messiah all along. And they were just as happy as Ichabod Cohen that the pretense was over. The calm of the first half of the Seven Year Tribulation would cease and desist. And now, the moment had finally come that the false messiah had been waiting for, that is, the utmost desecration of the Temple referred to as the Abomination of Desolation, where the devil incarnate declares himself to be God, and, in the process, freely persecutes the Jews as they never have been persecuted before. Violent persecution will be the trademark of the false messiah's uncompromising rule.

THE BOTTOMLESS PIT OF HELL – REVELATION 20:1-4
THE DEVIL'S HEADQUARTERS – REVELATION 11:7

And, every time that the false messiah broadcasted his vile messages from the Temple in Jerusalem, it was always directly after he had, literally, emerged from the Bottomless Pit of Hell. It was becoming quite apparent that a monster had been created to defy God and destroy all those who opposed the false messiah's empire.

The entire world had been turned topsy-turvy as a result of Bathsheba being kidnapped. To all outward appearances, hell was having its way on the planet of Earth.

KING DAVID AND QUEEN BATHSHEBA'S PALACE
THE CONFERENCE ROOM

It was just David and Jonathan sitting alone together in the conference room of the Royal Palace. These two old friends had chosen to shut out the entire world for a moment to try to figure out for themselves how to get Bathsheba out of harm's way. They had no desire to listen to the expert advice of the Israeli Military Joint Chiefs of Staff. They didn't care what the seemingly concerned politicians had to say. They didn't, at this point, hardly trust anyone. They would not be comforted reading any of the letters of sympathy pouring in from all around the world. David and Jonathan were determined to come up with a solution of their own. They figured that if it was ever time to really believe they were the God of Israel's Two Anointed Ones of the last days, it was definitely now. Revelation 11:1-19

Colonel Jesse Hartman, David's father, Major Ariel Rosenberg, Bathsheba's father, General Sarah Majesky – Commander-in-Chief of the Israeli Defense Forces (IDF), Brigadier General Aaron Felderman, and others were waiting outside the conference room for the king and Jonathan to invite them in for a debriefing meeting.

The dim darkness of Bathsheba's confinement had become her worst enemy. There was hardly any light in the place where she was being held hostage, with Bathsheba enduring conditions that were worse than a maximum-security isolation prison cell. There was no difference between day and night, and she had no idea if she would ever see the light of day again. Time had lost all meaning as well. Her kidnapping had become a nightmare that seemed to have no end or recourse. Cohen had placed her in a solitary dungeon. Bathsheba's body was tense, cramped, and screaming with pain, from spending most of her time suspended to a wall, being attached by chains. She fought to keep from fainting due to the agony she was in. Constantly entertaining the thought of seeing David again reinforced her focus on somehow escaping her plight.

When Bathsheba opened her eyes, she was surrounded by nothingness. It was so dark that she could not even make out the outline of the dungeon. All the memories between her and David kept flooding back. And Bathsheba, being the sweet, tender girl she is, wept time and time again.

Over and over, thoughts of her captivity gave Bathsheba involuntary shivers. She was determined not to be beaten by her plight, and her courage was succeeding in sustaining her. She was an innocent victim taken hostage by a madman.

When she was given something to eat, she forced down every morsel, with the faint hope of maintaining enough strength to be rescued. And Cohen prodded her to eat so he could "get that Ark from David." So, she ate every bit she could. But she was in a situation that anyone would have considered hopeless, especially considering the ruthless antagonist who had taken her hostage.

"I must survive." Bathsheba thought to herself. "I must fight to stay alive, just as my brave ancestors have survived."

In between not being chained up during meals, she would exercise, as much as possible, to keep her body strong, many times practicing the martial arts she had once trained in. From time to time, Bathsheba was allowed to take a shower. Then, it was right back into the dungeon where she was chained up again. And each time she took a shower, afterwards, it was the hardest thing imaginable to have to go back to solitary confinement. The isolation was unbearable. At certain points, Bathsheba found it difficult to breathe. Time went by slowly, because there was no way to keep track of time. Yet no matter what she may have been doing at any given moment in captivity, Bathsheba always managed to concentrate and focus on her education and all the romantic literature that David had quoted to her through the years, especially at Harvard. All of Bathsheba's thoughts burned and blazed to fight off overpowering fear, until her mind was empty of every other emotion excluding her love for David.

Bathsheba's head was pounding, and every muscle in her body ached. She was totally fatigued and exhausted. She calculated her options. Either she would be rescued, be killed, or just fade away. She knew escaping on her own could not even be considered as an option, merely a fleeting thought. And then, there was the extremely remote chance of being rescued. And it took every ounce of energy she could muster up just to get her through each passing day.

Yet Bathsheba had no illusions. The odds were against her. There was a faint hope of her being rescued. Even if David should choose to turn the Ark of the Covenant over to Cohen, there still wasn't any guarantee whatsoever that Cohen would return Bathsheba safely into David's care. Cohen had turned the Temple into his own impregnable fortress and headquarters. It more than appeared that Bathsheba would die at the hands of her captors, whether David turned over the Ark or not. There just didn't appear to be any realistic way of escape or rescue. And the noises she heard outside her dungeon cell were surrealistic and terrifying in the uncaring darkness.

The fact that Ichabod Cohen kept the Queen of Israel harnessed in chains, with the exception of allowing her to have meals and take showers, was a crystal-clear reflection of his cold, cruel hardness and rule with an iron fist disposition.

At this point, there was no difficulty reading sinister implications into all of Colonel Cohen's overtures. Cohen was capable of anything. And even with the prospect of David coming to Bathsheba's aid, there was the nagging doubt that she would not survive the circumstances of her situation. It was quite possible that Bathsheba's health would have withered too far for a good recovery after a potential, hypothetical rescue.

Anyone, objectively speaking, would have to concede that Bathsheba was engaged in one of the most intense spiritual dilemmas of all time. If the God of Israel had not miraculously equipped her from the time when she was first conceived to be the special lady of fortitude that had shaped her resilient demeanor, she would have never even survived this long. But the situation had culminated into a desperate, bleak, and unmerciful picture for the beloved Queen of Israel.

Being in the dungeon was a form of living in oblivion. Bathsheba was all alone in the dark. She had no idea how close she was to the edge of her sanity, considering all the constant bizarre sounds she had heard and horrific bedlam she had witnessed. And as Bathsheba reminisced about the conversation that she, David, and Jonathan had with Dr. Goldsmith at the Harvest Restaurant in Harvard Square near Harvard University, which served as one of her favorite memorable moments in life, she reflected upon Dr. Goldstein depicting her as the woman war of war in Song of Solomon 6:10. Bathsheba realized she was currently living the extremely critical moment that he had predicted would occur. Now, Dr. Goldstein was gone, and Bathsheba appeared to be in a hopeless situation. She knew, based on Dr. Goldstein's insight, that she was a special target of the enemy of her soul, the false messiah who held her hostage.

"Who is she that looks forth as the morning, fair as the Moon, clear as the Sun, and terrible as an army with banners?" Solomon referring to his mother, BATHSHEBA, THE QUEEN OF ISRAEL
SONG OF SOLOMON 6:10

Miraculously, a golden light appeared that caused Queen Bathsheba to lift her head up. As Bathsheba focused on the light, all of her despair immediately dissipated. The golden light saturated Bathsheba with a tangible inner peace, and each vector of light that brightened the once dismal dungeon served as rays of hope to penetrate the darkness. Every one of Bathsheba's fears subsided. And all of the scars that had been inflicted upon her in life were soothingly healed.

"And there appeared a great wonder in heaven, a woman clothed with the Sun, and the Moon under her feet, and upon her head a crown of twelve Stars." REVELATION 12:1
THE BLESSED VIRGIN MARY – THE QUEEN OF HEAVEN

And manifested before Bathsheba in the midst of the golden light was a strikingly beautiful, radiant lady dressed in a white robe, wearing a crown that displayed twelve distinct Stars, and she was carrying a Rosary in her right hand.

"Fear not, my precious child!" The vibrant lady admonished. "I am here to help you."

Bathsheba knew right away who the woman was standing right in front of her. She was not the least bit fearful at the sight of the Blessed Mary making an appearance. In fact, Bathsheba was totally relieved to witness this glorious confirmation that Dr. Goldstein was, indeed, a genuine Prophet of God.

"I am the Immaculate Conception, the mother of Jesus Christ." The virtuous lady asserted. "And you are the courageous, beautiful

Bathsheba, the Queen of Israel, the wife of King David, and the mother of Prince Solomon and Princess Charity."

Bathsheba burst out in tears. She was so thankful for the Blessed Mary's gracious visitation.

"I am honored by your presence, dear, majestic lady. These are tears of joy!" Bathsheba clarified.

"I understand." Mary responded with compassion and empathy. "You need to know that all of heaven is working on your behalf. You are on the hearts of many good people. God's angels are battling visual and unseen forces to secure your freedom. I am here to assure you that you have not been forgotten. Your captivity has signaled the Great Tribulation, and I am here to comfort you. You are greatly loved, Bathsheba. We intend to see that no harm comes to you and that you are safe. And I have much to share with you."

The Blessed Mary paused for a several seconds, in consideration of allowing Bathsheba to bask in the realization that she was in the presence of a wonderful friend. Just like Dr. Goldstein had predicted, the Queen of Israel would one day encounter the Queen of Heaven. The woman of Song of Solomon 6:10, the mother of Solomon, would one day meet the shining woman of Revelation Chapter Twelve, the mother of Jesus Christ. And today was that most eventful, supernatural day of divine intervention!

And in that dismal dungeon where Bathsheba was being held captive, the Holy Spirit was comforting Bathsheba. And the Holy Spirit was a gentle as a dove with a feminine quality, just like the Hebrew word for Spirit (also meaning breath or wind) is "ruach," denoting the character of a lady. Even the descending dove symbolizing the Holy Spirit at Jesu Christ's baptism was associated with feminine attributes. Matthew 3:13-17, Mark 1:9, 10, Luke 3:21, 22,

DAVID AND BATHSHEBA'S ROYAL PALACE
KING DAVID'S CONFERENCE ROOM
JERUSALEM, ISRAEL

"I wasn't quite sure if I was going to make it through Dr. Goldstein's funeral. It's one of the most difficult things I've ever had to face. And there's no way I could have made a speech to the people of Israel at this point while Bathsheba is still in captivity. All it would accomplish is adding fuel to the fire and putting Bathsheba in more jeopardy. I have to maintain a code of silence until she's safe." David said.

"I couldn't agree more, David." Jonathan concurred.

"There's only one way to rescue her, Jonathan." David exclaimed.

"The tunnel leading from the Royal Palace to the Temple." Jonathan responded. "It's a good thing you had that built on a top secret basis."

"That's right. We're going to take control of the roof for safekeeping, as a look-out point. But the underground tunnel that I secretly had built from the palace to the Temple is the only possibility of catching Cohen and his men off guard. But a serious problem does occur to me." David speculated.

"Yeah. How is it possible that the ruler of the underworld is not aware that the tunnel exists? And while we didn't include Cohen in on the planning and building of the tunnel, how can we be sure that he doesn't know anything about it. And even with the tunnel, taking Cohen and his men by surprise is going to be a stretch. But we have no other alternative. We sure can't rush any of the Temple doors. A stupid move like that would jeopardize Bathsheba's life." Jonathan broke in, having read David's mind.

"That's exactly right. If Cohen was a normal human being there would be no way he would know about the tunnel. But after what we witnessed in front of the Temple the other evening, it's difficult to say exactly what he knows and what he doesn't know. We could be setting ourselves up for an ambush. But we know for a fact that Cohen doesn't know everything. He, certainly, doesn't know the location of the Ark of the Covenant. Somehow, the God of Israel is pulling the wool over Cohen's eyes. It's the one and only explanation." David pointed out. "Otherwise, the Ark would definitely be in the Holy of Holies of the Temple right now."

"Well, I became convinced a long time ago that Israel has a pretty clever God. And based on that fact, we're going to have to take the chance of going through that tunnel connecting the palace and the Temple to rescue Bathsheba, David. It's the only possible way to get her out of there. At least we know the area of the Temple where she's located. They turned that room where they're holding her into a medieval dungeon. And when I viewed her on the security monitor, she looked very physically weak." Jonathan said, deeply concerned.

"Both of us have been trading notes with security. That's a very good thing. Because another consideration is that we may think those hidden cameras in the Temple are undetectable, but we may be underestimating the perspective powers of that monster, Cohen. I've seen Bathsheba in those chains. I can't bear the thought of her being in those conditions." David replied, seething with a wave of raging anger that overrode any propensity of fearing the bizarre circumstances he would encounter in rescuing Bathsheba.

"Speaking of monsters, David. The guys in security have been briefing me on what's going on in the Temple ever since Bathsheba was kidnapped. It appears that Ichabod Cohen is manifesting himself in true form from time to time." Jonathan remarked, with an underlying tone of fear.

"What are you talking about?" David asked.

"Well, do you remember when you, me, and Dr. Goldstein were at Mount Tabor, and Jesus made reference to the Red Drago, which is depicted in the Twelfth Chapter of Revelation?" Jonathan asked.

"You have got to be kidding me?" David said, in an alarmed manner.

"Cohen, in true form, is a fire breathing Red Dragon, David! Dr. Goldstein didn't lay down his life for nothing! I've seen that thing over the monitor myself! It's a strong reminder of the Red Dragon spoken of in the Book of Revelation. And that's not all. Cohen has practically turned the entire Temple into a dungeon. It didn't take him long. It's like the Middle Ages in there now. There are crushed bones of good Israeli soldiers on the floors of the hallways from when they made their hostile takeover of the Temple. Cohen's men knew far in advance about all the genuine Israeli soldiers in and around the Temple that they were going to have to bring down." Jonathan informed.

"And he's completely taken over Yitzhak Rabin Israeli Air Force Base as well. He took it right out from under us." David said with disgust. "Cohen goes way beyond being a narcissist."

"He's taken over the world overnight right under our noses." Jonathan responded. "David, Cohen is the narcissist to the narcissists."

"But I can't help but cling to Dr. Goldstein's last words to me, Jonathan. He said, with his last, dying breath, that I will be the one to get Bathsheba back to safety. I mean, Dr. Goldstein was always right on target where prophecies are concerned. He never missed it, not once. The Restored Samuel was always right on target with his predictions. And he assured me on his deathbed that Bathsheba would be rescued!" David said, with genuine hope.

"The man was an authentic latter-day prophet, all right, David, coupled with the knowledge of just how much you're in love with Bathsheba, he knew you'd find a way to get Bathsheba out of this mess. He knew your heart! God knows your heart! It doesn't take Ezekiel, the Prophet, to figure that much out. We have to rely on that. Dr. Goldstein was right the mark with his vision of the Mount of Transfiguration, and you and I were empowered. Dr. Goldstein was always completely accurate. He prophesied all of this was going to take place, and now, it's happening right before our eyes. So all of this has to be leading up to something positive. We just have to take it one step at a time." Jonathan heeded.

"Logically speaking, the God of Israel is fully aware of our situation. The entire world witnessed the Ark of the Covenant in heaven annihilate that Temple police guard devoted to Cohen, who was about to open fire on you. There was nothing left of that guy." David said. "Even Ichabod Cohen acknowledged that he saw the Ark of the Covenant in heaven."

"And we have to determine how many men to bring with us." Jonathan pointed out to David. "Too few or too many men could present a problem either way. Not having enough men could mean not counteracting the situation effectively, and going in there with too many men may make the situation too crowded."

"What bothers me the most, Jonathan, is that I was taken in by Cohen more than anyone, endorsing him as High Priest." David grieved greatly. "And that makes me directly responsible for Bathsheba's kidnapping."

"Come on, David." Jonathan retorted. "No one could have possibly seen that worldwide hocus-pocus stunt coming that Cohen pulled off, putting us all in a trance. That nut is sinister. And the creepiest thing about it is that he saved it precisely for his primo magic moment."

"My God!" David cried out in an emphatic manner. "We've got to move fast. We must get her out of there immediately, even before Cohen has a chance to make more demands for the Ark of the Covenant to be brought to him at the Temple. There's no way I can officially declare war on Cohen until Bathsheba is free. And when she is free, it's going to signal that we're on the road to Armageddon."

"Yeah. And we're going to at least have to be able to wash this dragon down with an intense spray of dry ice, using some kind of portable unit, because fire or water won't work. But that's just for defense. We'll have to take the chance it will hold Cohen off, should he choose to manifest himself as a dragon and start breathing fire at us. I've witnessed that fire-breathing dragon in action over the security cameras. It's not a pretty sight. So, we're going to need something for offense. Bullets would probably bounce right off that armor-plated dragon. Laser guns may be effective though." Jonathan instructed.

Jonathan opened the conference room door to welcome all those who had been patiently and understandingly waiting to be admitted in the meeting.

"General Majesky, you definitely feel that your paratroopers can take Cohen's guards posted on top of the Temple close to the second we enter the Temple through the tunnels?" David asked sternly, expecting a direct answer.

"That's exactly right, Your Highness." General Sarah Majesky, the Commander-in-Chief of the Israeli Defense Forces (IDF), assured the king. "All of my paratroopers are trained well enough to land on a shekel at just the precise second. Cohen's men won't even know what hit them. And from that point on, it will be my men on guard on the Royal Palace roof. And it will provide us with a good vantage point of the Temple while our other men are immobilizing and neutralizing Cohen's guerrillas outside the Temple. It will all combine to provide us with enough control outside the Temple until our queen is safe."

"And General Kunstadt," David continued, contriving and reviewing the overall plan, "you feel confident about putting Cohen's outside Temple guards out of commission without any detection at all?

"You can count on it, Your Highness." General Donald Kunstadt boldly responded. "We'll all move in together exactly on time. Between our camouflaging techniques and the tricks our security personnel are going to play on the cameras that Cohen has in use, no one will know the better."

"And Captain Tokajer," David turned Captain Eric Tokajer, maintaining a stern demeanor, "You and your personnel in Security somehow have the capability of giving Cohen's men, who are monitoring the interior cameras of the Temple, the impression that it's just regular business as usual, despite the fact that Israel troopers have penetrated the Temple via the tunnels?"

"Absolutely, Your Highness!" Captain Tokajer confidently responded. "Cohen's Security personnel will be monitoring a recording that our Security team will set up on the cameras in the Temple to give the appearance that everything is going smoothly. They will have no idea that you and your men are inside the Temple."

"We've got to gain as much control as possible, but whatever we do," David said emphatically, "we all have to keep in mind that we're not there to reclaim the Temple. We're there to rescue Bathsheba. We're going in to get her, and then, we're, immediately, moving back out. And we've got to count on the fact that we have the advantage that our God is capable of blinding this monster from perceiving the tunnel and our miniature cameras inside the Temple. We've got no choice but to count on it." David said. "Perhaps dependence upon the God of Israel is what this is all about!"

"You hit the nail right on the head, David! I feel the very same way. And there is one final issue I might bring up: Should we allow our king to participate in such a dangerous assignment?" Jonathan posing the question as his friend, fully aware that David wasn't going to miss being a component of this venture to rescue Queen Bathsheba.

"We've got to get her out of there, Jonathan!" David replied.

"And Jonathan said to David, 'Go in peace, forasmuch as we have sworn both of us in the name of the Lord God of Israel, saying, The Lord be between me and thee, and between my seed and thy seed forever.'" I Samuel 20:42 – The Eternal Covenant between David and Jonathan

"Then, Jonathan said to David, 'The Lord God of Israel be between me and thee forever.'" I Samuel 20:23

"The Lord's oath was between them, between David and Jonathan." II Samuel 21:7

THE TRIBULATION TEMPLE
JERUSALEM, ISRAEL
THE TEMPLE MOUNT

A hidden door to one of the back walls of the Temple electronically slid open. It was quite apparent that the engineers who possessed the savvy to design such a marvel door were born geniuses. David and Jonathan advanced with ten men right behind them. The total of twelve men seemingly represented one man for each of the Twelve Tribes of Israel. They darted quickly out of the dark void of the tunnel, wearing military issue camouflaged tan, brown, and green guerilla tactical uniforms, with black paint on their faces.

The wall automatically shut behind the Israeli guerillas as they advanced. They practically marched in disciplined cadence down the long, spooky corridor. The Israeli raiders, carrying portable, highly modernized dry ice units with nozzles and laser guns strapped around them, knew exactly where each one of Cohen's men were posted for that particular time of day. Hopefully, Cohen's men weren't on to them. Each one of Cohen's men on guard were standing at attention at their posts, with intense, watchful eyes.

It was all too apparent by the eeriness of the Temple interior that the building had without question been transformed from Solomon's Temple to the Tribulation Temple. It was a vast, horrible comparison, a horrific sight to behold, at the very least. The once beautiful, dazzling inner realm of Solomon's Temple Rebuilt had been reduced to a House of Horrors, hence, the Tribulation Temple.

"Now, I know how Daniel felt in the lion's den!" Jonathan muttered to David, as they entered the spook house.

The twelve men were just about to turn the corner where they knew one of Cohen's soldiers would be posted. Jonathan, being out in front to the right, was ready. And as he came around the corner to the new hallway, he gave the soldier a sharp jab to his stomach with his elbow, and then, a karate chop to the rear of the neck of Cohen's loyal henchman, putting the soldier down on the floor, rendering him unconscious.

David and Jonathan continued to move forward, as two of their men stayed behind long enough to tie up Cohen's blacked-out soldier and gag his mouth with tape.

David, Jonathan, and his men knew when they came around the next left turn, on the other side, there would be two more soldiers posted on each side of the door to the dungeon chamber where Bathsheba was being held hostage.

As David and his men rounded the corner, the two soldiers posted at the door were at attention with their rifles strapped on their right shoulders. The Israeli rescue team came around the corner so fast that it caught Cohen's two posted soldiers totally off guard.

"Hold it right there!" David shouted. "These are laser rifles. One wrong move, and you're going to be a couple of post toasties."

David's men quickly grabbed the two guards, disarmed them, gagged them with tape, tied them up, and got them out of the way.

"That was too easy." Jonathan keenly noticed.

David looked through the bars of the little window of the door to the room where Bathsheba was held captive. He could faintly see her on the other side of the dimly lit room, chained to the wall. David's heart completely broke in half. Bathsheba appeared completely lifeless, with her head hung down.

"Bathsheba! It's David. You're among friends now!" David declared, sounding as confident as he could. "We're getting you out of here right now!"

Up to this point, in a state of utter weakness, Bathsheba had felt the dungeon wall completely close in on her. She had become the defiant victim of a slowly unfolding ordeal. Her throat had become raw from screaming at the terrifying scenes that she had heard and witnessed. Except for the faint hope that David would rescue her, she was left with the mind-numbing prospect of being caged in this purgatory for the remainder of her days, at the hands of an unmerciful culprit. It was a modern form of medieval torture. The monument of the Temple that she herself had dedicated before all the people of Israel had now, in an evil twist of fate, become the catalyst to seal her doom. And had it not been for the timely, encouraging visitation from the Blessed Mary, Queen Bathsheba would surely be dead by now.

David once again used his laser handgun to destroy the lock on the door.

David and Jonathan ran up to Bathsheba, with five of their men covering their backs inside the room and the other five men posting themselves outside of the room.

"You came for me, David!" Bathsheba exclaimed. Her heart accelerated as David approached her.

"I had to come, Bathsheba. You're all I've got." David immediately replied.

"The people of Israel did not forget me in their prayers." Bathsheba stated in a rejoicing tone.

"We've all been most concerned about you, Bathsheba." David made it clear to her. "You're special in the sight of the Lord."

David pulled out a hand-held laser gun.

"Now, Bathsheba, stay perfectly still." David insisted.

"Anything you say, Your Highness." Bathsheba cheerfully responded.

David fired the laser pistol attentively at the shackles until they had broken free from both of Bathsheba's wrists. She slumped over David as the chains lost their grip upon her, being too weak to stand on her own.

David carefully held Bathsheba up, so that they were now face to face.

"Are you glad to see me?" Bathsheba said in a sparkling manner, successfully sounding upbeat despite her physical weakness. And all fragility aside, the sight of suddenly seeing David charged her with electricity.

"I'm always glad to see my favorite person!" David responded, quickly surmising that he had to get Bathsheba to the nearest hospital. "We need to rush you to a doctor to get your strength up. I want you to get on my back and ride piggy-back. Now, here's what I need you to do for me, Bathsheba. I'm going to hold your legs, but just in case I need to use my weapons, I'm going to have to depend on you to keep both your arms and legs wrapped around me as tight as you possibly can, because we're going to safely get you out of here. And everyone in Israel is going to be jealous of me, Bathsheba, because they will have wished that they had been the ones to have rescued you. Okay? Can you do that for me?" David instructed in an understanding manner. "Everyone wants to see the First Lady of Israel up close and personal."

"I can do that just for you, David." Bathsheba replied.

"That's my girl." David responded with a reassuring smile followed by a determined expression. "Now, here we go, okay? Let's get you to a safe place, my love."

"Okay, David. I'd go with you anywhere!" Bathsheba said in a helpless manner. "It's just nice to hear the sound of your voice."

David and Jonathan darted out of the room where Bathsheba had been held captive, surrounded by five of their men to the front and five to the rear, in protection of their queen.

They made it around the right turn without hindrance, but when they came to the next turn to the left that would take them directly to the wall leading to the tunnel, their worst fears came true.

There, in the middle of the hallway, was the single most hideous looking monster that anyone could possibly imagine, blocking the way to the tunnel of escape. It was, indeed, the Red Dragon, as depicted in the Twelfth Chapter of the Book of Revelation. Cohen's human demeanor was enough to give most people the creeps, but his manifestation in dragon form was abominable, appalling, dreadful, and outright terrifying.

The dragon had appeared out of nowhere in full fire-breathing fashion, and the men in front of David and Jonathan pulled out the nozzles to the advanced dry ice units, hoping to move the menace off to one side long enough to allow them to get by. All five of the men simultaneously focused the dry ice on the fire coming from the charging dragon, but it was to no avail. Even all twelve men shooting the dry ice at the fire breathing dragon at full force barely made a dent to quench the threatening fire.

The dragon was relentless. When the dry ice machines miserably failed to accomplish their purpose, all twelve of the Israeli men went for their laser weapons. The laser beams bounced right off the approaching Red Dragon, like the sun being deflected from a mirror.

And just when it seemed that David, Bathsheba, Jonathan, and the ten Israeli soldiers were about to be overcome with the fire coming from the dragon's mouth, two wonders appeared that could only be explained as coming from heaven. Just as it's stated in the Twelfth Chapter of the Book of Revelation, the Archangel Michael along with another Archangel, in this particular case, Gabriel, suddenly appeared along with other angels to do war with the Red Dragon. Michael and Gabriel bravely and gallantly stood between the dragon and David's party. "And Michael and his angels fought against the dragon." Revelation 12:7

THE RED DRAGON - REVELATION 12:3

"And there appeared a great wonder in heaven. A woman clothed with the Sun, and the Moon under her feet, and upon her head a crown of twelve stars. And she brought forth a man child. And there was a war in heaven. And Michael and his angels fought against the Red Dragon. And when the Dragon saw that he was cast down to the Earth, he persecuted the woman which brought forth the man child." Revelation 12:1, 5, 7, 13

"Who is she that looks forth as the morning, fair as the Moon, clear as the Sun, and terrible as an army with banners?"
Song of Solomon 6:10

Then, all of a sudden, the Archangel Michael said the dragon, "The Lord God of Israel rebuke thee, Satan!" Jude 1:9

"AND THERE WAS A WAR IN HEAVEN. AND MICHAEL AND HIS ANGELS FOUGHT AGAINST THE DRAGON."
REVELATION 12:7

With that said from Michael, it was just enough to not only cease the fire coming out of the dragon's mouth, but also render sufficient power to hurl and bounce the dragon off the interior Temple wall in a such a impactful fashion that the monster returned to the manifestation of a man, that is, Ichabod Cohen.

As Cohen, was lying there in disarray, the Archangel Michael said to David, Bathsheba, Jonathan, and the ten men as he pointed to the tunnel wall, their avenue of escape, "You may proceed."

It might as well have been an open invitation for Moses and the Israelite children to cross the parted Red Sea. Exodus 14:26-30

"Looks like we all really do have one common enemy." Bathsheba quipped to David, still securely riding on his back.

"Bathsheba, there's little wonder why you're the woman of war depicted in Song of Solomon 6:10." David exclaimed in all sincerity. "You are, indeed, God's chosen lady! You are special in the eyes of our Lord."

"I just take after my husband." Bathsheba replied, quite confidently and courageously.

The computer, connected to the sensors that were designed to detect the presence of David, Bathsheba, Jonathan, and their men, opened the wall, and all twelve of men with the Queen of Israel secured themselves safely into the tunnel that they would take to retreat back to the David and Bathsheba's Royal Palace.

"I'll see you in hell after I get the Ark of the Covenant away from you, David!" Cohen vehemently snarled contemptuously, after he had stood to his feet.

"And so it begins!" David yelled out in defiance, somewhat regaining his composure from all the high drama as the impenetrable wall to the Temple shut, officially signaling Bathsheba's rescue.

KING DAVID AND QUEEN BATHSHEBA'S ROYAL PALACE FRONT LAWN
KING DAVID ADDRESSES THE NATION OF ISRAEL AND THE ENTIRE WORLD VIA SATELLITE TELEVISION

The news of Bathsheba's freedom literally traveled faster through the grapevine via word of mouth than it did through all the various media broadcasts. And freedom was tangible again to Bathsheba. She would close her eyes, and continually relive the miracle of David rescuing her. No one was threatening her now. She was breathing fresh air. And after a time in the hospital to regain her strength, improve her composure, get some rest, and receive hospital antibiotics that the doctors recommended to fight off any infection to her body as she mended, the courageous, elegant smile that Queen Bathsheba radiated to everyone she greeted absolutely dazzled the nation of Israel.

"It has been with the utmost regret that I have not been able to address the nation of Israel since the dramatic, and even bizarre events that have taken place which have affected us all as a people." David said to open his message to Israel.

JACOB'S TROUBLE

JEREMIAH 30:7

As you know, our beloved queen has been held hostage, and to allow any sort of public communication would have put her life in further danger and jeopardy. This hindrance to be allowed to keep you informed has brought me immeasurable personal sorrow and pain. Yet it is with great happiness that I am able to officially report to you all that Queen Bathsheba has been rescued and in a very safe place now. And she would at this very moment desire to express her best wishes to all of you, and most sincerely thank you for your concern and prayers for her safe return. For that, both Bathsheba and I are, indeed, grateful to the good people of our nation, the apple of the God of Israel's eye. Deuteronomy 32:9, 10

I will not underestimate the challenge that is set before us all. Our country and our entire world is facing an extremely precarious situation. Many sinister undertakings have occurred in the course of years which have gone unnoticed because we have been under a spell of convincingly delusional smoke, screens, and mirrors. Now, for a host of various reasons, including the reenforcement of truth that our prophets of old foretold, we are fully aware of exactly what is taking place on Earth.

Now, there is no pretense, and we have become 100% enlightened to the precarious situation at hand. We are no longer influenced by any disillusionment. We see things now as they are in reality. And our perceptions now are not misconceptions any longer but are, indeed, the actual way that things are supposed to appear in our minds. And what we see and hear is accurate. We have been delivered from this veil of deception and entanglement. We have been awakened and revived by the God of Israel!" Ezekiel 37:10

Too many of the military establishments right here in our country have experienced a hostile takeover. An example of this would be that while Jerusalem Israeli Air Force Base and Golda Maier Israeli Air Force Base at the Temple Mount here in Jerusalem are both still intact. Yitzhak Rabin Israeli Air Force Base in Tel Aviv has been completely run over by our enemies, who are all led by Ichabod Cohen, a Jewish impostor of epic proportion. Considering the manner in which our adversaries have managed to gain control, it would not be an exaggeration to say that this travesty is transpiring all over the world, and the extent of these undesired, targeted takeovers is being thoroughly assessed.

We must rely, as we never have before, upon our God's provision. To think that we need to count on any outside resources from this monster we are dealing with would be a grave error. This archnemesis we are confronting would have us sell out to him, and I am here to assure all of our people that is not necessary. The Israeli people need not rely on Ichabod Cohen for anything. The God of Israel will provide for his people, and we have allies who love our nation, no country more than the United States of America.

I would implore the citizens of this country to be in close proximity of the bomb shelter that has been provided or reinforced for you. And keep your specialized, protective masks close at hand.

By the authority that has been invested in me, by the President of Israel, by the Prime Minister of Israel, the party members of our Parliament, the Knesset, and with the concession of the Joint Chiefs of Staff of the Israeli Defense Forces, all in unanimous agreement,

I, hereby, proclaim a Declaration of War in response to the clandestine forces that have deviously threatened our freedom. The shofar of Zion has sounded, and we must realize that this war is of God, and therefore, and it is God's battle. We are now at a great crossroads, and we are prepared to confront this situation in full force.

As the great Israeli Prophet, Jeremiah, predicted, Jacob's Trouble is upon us. Jeremiah 30:7 - All the forces of good and evil have merged together to engage in a final, ultimate showdown. And all those who run from this impending doom and gloom out of fear will run right into it.

But we must be confident that this new age Babylon will, in due time, become a deserted wasteland. And that all who pass by will be horrified and will gasp at the destruction they will one day see there. We count on the hope that modern-day Babylon will eventually become desolate forever.

Despite the bogus miracles this false messiah has projected to the world in cheap imitation style of our own true Messiah, and despite the fear he will attempt to continue to inflict upon of all good people within the sound of my voice, we will resist the oppressive rule of this brutal dictator and look forward to that day when we shall witness in amazement the coming of our Messiah, who will cause us to collectively overcome any and all adversity and deception. This must be our hope. We shall procure everlasting peace as a result after these dark days have passed. This perpetrator is the common enemy of us all. He is the very embodiment of all evil. He is a culprit who desires to create so much crossfire that we are fighting against each other. And when he is removed, everything else will fall back into its proper place, and the entire world will become properly aligned and in perfect order.

We are also here to pay our ongoing respects to our dear friend and fellow countryman, Dr. Samuel Goldstein. His death occurred in a noble effort to protect, defend, and enlighten the great country of Israel. Had it not been for Dr. Goldstein, the entire world right now may still be covered in an impenetrable shroud of deception. Dr. Goldstein did not consider his ultimate sacrifice to this cause to be a vain or empty one. And we shall question his profound wisdom in the face of the danger he bravely confronted on his own. Of all the people who have served as a mentor to me, Dr. Goldstein was the most human. And I am most confident that the God of Israel will allow me to see him again in a more glorious place.

And we are most thankful for the full recovery of our Royal Palace dog, Shalom, who belongs to all of Israel. His instinctive, heroic actions saved the life of my best friend and fellow comrade, Jonathan Diamond. And I, personally, believe Shalom's comeback power is indicative and most reflective of the recouping, comeback ability we all possess to be overcomers in this hour of despair. I would like to thank all of you who expressed sincere concern for Shalom's welfare.

In conclusion, considering the fact that we are, indeed, being confronted with hostile regimes diametrically opposed to Israel and her friends, it would be prudent for all of us to be reminded of the words of United States President John F. Kennedy, when he said:

'No government or social system is so evil that its people must be considered as lacking in virtue. For in the final analysis, our most basic common link is that we all inhabit this small planet. We all cherish our children's future. And we are all mortal. Confident and unafraid, we labor on --- not toward a strategy of annihilation, but toward a strategy of peace.'

Despite how evil a government system anywhere on Earth may appear to be, there are still innocent people within the borders of these countries desiring to be free from that evil.

Our forefather, Jacob, hoping in our Israeli Messiah to come, wrestled with an angel until the break of day, refusing to let the angel go until the angel blessed him. The angel blessed Jacob with the new name of "Israel." And just like Jacob, so too can we all have power with the God of Israel and power with men, as we prevail as one. And we can build an altar together at this place now, because our lives have been preserved. Genesis 32:24-30, Genesis 35:9-15

We must have faith that our God intends to restore Israel, and to restore unto us the years that the locust and the caterpillar have eaten, by the God of Israel's great army. Joel 2:25-32 - It is imperative that we believe that he will defend every city in Israel, especially Jerusalem, put his special mark of protection on us, and pour his Spirit out upon us. Joel 2:25-32, Acts 1:1-8, Acts 2:16, 17

The God of Israel has not forgotten his people, and the people of Israel have not forgotten him. May our God greatly bless you all."

There was no applause or fanfare at the conclusion of David's speech. The gravity of the situation weighed all too heavily upon the hearts of the people desiring to witness some resemblance of good again in the world. And the rescue of Bathsheba to many people represented that hope was still alive. David's words were taken quite seriously to all those who were within the sound of his voice. All sympathetic listeners were aware that they needed to be willing and active participants in bringing safety to their world. David's oration was a word to the wise.

It wasn't so much that people regained their power to correctly perceive the world all of a sudden that shook them so much. It actually was that people were shocked at how so many deceptive changes had taken place right under our noses, without them even realizing it. And their capability to now take it all in at one time and maintain complete composure was absolutely staggering. God's people took the words "Fear not" to heart. (Isaiah 41:10: "Fear not, for I am with thee. Be not dismayed. For I am your God." – "Fear not, little flock. For it is the Father's good pleasure to give you the kingdom." Jesus Christ, Luke 12:32) And their trust in the God of Israel gave them overcoming power in the face of so many negative, scary factors.

The Common Market of Europe, that is the European Union (EU), initially comprised of twelve nations of the European Economic Community on February 7th, 1992 at the signing of the European Union Treaty, paved the way for a European Ferderation that would go on to engulf all of Europe ("Tarshish" in the Hebrew Bible - The Old Testament), and eventually, the entire world. This union represents billions and billions of people. Technology had exceeded the maturity of mankind, and the dark side of the Internet was exclusively being utilized. In recent years, an undetected staggering explosion of computer and related electronic technologies all correlated with a one world computer that served to drive countries into a one world government, a one world church endorsed by the World Council of Churches, and a one world economy controlled by a single absolute ruler. The love of money (I Timothy 6:10 - the root of all evil) took complete precedence over the welfare of human beings. Greed will serve as the pervasive theme and mantra of the Great Tribulation.

The battle for the almighty euro-dollar, a new world currency, issued from the European Central Bank, a one world bank, would serve to choke out any and all remaining joy in life. Nations giving up control of their own money to an outside source caused them to lose control of their own future and independence. A one world financial system answering to a one world bank controlled people's lives and created a global community where everyone was accountable. Stations were set up around the world for people to have microchips implanted in their right hands or their foreheads to serve as a barcode for people to make transactions for goods and services. All those who did not receive the Mark of the Beast would be identified and either starve, live out in the streets, and/or be incarcerated or executed, as reflected in the Thirteenth Chapter of the Book of Revelation. The foundation of the new revived Roman Empire, also known as the modern, latter day Babylon or the United States of Europe, the single most evil system of government, had been firmly established. The super political state would track down, march over, and stomp out any good and decency on Earth in a militant fashion. Only an empty vacuum of void purposeless in life remained, placing people in the worst kind of bondage and tyranny imaginable. The false messiah, Satan's messiah of empty promises, would now be the great image to be bowed down to and worshipped. And all national identities and interests were fully expected to yield to one single global world view of this evil tyrant. An unmerciful false messiah was attempting to beat the people of God down into the ground over and over, until they submit or until they were pulverized.

The good news is that, according to Ezekiel 9:4, God has already placed his mark upon his own people. The God of Israel has poured out his Spirit. And the emphasis need NOT be placed on the Mark of the Beast. Total attention and significance should be totally focused on God's Mark upon his people.

"And the Lord God of Israel said unto the man clothed with linen, (Jesus Christ, the Son of God) who had the writer's inkhorn by his side, 'Go through the midst of the city, through the midst of Jerusalem, and set a mark upon the foreheads of the men that sigh and that cry for all the abominations that be done in the midst thereof." Ezekiel 9:3, 4

"That we should be the praise of his glory, who first trusted in Christ. In whom you also trusted, after that you heard the word of truth, the Gospel of your salvation, In whom also after that you believed, you were sealed with the Holy Spirit of promise." Ephesians 1:12, 13

"And there shall be no more curse. But the Throne of God and the Lamb shall be in it. And his servants shall serve him. And they shall see Jesus Christ's face (Matthew 17:8). And his name shall be in their foreheads." Revelation 22:3, 4

These fortunate souls will not be branded with the Mark of the Beast and will have no other alternative than to rely by faith upon God's provision. They will not depend on this evil world order, but they will look forward to the fair and peaceful government that the Israeli Messiah will offer. The fact that the false messiah's appearance on the scene has become a reality is enough to convince the Israelis that the true Messiah is soon coming. And yet, the obvious lack of love on the planet has enslaved mankind with a slow, agonizing torture. A Catch 22 lurks at every turn. The Great Tribulation has begun, officially signaling the point of no return.

The most compelling ray of hope in the Great Tribulation is that the God of Israel has raised up the Restored David and Restored Jonathan of the last days. As representatives of all the Israelis, these "Two Anointed Ones" of the Book of Zechariah paint a picture of both invincibility and vulnerability. They win, they lose, and they win again. Clothed in sackcloth, these "Two Witnesses" of the Book of Revelation mourn the persecution of God's people and the evil that is running rampant in the world.

THE GREAT TRIBULATION
JACOB'S TROUBLE
JEREMIAH 30:7, DANIEL 9:27, REVELATION 11:3

"There shall come a man who will oppose and exalt himself above God, so that he will be worshipped as God. He will sit in God's Temple, convincing others that he is God." II Thessalonians 2:4

"And in the midst of the week (The Seven Year Tribulation) the false messiah shall cause the sacrifice to cease, and for the overspreading of abominations, he shall make it desolate." Daniel 9:27 – The Great Tribulation – The Abomination of Desolation

"And I, Jesus Christ, will give power unto my Two Witnesses. And they shall prophesy a thousand, two hundred, and three score days (three-and-a-half years – The second half of the Seven Year Tribulation – The Great Tribulation), clothed in sackcloth." Revelation 11:3

"When you, therefore, shall see the Abomination of Desolation spoken of by Daniel, the Prophet, stand in the Holy Place." Jesus Christ – Matthew 24:15

Every last bit of the evil that the false messiah perpetrated upon God's people was quite intentional. He did it on purpose. He knew exactly what he was doing.

Pandemonium, fear, and confusion will impact the entire global community. The ensuing outcry of sorrow, loss, and panic will result in a titanic tidal wave (tsunami) of chaos. World economies, the Stock Market, the work forces, the militaries, and police forces will all be affected, resulting in global political, social, economic, and spiritual upheaval. It would be impossible to estimate the financial impact on the global economy. The Stock Market will plummet. New alliances, political shifts, and emerging leadership will arise on the planet. This will pave the way for the false messiah to rise to power in Europe. There is little wonder that a superior power (a sinister, power-hungry fiend) would find this to be an opportune occasion to take control of the global network of international commerce, not to mention political, religious, and military manipulation of the entire world. Desperate people would gladly welcome any recovery that would bring about some resemblance of stability from the ongoing chaos. Everything will give way and be dominated by materialism, atheism, secularism, humanism, relativism, superstition, and mysticism, all serving to induce fear in the public at large.

A godless worldwide state will become the environment successful in justifying war for the common good of the state only, with total disregard for its "citizens." As our culture continues to become more secularized, the stage will be set for the endorsement of war against all those who oppose the will of the state. Israel will have a central role in colliding with this world state. And the genuine Israeli Messiah (Mashiach ben David, who is, Jesus Christ) is expected to be the one to set the stage for what may be safely considered as the Battle of Armageddon in the Figurative Valley of Megiddo (which means involving all the nations of the world).

There will be an ongoing crisis in the Middle East. And at a certain critical point during this turmoil, all Israelis will have no other choice than to accept the reality that there will be absolutely no hope for lasting peace without the true Jewish Messiah appearing on the scene to rescue Israel from a horrific, inevitable plight.

And so far as the culprits who are responsible for the Church of Jesus Christ losing its simplicity, they will pray for the mountains and rocks to fall upon them because they will never be able to find the salvation (freedom from evil – Luke 23:28-30, Revelation 6:15-17) that's freely available only through the Israeli Messiah. Salvation will elude them for all eternity, and they will never have God's Mark upon them. Ezekiel 9:4, Ephesians 1:12, 13, Revelation 22:3, 4

And just as much as there was a war in Heaven, so too, in a reflection of direct correlation, there was a war on Earth. And Michael the Archangel, and all the angels of God will choose to do battle against the Red Dragon. Revelation 12:7

All good leaders of the nations of Earth were tense. And all were ready to take up arms against anyone they considered to be a threat.

"And I heard a voice in the midst of the four beasts say: "A measure of wheat for a penny, and three measures of barley for a penny.'" Revelation 6:6

"And I beheld and heard an angel flying through the midst of heaven, saying with a loud voice, 'Woe, woe, woe to the inhabitants of the Earth.'" Revelation 8:13 – The First Woe of the Book of Revelation

"These are the Two Witnesses, Two Olive Trees, and the Two Candlesticks standing before the God of the Earth. These two have the power of Elijah and Moses. And if any man shall hurt them, fire proceedeth out of their mouths. And when the Two Witnesses shall have finished their testimony, the Beast that ascends out of the Bottomless Pit shall make war against them, and shall overcome them, and shall kill them. And after three-and-a-half days, the Spirit of Life from God entered into the Two Witnesses, and they stood upon their feet. And great fear fell upon them which saw them. And the Remnant of Israel gave glory to the God of heaven. The second woe has passed. And the third woe will come quickly. And the second angel sounded. And there were great voices in heaven, saying, The kingdoms of this world are become the kingdoms of the

Lord God of Israel, and his Christ. And he shall reign forever and ever."" Revelation 11:4-7, 11-15 – The Second Woe of the Book of Revelation

"Woe unto the inhabitants of the Earth! For the devil has come down upon you, having great wrath, because he knows his time is short." Revelation 12:12 – The Third Woe of the Book of Revelation

All roads were pointing toward Jerusalem, Israel, the most fought over city on Earth. The Temple Mount, the most volatile soil in the world, as always, is the focus of concern. The obsession was continuing in unhindered fashion of who would be in control of this sacred ground.

The war had escalated to such an extent, that it required the full-time attention of all Israeli and American military personnel. Even David and Jonathan had become so involved in the escalation leading up to Armageddon that it had gotten to the place where they were being taken away from their loved ones more and more for an undetermined amount of time.

An Israeli Press Conference was held. The Israeli and American TOP GUN Fighter Pilots were being interviewed just prior to them taking to the skies. The remainder of the Israeli Defense Forces were promptly reporting to their posts.

"We're not out to look like heroes." Jonathan stated to the reporters at the Israeli Press Conference. "We're just wanting to get Israel out of this crazy mess."

"I suppose we haven't done enough." David added to Jonathan's remarks.

Air raid warning sirens were sounding all around Israel to warn her citizens of air raids, missile attacks, and offensive ground maneuvers imminent, directed against the civilian population. The air raid siren's alarm was deafening, consisting of a continuous ascending and descending tone.

Israel also declared a chemical-weapons civil defense alert. Civil Defense authorities instructed the public to don their specialized, protective masks and be prepared to take cover in their assigned bomb shelters.

The Muslim audible speakers positioned all around Jerusalem were going off its usual five times a day, leading people to prayer, but now, with much more urgency.

Jerusalem was under attack, and unfriendly armies from other nations were making advances toward the ancient city. The insistent sound of the loud sirens, piercing abruptly through the silence, indicated the obvious danger to the public.

"Behold, the day of the Lord comes. For I will gather all nations against Jerusalem to battle. And the city shall be taken. And half of the city shall go forth into captivity, and the residue of the people shall not be cut off from the city. Then, shall the Lord God of Israel go forth, and fight against those nations, as when he fought in the day of battle. And Jesus Christ's feet shall stand in that day upon the Mount of Olives, which is before Jerusalem on the East, and the Mount of Olives shall cleave in the midst thereof toward the East and toward the West, and there shall be a very great valley."
Zechariah 14:1-4

"Take heed that no man deceives you. For many shall come in my name, saying I am Christ. And shall deceive many. And you shall hear of wars and rumors of wars. See that you be not troubled. For all these things must come to pass, but the end is not yet. For nation shall rise against nation, and kingdom against kingdom. And there shall be famine, and pestilences, and earthquakes, in divers places. All these are the beginning of sorrows. Then, shall they deliver you up to be afflicted, and shall kill you. And you shall be hated of all nations for my name's sake. And then, shall many be offended, and shall betray one another, and shall hate one another. And many false prophets shall rise, and shall deceive many. And because iniquity shall abound, the love of many shall wax cold. But he that shall endure unto the end, the same shall be saved. And the Gospel of the kingdom shall be preached in all the world for a witness unto all nations. And then, shall the end come. When you, therefore, shall see the Abomination of Desolation, spoken of by Daniel, the Prophet, stand in the Holy Place (The Holy of Holies), then let them which be in Judaea flee into the mountains. For then shall be the Great Tribulation, such as was not since the beginning of the world to this time, no, nor ever shall be." Matthew 24:4-16, 21

"And when you shall see Jerusalem compassed with armies, then know that the desolation thereof is near." Jesus Christ, Luke 21:20

"Behold, I come as a thief. Blessed is he that watches and keeps his garments. And Jesus Christ gathered them together into a place called in the Hebrew tongue, Armageddon." Revelation 16:16

And at the Western Wall where the Jews prayed, mourned, and cried out to the God of Israel, it was standing room only. Everyone had an inclination of giving into fear knowing that a monster as sinister as the false messiah was lurking somewhere out there in the world, using the Israeli Temple as his base headquarters. David had admonished his people in earlier speeches to not give into that tendency.

"CALL UNTO ME, AND I WILL ANSWER THEE, AND SHOW THEE GREAT AND MIGHTY THINGS."
THE GOD OF ISRAEL - JEREMIAH 33:3

In the midst of all the panic and the wailing sirens, David and Bathsheba would say their final goodbyes to each other. Being the Queen of Israel and David's wife, she was allowed admittance nearby to where David would be mounting his F-22 Raptor. Bathsheba reasoned in her mind over the situation the best way she knew how.

A Pre-Flight Briefing had been held. The main distinction between this battle and the Battle of Gog and Magog would be that there would be many dogfights with unfriendly fighter jets, therefore, a great deal of communication would be required among TOP GUN Fighter Pilots during the Battle of Armageddon, along with making reports to and receiving orders from Israeli Command (Joshua). Another major distinction is that the Battle of Armageddon would involve every single nation on Earth, while the Battle of Gog and Magog engaged Israel with those hostile nations in and surrounding the Middle East. The Battle of Armageddon safely qualified as a world war.

David and Jonathan had been ordered to stay close to the perimeter surrounding Jerusalem. Armageddon, indeed, would prove to be a nightmare, but it was a nightmare that was actually happening.

JERUSALEM ISRAELI AIR FORCE BASE

Air raid sirens were blaring all over Israel. David was suited up to board his F-22 Raptor Stealth Fighter Jet. Bathsheba came to send David off at Jerusalem Israeli Air Force Base, which David had established as king years ago. Military personnel scurried all over the base, preparing for the war to end all wars. The royal couple were embraced just outside a hanger not far from David's F-22 Raptor. It was beginning to rain. Bathsheba had no idea if she was saying farewell to David for the last time. It was reminiscent of the final scene in the movie, "Casablanca," starring Humphrey Bogart and Ingrid Bergman.

Bathsheba: "You cheat death, don't you, David? You approach death like a poker game with high stakes. And even though the deck of cards is stacked against you, you insist on playing to win."
David: "Yes, Bathsheba. I cheat death."
Bathsheba: "You've played your last card quite a few times, haven't you, David?"
David: "That's perhaps a good way of putting it. War is the trade of all kings, Bathsheba."
Bathsheba: "No one knows you the way I do, David! I wish I could be with you when you're fighting in combat up there in the not quite so blue sky."
David: "You are with me, Bathsheba!"
Bathsheba: "When you're in battle, David, I contact Israeli Command every day and ask the Commander on Duty: 'Where's David? What's he doing?' So, go placidly, my Love, amidst the noise and confusion. You and I are so involved. You come back to me safe, David. We have a long way to go watching our children grow together. I will be right here waiting for you. Good things come to those who wait. When will we meet again, David?"
David: "I look forward to seeing you when the Israeli war is over!"
Bathsheba: "Until then."

    David walked away from Bathsheba, heading toward his fighter jet, considering how he never really believed in unconditional love until he had gotten to know her.

    Bathsheba couldn't help but think to herself about how that she and David were being separated from each other for an undetermined amount of time in such a melodramatic fashion. It was a heart-wrenching scene. She was so deeply absorbed in her thoughts that a loud clap of thunder in the midst of the falling rain didn't even shake or distract her total focus on David. Bathsheba's heart soared as she watched David walk away.

    The scene of observing these two being separated under such circumstances was absolutely devastating, heartbreaking, and gut-wrenching. All Bathsheba could do is watch David as the canopy to his F-22 Raptor went up, he positioned himself in the cockpit, and the canopy came back down. The engine to his jet fighter began to roar, and David was about to get back into the most dangerous game in the world on a full-time basis, in the single most treacherous war that would ever be fought. David took one last look out of the cockpit of his F-22 Raptor Fighter Jet only to get a final glimpse of Bathsheba in between the raindrops on his canopy as he prepared to take off.

From the very outset of Israel becoming a nation in 1948, the doomsday clock had measured the time it would take for the apocalypse to take place. Now, in the hearts and minds of so many people around the world, it was felt that the best way to gauge the potential length of the apocalypse would be to correlate Armageddon in terms of how long it would take for the King and Queen of Israel to finally be reunited once again.

"And the Lord Jesus Christ gathered them together into a place called in the Hebrew tongue, Armageddon." Revelation 16:16

CHAPTER SEVEN
THE BATTLE OF ARMAGEDDON

Revelation 16:16 KJV
And he gathered them together into a place called in the Hebrew tongue Armageddon.

DAVID AND JONATHAN SURROUNDED
BY THE APOCALYPSE

Commander David Hartman: "Joshua, Soaring Eagle airborne."
Commander Jonathan Diamond: "Joshua, Greased Lightning airborne."

DAVID AND JONATHAN TAKING OFF FROM
JERUSALEM ISRAELI AIR FORCE BASE

Joshua: "Roger, Soaring Eagle and Greased Lightning airborne."

Jonathan and David's fighter jets are in a parallel 45-degree tactical turn together in the upper atmosphere at 50,000 feet over Jerusalem, Israel.

Israel's version of the United States Strategic Defense Initiative, having the nickname of "Star Wars" missile killer system (proposed by President Ronald Reagan on March 23rd, 1983 – SDI), is called the Arrow-3 Ballistic Missile Interceptor. Israel's upgraded ballistic missile shield became operational to the extent that incoming nuclear missiles can safely be destroyed. The system was developed by Israel Aerospace Industries and the United States aviation giant, Boeing, and became operational in January 2017. The Arrow-2 has been in use even longer since 2000. The Arrow-2 is designed to intercept projectiles high and low within the atmosphere. The Arrow-3 rocket system is designed to intercept the longest-range missiles, including missiles traveling outside the atmosphere. Arrow-3 missiles will fly into space, where their warheads detach to be "kamikaze satellites" that track and slam into their targets. The Arrow-3 serves as the top tier of the integrated Israeli shield, built to withstand various simultaneous missile or rocket attacks.

The middle tier of the Israeli Missile Defense System is called, "David's Sling." This system, also referred to as, "Magic Wand," was developed to shoot down the newest generation of tactical ballistic missiles, mid-range, lower altitude rockets and Cruise Missiles.

Iron Dome is an Israeli land based mobile defense system that is designed to intercept short-range rockets and artillery, including Cruise Missiles. The Iron Dome interceptor is the bottom tier of the multi-layered Israeli Missile Defense System.

When all the multi-layered defense systems work together, they are, collectively, able to handle a number of threats and different types of threats at the same time, providing much better protection to the State of Israel.

Sophisticated space-based anti-ballistic systems were set up at orbiting laser battle stations, with the purpose of detecting and targeting a large swarm of ICBM warheads in and out of the Earth's atmosphere. But it was deemed more reliable to utilize friendly fighter jets with laser defense systems who were located in the regions of risk.

The Anti-Ballistic Missile (ABM) is the theater missile developed by Israel and the United States, specifically designed and built to intercept and destroy Intercontinental Ballistic Missiles (ICBMs) and submarine-launched ballistic missiles. An interceptor missile aimed at destroying a ballistic missile just by colliding with it is referred to as "Kinetic Kill Vehicles" or KKV.

The Aegis Ballistic Missile Defense System (Aegis or ABMDS) is the United States Department of Defense Missile Defense Agency's program that was developed to intercept short to intermediate-range ballistic missiles in their post-boost phase (not recommended to blow up a nuclear missile on the launch pad). This defense system employs interceptors that are most effective in destroying nuclear missiles just prior to their reentry into Earth's atmosphere from space. The American made Patriot System is used to shoot down enemy aircrafts. And of course, the United States have fighter jets with laser beam technology (Strategic Defense Initiative - SDI). This advanced defense system developed from the United States Air Force's Self-Protect High Energy Laser Demonstrator program, is also known as SHiELD.

The United States Department of Defense has declared Israel's effective multi-tiered defense system, capable of communicating effectively with each layer to shoot down targets, as a phenomenal success, hailing it as one of the most advanced defense networks in the world.

However, even with the impressive capabilities of Israel's missile defense systems, top Israeli officials warn that the defenses will not hold a complete, airtight seal in the case of all-out war, and some rockets will inevitably slip past the defenses. Despite all of the world-renowned defensive measures that Israel has in place, there is still no full proof guarantee that nuclear missiles, chemical weapons, and otherwise won't get through.

David and Jonathan were adjusting themselves to the mission ahead of them, determining how sophisticated the threat is, and the enemy's capabilities. In this case, the situation was extremely dynamic. It was imperative that David and Jonathan maintain their edge to be combat ready. No one had to remind them that their purpose was to gain control of the flying skies above and the territory below. Both David and Jonathan had integrated themselves into their fighter jets, men on board their machines, and had evolved together with the sole objective of that very purpose. To be successful in their respective, assigned roles, with David as the Squadron Flight Leader and Jonathan as his Wingman, their ambitions must be singular and primary. They would have to render a cool, calculated response to an unpredictable enemy at every turn.

One obvious task would be to quickly distinguish friends from foes. Other tasks include attacking multiple targets with beyond visual range missiles, use guns in close situations, manage advanced radar and electronic warfare gear, do it all in seconds, sustain G levels that push pilots to their physical limitations, and fly the complex Mach speed fighter jet from a cockpit containing primary and secondary control systems, requiring the pilots to make thousands of split-second decisions in the course of their day.

Since the beginning of the twenty-first century, air warfare has dramatically changed. Without the technology of a modern cockpit, the friendly fighter pilot would not be able to survive. In the closing speeds of Mach 2 and higher, pilots cannot hesitate to the merge and to attack. They have radar and weapons that make a kill more certain.

With an attack coming in that may provide as little as 10 seconds to react, sometimes less, there is no time to be looking around, inside the cockpit. The pilot's view is looking forward through the windscreen of his cockpit. This is the HUD, or the Head Up Display. It presents everything the pilot needs to see in order to fly. Precious seconds, otherwise spent looking down at his instruments, are now focused on looking outside, alert to potential threats.

Hands On Throttle And Stick (HOTAS) allows the pilot to manage every aircraft weapon task he needs without having to take his hand off either the throttle or stick. Microswitches allow him to take any action he needs. The HUD combined with HOTAS allows the pilot to control his destiny and win the fight.

No modern fighter pilot can win without the best and most complete information displayed on the HUD (HMDS – Helmet Mounted Display System), a bright window to look through, based on computer technology, day or night. For enemy forces, there's nowhere to hide. The HUD provides the pilot with real, continuous situational awareness, the key to a pilot's life or death. What's happened? Where are the threats? What are the weapon's envelopes? Can I kill? Am I vulnerable? Where is the danger coming from? The pilot must know what's going on, and the HUD tells him, with flight data, with radar data, with lock-in confirmation when he has a target in his sights. In every essential scenario for flying and fighting, the answers are there on the HUD.

The idea is to enhance the squadron's proficiency to do their combat maneuvering. The entire squadron must be combat ready, so when the pilots deploy, they will be the best they're going to be, that is, the best of the best. These brave fighter pilots are trained, at the peak level of confidence and skill, to master a machine that, perhaps, has reached the highest order of technological complexity. The aim is to win consistently in battle, at the risk of their lives every single day. There is little wonder why fighter jet combat is the single most dangerous "game" in the world.

Commander Ariel Rosenberg (Chief Israeli Defense Forces Commander at Israeli Command - Joshua): "Who's up there right now, Captain?"

Israeli Operations Officer: Soaring Eagle and Greased Lightning, Commander. They're in a 45-degree tactical turn in parallel as we speak."

Commander Rosenberg: "Soaring Eagle and Greased Lightning, up to their usual acrobats, I see. Chances are that it won't be a boring day."

Israeli Operations Officer: "All bets are off, Commander."

"This is very peculiar." Soaring Eagle (David) communicating with Greased Lightning (Jonathan), his Wingman.

"Joshua, Soaring Eagle and I are picking up an all-out invasion on radar. We have been detected --- Greased Lightning."

David banked left and dived down fast, in an effort to confuse the radar of incoming bandits. Radar is meant to look out into a blue sky where there is little clutter, and David was forcing the bandits to focus on the ground environment. So, now, the bandits have to recalculate their math to deliver any weapons.

David suddenly found himself in a 100% pure defensive, survival mode, and both David and Jonathan are in the deadly grip of the incoming bandits going for a lock-in with their weapons.
Jonathan: "Eagle, you're spiked! I've got an indication of a missile threat on my radar warning receiver. Break that bandit's radar lock by minimizing the Doppler signature of your jet."

"Jerusalem, we officially have a problem." David reported to Joshua (Israeli Command).

David, being in the extremely vulnerable position of losing everything, had no choice but to turn it all over to his Wingman. It looked like David didn't have a chance. He was in a purely defensive mode, trying to avoid being blown out of the sky, and had no choice but rely on his Wingman for survival. Jonathan was David's best hope of escaping the threatening bandit's deadly grasp.

Jonathan, being behind David, sees the situation, locks in on the lead bandit, and fires a Heat Seeking Aim 7 Missile. The missile reached the lead bandit on David's tail, resulting in a powerful explosion, and the fiery clutter of his aircraft descending toward the Earth.

Then, both David and Jonathan wondered, "What's next?" It was as vulnerable a situation as you could get into via an air-to-air dogfight.

There was little wonder why David was initially targeted by the enemy. Their rationale is probably that the king of Israel going down means that all of Israel will go down with him as well. David and Jonathan were playing a game of poker, and the enemy bandits were playing a game of chess.

David and Jonathan had two choices: Turn around and head in the other direction to run away from the incoming cloud of bandits or maintain a heading directly at them and fight the unexpected intruders. Considering how badly they were outnumbered at that bearing, they couldn't be blamed for retreating. But David and Jonathan flew straight ahead to confront the enemy. They took the path of greatest resistance.

David and Jonathan found themselves in an intense, continual aerial spiral with the invading aircrafts.

"They are coming out westbound as well, Soaring Eagle." David relayed to Israeli Command. "Tally, Joshua. We have more enemy bandits in sight, and then, some."

But there's still much more trouble. David and Jonathan are quickly configuring what's next. Broadcast Control alerts Soaring Eagle and Greased Lightning of four more bandits closing in fast, two from just eight miles away. One thing's for sure on the next go around. David and Jonathan would not be caught off guard again.

Soaring Eagle and Greased Lightning chose to turn and fly right at the bandits, to fight their way through.

David and the lead bandit that he was confronting faced off in an intense aerial spiral, and then went back and forth chasing each other's tails. Suddenly, the lead bandit, detecting David locking in on his aircraft with a weapon, flew directly down towards the Earth trying to out-maneuver the warrior-king fighter pilot. The bandit attempted to make a hard turn back up, but it was too late to escape his momentum downward. The bandit's afterburners were cooking, and he was doing everything he could to bring the nose of his jet level to the horizon, but it just didn't happen. The bandit had put himself into a no-win scenario that translated his fighter jet into an exploding fireball upon hitting the ground. David, immediately, reported to Joshua about the bandit having splashed.

"Splash! Splash One! That bandit hit the ground." David reported to Israeli Command (Joshia).

Suddenly, Israeli Command (Joshua) was receiving communications from members of the Israeli fleet with a massive amount of priority radar information regarding an imminent invasion that affected the entire world. The top secret information was all being channeled through Broadcast Control. It seemed like the entire allied fleet on duty had something vital to say to the friendly Command Structure. Situational awareness, for all good guy fighter jet pilots, was lighting up like a Christmas tree. Whether they were of military or civilian status, all those fighting the good fight of faith, that is, persevering through hardship and difficulty, certainly qualified as "troopers."

Jonathan: "Joshua, all airborne fighter pilots that are in the fleet in our perimeter are getting red flags. Battle lines are officially being drawn. This is not a drill! We have employment, many groups of bandits within range."

Joshua: "We're assessing the overall situation now, Lightning. The fleet has orders not to fire unless there is an imminent threat. That is an order to both the TOP GUN Fighter Pilots and the entire Israeli fleet. We are determining what kind of theater we're in and how busy it is. We are also surmising what nations these bandits represent. It's not a theory that this is a conspiracy. But obviously, Lightning, this order not to fire does not apply to you and Eagle. These bandits saw you and Eagle coming. Stand by."

Jonathan: "Wilko, Lightning standing by."

Soaring Eagle: "It's quite apparent Cohen is directly behind all this activity. It's the trademark of his commands. I can see his wheels turning now. He's in the sky now, dishing out orders."

Jonathan: "Heads up, Eagle. Joshua, Eagle is under fire! Man, that was close!"

David: "Horseshoes and grenades."

Jonathan: "Joshua, these bandits are coming at us like World War II Kamikaze Zeros. I repeat, they're approaching all of us like suicide fighter jets! They're determined to harm our king!"

Joshua: "We read you, Lightning. We're alerting the entire fleet to take their positions and stand-by for offensive action. We have reinforcement pilots headed your way. ETA is 3 minutes. We're continuing to access the big picture."

Jonathan: "Wilko, Joshua."

Israeli Commander Ariel Rosenberg: "It is official. The entire Israeli fleet is at major red alert status. We have some busy airways, people.

Keep your transponders on. Right now, consider yourselves to be in International Airspace. There are no boundaries in this situation."
Jonathan: "Looks like the big picture assessment is turning into one gigantic superpuzzle. Talk to me, David."
David: "Lightning, we have bandits inbound, Vector 070. And that's just to mention the enemy aircrafts coming from that particular heading."
Jonathan: "Received. I'll take the one at Contact 50, left at 20 miles with rapid closure. I'm going for my guns to start."
Mulholland Drive: "Joshua, we have bandits like fireflies all over the sky. Clouds of them."
David: "Joshua, this is Soaring Eagle. I have inbound aircrafts, identified as unfriendly, heading 5,7,2 at 15 miles, closing fast!"
Joshua: "Roger that, Eagle. We have it on radar as well. These bandits are coming in from all directions, all points west! That is confirmed.
Bethlehem Hawkeye: "Let's see how many of these things come out of the woodwork. Can you see any trailers?"
David: "I'm getting radar data, clearly showing a supernatural phenomenon that's working on our behalf, against these bandits."
Galilee Ghost: "It's like a swarm of locusts coming in from all sides, courtesy of Moses!" (The Tenth Chapter of Exodus) That means that the first woe of the Book of Revelation has pasted."
Geronimo: "The visual looks endless."
Tiberius Concorde: "They're the equivalent of Harriers and Boeing AH-64 Apache Helicopters. And even though these locusts originated from the Bottomless Pit like the plague, just as it happened in Exodus of the Torah, Moses has power over them."
David: "That's right. They're ours. And they're ordered not to attack anyone except those without the Mark of God on their foreheads, causing Cohen's directive to backfire. Revelation 9:1-12 - Moses definitely had a hand in this maneuver!".
Tel Aviv Baron: "Yeah. Moses is still in top form today, all right!"
Ezekiel: "No complaints from me. We'll gladly take the assistance."

The Pathway: Color Picture Photo Edition

By this crossroads in the battle, all of the Israeli TOP GUN Fighter Jets, the Israeli Defense Forces, and all of Israel's allies were absorbed in offensive and defensive basic fighter maneuvering.

David: "Lightning, I'm going head-to-head with these bandits to see how much company they've got! I'm going to break high and right and try to get a glimpse of how much backup these front runners have."

Jonathan: "They're nose-to-nose with me at 45 seconds closure, Eagle. They're coming right at us! Looks like they want to play chicken! Some of these bandits are on suicide missions, emerging right at us from the ground undetected. They're clustering our radar. That one bandit's afterburner passed across my nose, putting me at risk."

David: "You're the closest alligator to the canoe, Lightning."

Jonathan: "It's showtime, Eagle."

Israeli Commander Rosenberg: "Keep doing the math until we get an exact number of how many bandits are moving in. And let's get an accurate position on every last one of them."

Operations Officer: "We're working on it, Commander. Sensors are reading and calculating data to the quantum computer now for an overall assessment. We'll have complete computations very shortly, in several seconds."

Israeli Commander Rosenberg: "Let's get the stats on any and all the various computations complied as quickly as they come in and prioritize those scenarios. Collectively, we'll determine which groups are more tactically important to go after and where the attention needs to be focused."

Israeli Operations Officer: "I don't think any of us were expecting such an action-packed day, Commander."

Israeli Commander Rosenberg: "They don't call it Armageddon for nothing, Captain!"

David: "Lightning, you take Black Angel One. I'm going after Black Angel Two. I'll catch you on down the road."

Jonathan: "Sounds like a plan to me. And I'll be in Jerusalem before you. Wait a minute! I lost Black Angel One in the sun! Hold on. There he is. He's doing a 360-degree turn, and he's right on our tail!

This bandit is all over us! Joshua, we are under missile lock from the rear courtesy of the enemy, but we have a course of action."
Joshua: "Go with the flow, Lightning and Eagle. Focus your energy. You guys know the drill. Push the envelope."
David: "Acknowledged, Joshua. Lightning and I are going for a Bracket now."
Jonathan: "The Split worked, Eagle. Let's turn the tables and get them in a Bracket."
Commander Ariel Rosenberg: "Launch the Alert Six Aircrafts!"
Israeli Operations Officer: "Yes, sir!"
Jonathan: "Go get him, Eagle."
David: "I'm going for missile lock on Black Angel Two. Come on, Baby. I've got a lock on him! Bingo! He didn't even know what hit him."
Jonathan: "You got him, all right, Eagle! No shortage of work ahead."
David: "We're on the cutting edge."
Jonathan: "Yeah. We're definitely earning our paychecks today."
Commander Rosenberg: "Where are Lightning and Eagle right now?"
Operations Officer: "They're at heading 0, 9, 5 in yet another 45-degree tactical turn in parallel together, Commander Rosenberg."
Commander Rosenberg: "Armageddon doesn't even put a damper on those two acrobats!"
Jonathan: "Here comes another troublemaker! If I reverse on a hard cross, David, I could immediately go to laser guns on him."
David: "You're clearly in proper range for laser guns, Lightning."
Jonathan: "Done deal! That bandit is past tense now, Eagle."
David: "Gutsiest move I've ever seen. You're a hard act to follow. Joshua, we have bandits, right, at 10 o'clock. We're incognito at this bearing."
Jonathan: "Eagle, you've got the lead. You're covered! Break now."
David: "He's too close for missiles, Lightning. I'm switching to laser guns. That bandit is history!"
Joshua: "Israeli Command to the entire fleet. Just in case you suspected that we are engaged in Armageddon, you definitely have

it confirmed from us now at this bearing. Revelation 16:16 is upon us."

David: "Lightning, you've got a bandit hot on your tail. He's still back there. It's your old nemesis, Black Angel One once again."

Jonathan: "Yeah. I've got him in my rear sight. It's Black Angel One again, all right. I'd recognize that demon anywhere. Eagle, I'm gonna hit the brakes, and let him fly right by me. I'll wait for the Bullseye Point. Here it goes."

Jonathan slowed down to draw the bandit closer. Then, he did an abrupt pull up to slow down rapidly, which forced the bandit to overshoot and fly right in front of Jonathan, where a missile shot from Greased Lightning's fighter jet quickly nipped the fight in the bud.

David: "You're in charge, Lightning! You're the man."

Jonathan: "As promised, Black Angel One was all mine. That demon is washed up, Eagle! Thanks for the heads up."

David: "You are one cool cucumber, Lightning."

Jonathan: "It was butter. Just like that Eagle. I hit the high note."

David: "Smooth. Like butter. What a game changer!"

Jonathan: "I can't wait for tomorrow, Eagle."

David: "Why's that, Lightning?"

Jonathan: "Because I get more handsome every day."

David: "I somehow saw that coming, Lightning."

Commander Ariel Rosenberg: "We are officially at battle stations, all the way around. Maintain your firing positions. All Israeli TOP GUN Fighter Jet Pilots will adhere to details and directives coming only from the Israeli Messiah, Joshua, and Israeli Air Traffic Controllers. Listen to our directions to intercept on a designated track. You are all programed to the system and joined together in a network of information, like a giant jigsaw puzzle. Maintain your Link 16 360-degree view of the battlespace. It will provide you with more situation awareness of what's happening out there. We are all in this together. And as for you, David and Jonathan: Keep your head about you, Mates."

Commander Rosenberg's advice could not have come at a more opportune moment. As David and Jonathan aptly demonstrated in the Battle of Gog and Magog, they had the capability to destroy nuclear weapons, at a proper altitude, in mid-flight. The very same challenge arose in the Battle of Armageddon, with David, Jonathan, and other TOP GUN Fighter Pilots confronted with the dilemma of ballistic Surface-to-Air Missiles and ICBMs (Intercontinental Ballistic Missiles) being launched and heading, for the most part, toward Israel and the United States. This required maneuvers to intercept these nuclear weapons with as little harm as possible to the civilian population.

The TOP GUN Fighter Pilots successfully managed to intercept every, single last one of these weapons, with the assistance of satellites spanning the entire globe. The pilots counteracted these missiles using sophisticated lasers serving as particle beam weapons, along with high performance computer systems, and a great deal of command and control on the part of the pilots. Not one innocent person was harmed on the ground in the face of this extreme danger. Even at the very beginning of Armageddon, Mutually Assured Destruction (MAD) had become a potential probability. The pilots fired Ballistic Missile Interceptors at ICBMs to feasibly put these missiles out of commission, without any serious repercussions. Sensor systems on board the fighter jets and built in the satellites in space provided detection of the infrared signatures of the boosting missiles and accurate, reliable targeting data. Computers assisted in identifying the missile's exact location. These new, modified, digital interceptors were capable of shooting down adversary missiles at any point in its flight, including the boost phase when the rocket launch motors are firing. The pilots focused on intercepting ICBMs in space during their mid-course phase, in an effort to prevent civilians from being harmed.

Very fortunately, capable Israeli and allied fighter pilots were positioned all around the world, making it possible for them to be in the vicinity of the missiles when their launches occurred. This allowed the respective pilots in the air to penetrate deeply enough into enemy airspace to execute the intercept. The friendly fighter pilots would be able to avoid unfriendly anti-aircraft fire thanks to its stealthy design. Certain TOP GUN Fighter Pilots were specifically designated to intercept the nuclear weapons, while other TOP GUN Fighter Pilots were assigned to protect them from interfering enemy aircrafts utilizing their weapons.

The sheer number of nuclear weapons launched against Israel and her allies from nations with rogue governments left little doubt that the war being waged was unmistakably Armageddon.

CHAPTER EIGHT
THE PRESIDENT OF THE UNITED STATES' ADDRESS TO THE NATIONS OF THE WORLD

"Good evening, my fellow citizens of the United States, and all allies of America on the planet of Earth. The United States Government, as promised, has maintained the closest surveillance of a military build-up in our world. Unmistakable evidence has established the fact that a series of ongoing offensive nuclear attacks is now in preparation, endangering all of mankind.

The purpose of these unrelenting strategies can be none other than to provide further nuclear strikes from certain evil forces, attempting to undermine any and all safety that we cherish in our world. It has become quite apparent to everyone around the entire world that we all, at this present moment, are being faced with a devastating crisis of unparalleled proportion. The United States is currently on a MILITARY DEFCON ONE ALERT STATUS unprecedented in the history of our country, indicating that we are at maximum readiness and that an all-out nuclear war is imminent. As evidence of this build-up was already in my hand, it became quite apparent that all the nations of Earth are preparing for a war in which no man, woman, and child will be unaffected.

Those who are in opposition with each other on Earth can be divided into two distinct factions: The forces of good and the forces of evil. The opponents of good confront us on a battlefield composed of many confusing elements, mixed signals, and demoralizing crossfire. This conflict provoking the proponents of good has existed throughout all time. It has been an ultimate tragedy for all generations from the beginning of history leading up to our generation.

Ladies and gentlemen, we all stand at a critical, devastating crossroads at this very moment. I am speaking in no uncertain terms. We are all, now, at this very point in time, witnessing the unfolding of whether the forces of good or the forces of evil, with dyer and eternal consequences, will ultimately prevail and dominate the world, as we know it, once and for all.

It is the position and intention of the United States of America, in reaction to these clandestine, underhanded, and treacherous assaults that have been perpetrated upon us all, to bring about an unwavering, ultimate victory resulting in freedom from the tyranny of our enemies.

Therefore, acting in the defense of the security of the United States and all of our allies around the entire world, under the authority entrusted to me by the United States Constitution, as endorsed by Congress, and supported by the United Nations, the Joint Chiefs of Staff of the NATO member nations, and top-level supportive military leaders here in our country and throughout the entire planet of Earth, we will unanimously and officially remain at our highest military alert level as an integral part of our strategy to maintain protection from all of our minions, out of sheer self-preservation. In addition, I have directed that the following recommendations be taken immediately:

The United States is making an appeal, with a sense of urgency, that all of our allies around the world join forces with us to ultimately seek peace on a global basis. We implore the nations of Earth, who are committed to the good, common values that keep us content, prosperous, and thriving, to set aside conflicting political differences and perspectives long enough to connect with each other. I would consider it imperative that we take any and all opportunities to rally together as one in a unified effort to eradicate, once and for all, the evil that has plagued our world and inflicted pain upon so many harmless, innocent people. The expressed purpose of the United States, joining forces with all of our allies, is to conclusively put an end to this senseless suffering.

It shall be the policy of this nation to regard any offensive attack launched by our opponents upon our allies, especially Israel, as an attack on the United States, requiring a full retaliatory response.

Let there be no misunderstanding to anyone concerned within the sound of my voice. We are engaged in a campaign in which the outcome will result in either total victory or utter doom. May the human race be allowed to experience a future of peace. And may our prize, therein, be life, liberty, and the eternal pursuit of happiness.

I look forward to a great future for America. A future in which our country will match its military strength with our moral restraint. Its wealth with our wisdom. Its power with our purpose. I look forward to an America which will not be afraid of grace and beauty, which will protect the beauty of our natural environment. And I look forward to a world which will be safe, not only for democracy and diversity, but also for personal distinction.

It is the sincere hope of the United States of America that all nations committed with us as participants in this precarious endeavor will triumph in what should be considered to be the Battle of Armageddon."

The Pathway: Color Picture Photo Edition

AMERICA JOINS ALL THEIR ARMED FORCES
WITH ISRAEL --- FULL FORCE

THE WAILING WALL/THE WESTERN WALL
JERUSALEM, ISRAEL – PSALM 122:6

"The Lord bless you, and keep you. The Lord make his face to shine upon you, and be gracious unto you. The Lord lift up his countenance upon you and give you peace. And the Lord shall put his name upon the children of Israel. And he will bless them." Numbers 6:24-27 --- The Jews praying for the coming of the Messiah and his Millennial reign ---

No evil force on Earth could keep the Jews from overrunning Colonel Ichabod Cohen's armed troops stationed at the Western Wall. The Orthodox Jews were especially demanding to exercise their inherent right to freely cry out to the God of Israel at the Wailing Wall of what was once the Restored Solomon's Temple. Now, the Israelis were praying for the Messiah to come, knowing that he alone was fully capable of manifesting the Millennian Temple. And the trademark of this promised, permanent Temple is intended to be the everlasting international peace that's accompanied with it.

"Nevertheless, when the Son of God comes, shall he find faith on the Earth?" Jesus Christ, The Son of God, Luke 18:8

CHAPTER NINE
THE COMING OF THE ISRAELI MESSIAH, JESUS CHRIST
Matthew 24:27-31

"But they shall serve the Lord their God, and David their king, whom I will raise up unto them." Jeremiah 30:9

Israeli Commander Ariel Rosenberg to all Israeli TOP GUN Fighter Jet Pilots: "All right, gentlemen. We have had enough time to calculate the severity of the campaign that we are currently engaged in. The forces of evil have pulled out all the stops. This is the big one. In each combat sequence, you're going to continually be met with yet another original, different challenge. Each and every new encounter is going to get even more and more difficult. We will be guiding you in this battle to fly right on the cutting edge of the envelope, faster and more dangerously than you've ever flown before. Israeli TOP GUN Fighter Jet Pilot Rules of Engagement exist for your safety, gentlemen, and for that of your team. They are not flexible, nor is Israeli Command – Joshua (which means "Jesus"). You are the elite. You are all the best of the best. And at this very crossroads, you are going to have to be even better. This is the real thing. This is what you've been trained for. You are Israel's hope for peace, with the Israeli Messiah's blessing upon you all. The code name for this colossal operation is officially: "Crossing Over the Jordan River." That code name has been encrypted into your quantum computers onboard your fighter jets. Needless to say, this will be the colossal operation of all colossal operations for Israel. It will be an immense endeavor. This will be Armageddon unfolding right before our very eyes, that is, biblical prophecy in the making. And we need to ensure that this War of Armageddon, gripping our world today, is the war to end all wars, giving us the advantage.

Blood may come up to the horse's bridle in this battle. Revelation 14:14-20 - That's what we're up against. Let's make sure that the blood which is shed in this particular theater is not the blood of any Israeli or that of our allies. Keep in mind that you are God's chosen in battle, and that you are his anointed. And as the God of Israel's anointed, you cannot be touched by your adversaries. Psalm 89:20-23; Psalm 105:15; Isaiah 54:17 - You are filled with God's Spirit, endued with his power, and baptized with fire. Just like the Israeli Messiah, Jesus Christ, you are all Lions of the Tribe of Judah, whether it be by heritage or honorarily bestowed upon you. Nevertheless, you are all the warriors of Israel. And the Lion is not bothered by the thoughts of the leopard. You all have your assignments, gentlemen. Show us what you've got and make us proud."

"Jesus Christ shall baptize you with the Holy Spirit and with fire." John, the Baptist, Matthew 3:11

"That you may be mindful of the words which were spoken before by the Holy Prophets and the commandments of us, the Apostles, of our Lord and Savior, Jesus Christ. Knowing this first, that there shall come in the last days scoffers walking after their own lusts. And saying, 'Where is the promise of his Coming? For since the fathers fell asleep, all things continue as they were from the beginning of creation." II Peter 3:2-4

"The Day of the Lord will come when the nations of the Earth are gathered together against Jerusalem, Israel." Zechariah 14:1-4

"And the Israeli Messiah, Jesus Christ, gathered them together into a place called, in the Hebrew tongue, 'Armageddon.'" Revelation 16:16

"But they that wait upon the Lord shall renew their strength. They shall mount up with wings of eagles. They shall run, and not be weary. And they shall walk, and not faint." (Isaiah 40:31 - Israeli TOP GUN)

"Then shall there enter into the gates of Jerusalem kings and princes sitting upon the Throne of David, riding in chariots and on horses, and the men of Judah, and the inhabitants of Jerusalem. And this city (Jerusalem) shall remain forever." Jeremiah 17:25

"Comfort ye, comfort ye my people," says your God. "Speak comfortably to Jerusalem, and cry unto her, that her welfare is accomplished." Jesus Christ, Isaiah 40:1, 2

"O, Jerusalem, Jerusalem. Thou that killest the prophets and stonest them that are sent unto thee. How often would I have gathered thy children together, even as a hen gathereth her chickens under her wings, and ye would not!" Jesus Christ, Matthew 23:37

The very first words that were uttered from a distance in a most commanding, authoritative voice were: "Touch not my anointed!!!"

"And from Jesus Christ, who is the faithful witness, and the first begotten of the dead, and the prince of the kings of the Earth. Unto him that loved us and washed us from our sins in his own blood. And has made us kings (and queens) and priests (and priestesses) unto God and his Father. To him be glory and dominion forever and ever. Amen. Behold, he comes with the clouds. And every eye shall see him. And they also which pierced him. And all kindreds of the Earth shall wail because of him." Revelation 1:5-7

The entrance of Jesus Christ was sudden, instantaneous and without warning in catching everyone by surprise. No one knew the hour when the Israeli Messiah was going to appear. It occurred quickly and suddenly. In the twinkling of an eye, Jesus came out of nowhere. This is an event whose time has come. Zechariah 14:1-4, Malachi 3:1-4, I Corinthians 15:51-58, II Peter 3:3-13

In the midst of all the calamity of Armageddon, the brightest streaks of lightning ever witnessed began striking in and around Jerusalem, followed by the loudest thunder anyone had ever heard. Before the source of the voice could be determined as that of Christ, with each streak of lightning came words that could be recognized as scripture from the Holy Bible. From the very essence of Jesus, the Word of God came forth naturally, for he is the Word of God. John 1:1

"Behold, the Day of the Lord comes. He shall gather all nations against Jerusalem to battle, and he shall fight against those nations. And he shall stand upon the Mount of Olives." Zechariah 14:1-4

THE COMING OF JESUS CHRIST – MATTHEW 24:21-36
"PRAY FOR THE PEACE OF JERUSALEM" PSALM 122:6
MATTHEW 24:1-44

"Blow ye the trumpet (shofar) in Zion and sound an alarm in my Holy Mountain (Mount Moriah, The Temple Mount). Let all the inhabitants of the land tremble. For the Day of the Lord has come. For it is here. Joel 2:1

"'For, behold, the day has come that shall burn as an oven. And all the proud, yea, and all that do wickedly shall be stubble. And the day has come that shall burn them up.' saith the Lord of hosts. 'But unto you who fear my name shall the Sun of Righteousness (The Son of God) arise with healing in his wings. And you shall tread down the wicked. For they shall be ashes under the soles of your feet in the day that I shall do this.' saith the Lord of hosts. 'Remember the law of Moses, my servant, which I commanded unto him in Mount Horeb (Mount Sinai) for all Israel, with the statues and judgments. Behold, I will send you Elijah, the Prophet, before the Coming of the Great and Dreadful Day of the Lord Jesus Christ.'" Malachi 4:1-5

Suddenly, as an unprecedented event, and at the sound of a trumpet, Jesus Christ, the Israeli Messiah, came forth in the clouds with a host of angels and saints behind him, causing the inhabitants of the nations of Earth to be in absolute awe of the sight. And Jesus opened his mouth, and the Word of God continually came out in great power, destroying all those who had brought harm and injustice upon his people.

"'And the Lord Jesus Christ, whom you seek, shall suddenly come to his Temple, even the Messenger of the Covenant – Jesus Christ – whom you delight in. Behold, he shall come.' saith the Lord of hosts. 'But who may abide the Day of his Coming? And who shall stand when he appears? For he is a refiner's fire!" Malachi 3:1, 2

"For, then, shall be the Great Tribulation, such as was not since the beginning of the world to this time, no, nor ever shall be. And except those days be shortened, there will be no human being to save. But for the elect's sake, those days shall be shortened. For as the lightning comes out of the east, and shines even unto the west, even also the coming of the Son of God shall be. Immediately after the Seven Year Tribulation of those days shall the Sun be darkened, and the Moon shall not give her light, and the Stars shall fall from heaven, and the powers and the heavens shall be shaken. And then, shall appear the sign of the Son of God in heaven. And then, shall all the tribes of the Earth mourn, and they shall see the Son of God coming in the clouds of heaven with power and great glory. And I shall send my angels with the great sound of the trumpet (a Jewish shofar). And they shall gather together my elect from the four corners of the wind, from one end of heaven to the other. Verily, I say unto you, This generation will not pass away, until all things are fulfilled. Heaven and Earth shall pass away, but my words shall not pass away. But of that day and hour no man knows, no, not even the angels of heaven, but my Father only." Jesus Christ, Matthew 24:21, 22 27-31, 34-36

"In that day shall the Lord defend the inhabitants of Jerusalem. And he that is feeble among them at that day shall be as David. And the House of David shall be as God, as the angel of the Lord before them. And it shall come to pass in that day, that I will seek to destroy all the nations that come against Jerusalem. And I will pour upon the House of David, and upon the inhabitants of Jerusalem, the Spirit of grace and of supplications. And they shall look upon me whom they have pierced." Jesus Christ, Zechariah 12:8-10

"And they shall look upon the Israeli Messiah, Jesus Christ, whom they have pierced." Zechariah 12:10, Revelation 1:7

"Behold, he (The Israeli Messiah) comes with clouds. And everyone shall see Jesus Christ, and they also who pierced him. And all kindreds of the Earth shall wail because of him. Even so. Amen." Revelation 1:7, Zechariah 12:10

The very first words that were uttered from a distance in a most commanding, authoritative, protective voice were: "Touch not mine anointed!!!" Psalm 105:15 – The intensity of Christ's words did reverberate all over Earth.

"And whosoever shall offend one of these little ones which believe in me, it would be better for him that a Millstone were hanged around his neck, and that he were drowned in the depth of the sea. Woe unto the world because of offences! For it must needs be that offences come, but woe unto that man by whom the offence comes!" Jesus Christ, Matthew 18:5-7

"Fear, and the pit, and the snare, are upon thee, O, inhabitant of the Earth. And it shall come to pass, that he who flees from the noise of the fear shall fall into the pit. And he that comes up out of the midst of the pit shall be taken in the snare. For the windows from on high are open, and the foundations of the Earth do shake. The Earth is utterly broken down, the Earth is clean dissolved, the Earth is moved exceedingly." Isaiah 24:17-19

"And I beheld when he had opened the sixth seal, and lo, there was a great earthquake. And the Sun became black as sackcloth, and the Moon became as blood. And the Stars of heaven fell unto the Earth, even as a fig tree casts her untimely figs, when she is shaken of a mighty wind. And the heavens departed as a scroll when it is rolled together. And every mountain and island were moved out of their places. And the kings of the Earth, and the great men, and the rich men, and the chief captains, and the mighty men, and every bondman, and every free man, hid themselves in the dens and in the rocks of the mountains. And they said to the mountains and rocks, 'Fall on us, and hide us from the face of him that sits on the Throne, and from the wrath of the Lamb. Jesus Christ, John 1:29 - For the Great Day of his Wrath has come, and who shall be able to stand?'" Revelation 6: 12-17

The entrance of Jesus Christ followed by the angels and saints was sudden, instantaneous, organized, and without warning, catching everyone by surprise. No one knew the hour when the Israeli Messiah was going to appear. Matthew 24:36 – It occurred quickly and suddenly. In the twinkling of an eye, Jesus came out of nowhere with his entourage behind him. This is an event whose time has come. Zechariah 14:1-4, Malachi 3:1-4, I Corinthians 15:51-58, II Peter 3:3-13

In the midst of all the calamity of Armageddon, the brightest streaks of lightning ever witnessed began striking in and around Jerusalem, Israel, followed by the loudest claps of thunder anyone had ever heard in history that resonated and echoed all around the world. Before the source of the voice could be determined as that of Christ, with each streak of lightning came words that could easily be recognized as scripture from the Holy Bible. From the very essence of Jesus, the Word of God came forth naturally, for Jesus is the Word of God. John 1:1

"The Earth shall quake before them. The heavens shall tremble, The Sun and Moon shall be dark, and the Stars shall withdraw their shining. And the Lord shall utter his voice before his army. For he is strong the executeth his word. For the Day of the Lord is great and terrible. And who can abide it?" Joel 2:10, 11

"A wonderful and horrible thing is committed in the land!" Jeremiah 5:30

"And I saw heaven open, and behold, a white horse. And he (Jesus Christ, the Israeli Messiah) who sat upon the white horse was called, 'Faithful and True.' And in righteousness did he judge and make war. His eyes were as a flame of fire, and on his head were many crowns. And he had a name written, that no man knew, but he himself. And he was clothed with a vesture dipped in blood. And his name is called, 'The Word of God.' - John 1:1 - And the armies which were in heaven followed him upon white horses, clothed in fine linen, white and clean. And out of his mouth went a sharp

Sword, - Hebrews 4:12 Revelation 19:15, 16 - that with it he could suddenly attack the nations. And he shall rule them with a rod of iron, as he treads the winepress of the fierceness and wrath of Almighty God. And he had on his vesture a name written, 'KING OF KINGS AND LORD OF LORDS.' And the Remnant of Israel was empowered with the Sword of him who sat upon the horse, that is, the Sword that proceeds out of his mouth." Revelation 19:11-16, 21 - By the Testimony of John, the Apostle – The Coming of the Lord Jesus Christ, AKA, The Great and Terrible Day of the Lord. Who can abide it? Joel 2:11, Nahum, 1:6, Malachi 3:1, 2

"I am the Light of the World." Jesus Christ – John 9:5

"Behold, the Day of the Lord has come. I have gathered all nations unto Jerusalem to battle. And I shall go forth, and fight against those nations." Zechariah 14:1, 2

Even by the first utterances of the one who was yet to be totally recognizable, the entire world heard the explosion that came with intense, assertive power. All of the people of Earth stood absolutely still as the entire planet shook. A phenomenon of unparalleled proportion was taking place in full force. It was all happening so furiously fast that people had extreme difficulty maintaining their composure.

"In the beginning was the Word. And the Word was with God, and the Word was God." John 1:1, Revelation 19:11-13 – Jesus Christ is the Word of God.

Then, came yet even more verses from the Bible, declared boldly from a distance. And the source of these biblical quotations was moving in quite fast.

"So shall my Word be that goes forth out of my mouth. It shall not return void. But it shall accomplish that which I please, and it shall prosper in the thing whereunto I sent it." Isaiah 55:11

"For the Word of God is quick and powerful, and sharper than any two-edged Sword, piercing even to the dividing asunder of soul and spirit, and of the joints and marrow, and is a discerner of the thoughts and intents of the heart." Hebrews 4:12

"I am the Pearl of Great Price." Jesus Christ, Matthew 13:45, 46

"Surely, I have seen the affliction of my people."
The God of Israel, Exodus 3:5-7

"Prepare for war. Wake up the mighty men. Let all the men of war draw near." Joel 3:9

"Multitudes, multitudes in the Valley of Decision. For the day of the Lord has come in the Valley of Decision. The Lord shall roar out of Jerusalem. He shall utter his voice from Zion. The Sun and Moon shall be darkened, and the Stars shall withdraw their shining. And the heavens and Earth shall shake. But the Lord will be the hope of his people, and the strength of the children of Israel. And you shall know that I am the Lord your God dwelling in Jerusalem, upon the Temple Mount. Then, shall Jerusalem be holy. For in Mount Zion shall there be deliverance. The Remnant of Israel shall call upon their Messiah. And I will restore the years that have been stolen from you. For I dwell in Jerusalem." Joel 3:14-17, 21, The Restoration of the Throne of David, Isaiah 9:6, 7

Then, the Earth began to quake. The heavens were trembling. The Sun began to darken, and the Moon and the Stars refused to shine. The only bright source of light that engulfed the Earth was coming directly from Christ and his army, demonstrating clearly that Jesus is the Light of the World!

"No weapon that is formed against you shall prosper. And every tongue that shall rise against you in judgment you shall condemn. This is the heritage of the saints of the Lord, and their righteousness is of me." Isaiah 54:17, The Lord Jesus Christ

More and more and more of God's Word blasted the entire Earth, as Christ's approach became closer and closer. Jesus advanced toward the Earth faster and more furious than the speed of light.

Before long, it became all too apparent that Jesus Christ was the very one quoting these Bible verses that were striking the Earth as intense bolts of lightning. Heaven had, literally, opened, and Jesus Christ emerged, sitting on a white horse with a crown on his head, prepared to make war. And the armies of heaven followed him, also seated upon white horses and clothed in fine, white linen.

And the Word of God came out of Christ's mouth like a sharp Sword, ready to do battle against his enemies, so that he would rule the nations with a rod of iron, bringing about the Restoration of the Throne of David. And Jesus came in the fierceness and wrath of Almighty God. And he had on his vesture the name written, "KING OF KINGS AND LORD OF LORDS." The greatest Israeli warrior of all time is, now, intervening in the Battle of Armageddon.

And the false messiah, the kings of the Earth who followed him, and all the armies on the planet, gathered together to make war against Jesus Christ and his army. Zechariah 14:1-4, Luke 21:20, Revelation 19:11-17, 19-21

Then, another verse of affirmation hurled toward the Earth as Christ approached ever closer: "The God of Israel's Habitation is in Jerusalem." Ezra 7:15

"Afterward, the children of Israel shall return, and seek the God of Israel, and David, their king. And they shall fear the Lord and his goodness in the latter days." Hosea 3:5

And it was at this very point when the inhabitants of Earth could vividly see Jesus Christ and his army. The entire world, especially Jerusalem, became totally bombarded with Bible scripture that appeared to be counteracting the negative forces that were involved in this spiritual war. Revelation 12:7 - Each one of the portions of scripture was accompanied by magnified, profound streaks of lightning followed by blaring, booming, deafening thunder.

One declaration after another was hurled at all the residents of the planet. And no one had any other no choice but to listen and heed. The entire Earth, with Jerusalem receiving the most intensity, was being bombarded with God's Word, hard, fast, and continuous, coming directly from the mouth of Jesus Christ. Loud and clear, everyone on Earth could miraculously hear Jesus in their own language. On and on and on it went.

"Behold, I have set the land before you. Go and possess the land which I have sworn unto your fathers, Abraham, Isaac, and Jacob, to give unto them and their children after them. The God of Israel has multiplied you. And behold, you are this day as the Stars of heaven. And I will bless you, as I have promised."

"Where sin abounds, grace does abound much more." Romans 5:20, Jesus Christ

"Now, the glory of the Lord appears to all the nations of Earth." Isaiah 66:18

People of all backgrounds were falling on their faces at Christ's appearance. There had been many who mocked the Coming of Jesus Christ, saying, "Where is the promise of his coming?" But no one was mocking now. II Peter 1:16-18 – II Peter 3:12, 13

It was all happening so fast. There was no time for anyone to question what was going on. There was no room to debate, argue, or analyze the situation. And it could not be disputed that the source of all the power backing up this unprecedented phenomenon was the Son of God himself. Revelation 19:11-16 - Even the most dedicated atheistic scientist, despite all the knowledge acquired to rationalize that there is no God, could not deny that the only explanation for what was taking place was the Coming of Jesus Christ.

"Remember all the commandments of the God of Israel. Numbers 15:39-41

"Hear, O, Israel. The Lord our God is one Lord. And you shall love the Lord your God with all of your heart, with all of your mind, with all of your soul, and with all of your strength." When Jesus made this statement, such an intense tremor resulted that the Earth practically fell off its axis. Deuteronomy 6:4, 5, I John 5:7

"Let my people go!!!" The Book of Exodus, Jesus Christ

"Make bright the arrows. Gather the shields. For the Lord's device is against Babylon, to destroy it. Because it is the vengeance of the Lord, the vengeance of his Temple." Jeremiah 51:11

"And if you be Christ's, then you are Abraham's seed, and heirs according to the promise." Galatians 3:29

"Now, I will remember my Covenant with Jacob, and also my Covenant with Isaac, and with Abraham I will remember. And I will remember Israel." Leviticus 26:42

"A day with the Lord is as a thousand years and a thousand years as one day." II Peter 3:8

"Behold, I come quickly!" Jesus Christ, Revelation 22:7, 12, 20

"In that day shall the Lord defend the inhabitants of Jerusalem. And he that is feeble among them at that day shall be as David. And the House of David shall be as God, as the angel of the Lord before them. And it shall come to pass in that day that I will seek to destroy all the nations that come against Jerusalem. And I will pour upon the House of David, and upon the inhabitants of Jerusalem, the Spirit of grace and of supplications. And they shall look upon the Israeli Messiah, Jesus Christ, whom they have pierced, and they shall mourn him, as one mourns for his only son." Zechariah 12:8-10, Revelation 1:7

"Peace, be still, and know that I am God. My peace I give unto you. The peace of God that passes all understanding. Let not your heart be troubled, neither let it be afraid. Be of good cheer. I have overcome the world." Psalm 46:10, John 14:1, 27, John 16:33, Philippians 4:7

"In my Father's house are many mansions. If it were not so, I would have told you. I have prepared a place for you. And I have come again to receive you unto myself." John 14:2, 3, Jesus

Relentlessly and strategically, Jesus continued to bombard the Earth with powerful projectiles of God's Word.

Jerico Knight: "Looks like a modern-day holy crusade."

Jonathan: "Give me a picture, Eagle."

David: "Up ahead, Lightning. I'm open to modification. Most of these bandits have very capable missiles."

Jonathan: "Okay. I see them, Eagle! Let's keep our immediate focus on the bandits who are attacking. You've got the lead. I'll cover you. Break now, David!"

David: "Received."

Jonathan: "Joshua, we have multiple bandits, 2, 6, 9, two miles away. Looks like they're heading away from us. Wait a minute. They're turning around. They're boomeranging and coming right at us! Those demons just cut me off! Where did these bandits learn how to drive? I've just been side swiped, Eagle! I'm not going to let them get in my face like that again! You take your pick of the litter of bandits, Eagle, and that one will be all yours."

David: "I can't take the shot from here. That's the Big Kahuna, you know? The false messiah himself. The international incident from hell waiting to happen. We have an official I.D. on Cohen. He's in true form now, I see, looking as hideous as ever."

Jonathan: "Yeah. Bad hair day, for sure. That's the legend in his own mind, all right. I've seen that look in his eyes in every Alfred Hitchcock movie. Eagle, go with him hard right. Get in there and engage."
David: "Cover me, Lightning."
Jonathan: "Not a problem, Eagle. I'm your Wingman. I'm right behind you, and I'm not going anywhere. I'm sworn to protect your back, and, right now, your back is covered better than ever."
David: "That's comforting to know. These demons are nothing but a bunch of control freaks! I'm telling ya: 'Satan's strategy is to irritate us all to death, by attacking our emotions.'"
Jonathan: "Looks like blue sky for you at this bearing. We'll improvise as we go along. We're not strangers to that."
David: "I'm playing this out, my friend."
Jonathan: "You call all your Israeli comrades your friends, Eagle."
David: "Roger that, Lightning. But I only call one of my comrades my best friend."
Jonathan: "Back at ya, Soaring Eagle."

"And the Lord shall utter his voice before his army. For his camp is very great. For the Lord God of Israel is strong who executes his Word. For the Day of the Lord is great and very terrible. And who can abide it?" Joel 2:11

"And David said unto his men, 'Gird ye on every man his Sword.' So, every man girded on his Sword, and David also girded on his Sword." I Samuel 25:13

"The entire army of Israel aligned right behind David in formation when he went to do battle with Goliath."
I Samuel 17:1-58

"Then said the Lord God of Israel unto me, 'Prophesy unto the wind, prophesy, son of man, and say to the wind, Thus says the Lord God of Israel, Come from the four winds, O breath, and breathe upon these slain, that they may live.' So, I prophesied as he commanded me. And they lived, and stood up upon their feet, an exceeding great army." Ezekiel 37:9, 10

"I am the Resurrection and the Life. He who believes in me, though he were dead, yet shall he live. And whosoever lives and believes in me shall never die." Jesus Christ, John 11:25, 26

The Restored David of the last days is the servant of the Israeli Messiah, Jesus Christ, and the people of Israel.

David: "The Ark of the Covenant is against you, Cohen!"
Colonel Ichabod Cohen: "From hell's heart, I stab at thee."

"Woe unto them that call evil good, and good evil. That put darkness for light, and light for darkness. That put bitter for sweet, and sweet for bitter." Isaiah 5:20

IAI Arava VII: "It's high time that we rebuked Satan once and for all." Jude 1:9

"Yet Michael the Archangel, in contending with the devil, said. 'The Lord rebuke you, Satan.'" Jude 1:9

Jonathan: "They're coming, all right. They're coming in droves!"
David: "Wait for the volley. I've got open sky now, Lightning."
Jonathan: "Joshua, Eagle is engaging and preparing to lock-in, focused on the archnemesis."
Joshua: "Received, Lightning, and understood."
David: "I just need to turn the corner. Now, I've got the Chief Bandit in my pipper."
Israeli Command: "Keep in mind the definition of happiness according to the Greeks, Commander: 'The full use of your powers along the lines of excellence.'"
David: "Wilko, Joshua. This whole thing started out as a lark. But now, it's turned into a Holy Grail."

"'Not by might, nor by power, but by my Spirit (The Holy Spirit),' says the Lord God of Israel." Zechariah 4:6

"Then said David to the giant (Goliath), 'You come to me with a sword, and a spear, and with a shield. But I come to you in the name of the Lord of hosts, the God of the armies of Israel, whom you have defied. This very day will the Lord deliver you into my hand. And I will smite you so that all the Earth may know that there is a God in Israel. For the battle is the Lord's, and he will give you into our hands.'" I Samuel 17:45-47

"Fight the good fight of faith. Lay hold on eternal life. Keep this commandment until the Appearing of our Lord Jesus Christ." II Timothy 6:12-14

"Put yourselves in array against Babylon (The New Roman Empire – The Modern-Day Babylon) round about. All of you that bend the bow, shout at Babylon, spare no arrows. For Babylon has offended the Lord God of Israel. Shout against her round about. Her foundations are fallen, her walls are thrown down. For it is the vengeance of the Lord. Take vengeance upon Babylon (The New Modern Babylonian Empire - The land of hedonists). All she has done, do unto her." Jeremiah 50:14, 15

David: "Could I make a quick statement, off the record, to you, Lightning?"

Jonathan: "Whatcha got?"

David: "More than anything, you know my main inspiration for getting through all this is Bathsheba, because her and I mean so much to each other. My kingdom for Bathsheba!'

Jonathan: "Received, Eagle. You'll see Bathsheba soon. You are right on the verge of it. I know you well enough to know that you're not going to allow anything to jeopardize her slipping through your fingers. Now, let's get the world back in proper alignment, where it belongs."

David: "God knows my heart, Lightning." I Samuel 13:14

Jonathan: "That's something I know I can count on, Eagle."

"Blow ye the trumpet in Zion (Jerusalem, Israel), and sound an alarm in my holy mountain. Let all the inhabitants of the land tremble. For the Day of the Lord has come, for it is at hand, a day as there has never been the likes of it. A fire devours before God's people, and behind them a flame burns. The land is as the Garden of Eden before them, and behind them desolate wilderness. Yea, and nothing can escape them. The appearance of them is as the appearance of horses. And as horses, so shall they run. Like the noise of chariots on top of the mountains shall they leap, like the noise of a flame of fire that devours the stubble, as a strong people set in battle array. They shall run like mighty men. They shall climb the wall like men of war. And they shall march everyone on his ways, and they shall not break their ranks. Neither shall they thrust one another, and everyone shall walk in his path. And when they fall upon the sword, they shall not be wounded. The Earth shall quake before them. The heavens shall tremble. The Sun and Moon shall be dark, and the Stars shall withdraw their shining. And the Lord God of Israel shall utter his voice before his army. For his camp is very great. For he is strong who executes his Word. Alas, for the Great and Terrible Day of the Lord is at hand. As a destruction from the Almighty it shall come! And who can abide it?" Joel 2:1-11

I have made a Covenant with my chosen. I have sworn unto David, my servant. Your seed will I establish forever and build up your Throne to all generations. Selah. I have exalted one chosen out of the people. I have found David, my servant. With my holy oil I have anointed him. With whom my hand shall be established. My arm also shall strengthen him. The enemy shall not exact upon him, nor the son of wickedness afflict him. And I will beat down his foes before his face, and plague them that hate him. My Covenant will I not break, nor alter the thing that has gone out of my lips. Once I have sworn by my holiness that I will not lie unto David. His seed will endure forever, and his Throne as the Sun before me. It shall be established as the Moon, and as a faithful witness in heaven."
Psalm 89:3, 4, 19-23, 34-37, Acts 13:22, 23

"At that day, you shall know that I am in my Father, and that you are in me, and I am in you." Jesus Christ, John 14:29

"For it is the day of the Lord's vengeance, and the year of recompenses of the controversy of Zion (Jerusalem)." Isaiah 34:8
Joshua: "Collective fire at the Israeli Messiah's command."
David: We're firing on all cylinders, Joshua! I have that Red Dragon in my scope, and locking-in on him right now!"
Commander Ariel Rosenberg: "Rev up your engines, Israeli TOP GUN. I hear the collective roar of fighter jets on red line overload! The Israeli Messiah has assigned angels with gossamer wings to be posted all over Earth. So, shove it into overdrive."
Jonathan: "Steady. God's speed, Eagle. We're going to set the world on fire with collective firepower. Joshua, Eagle and I are accelerating to firewall (full power). Our throttles are all the way to

their forward limit. Pedals to the metal. No turning back. All of TOP GUN is close behind us."

"'Vengeance is mine. I will repay." Jesus Christ, Romans 12:19

"I will build my Church. And the gates of hell shall not prevail against you!" Jesus Christ, Matthew 16:18 --- The Worldwide Church of Jesus Christ

"BEHOLD, A GREAT, RED DRAGON" ---REVELATION 12:3

"And there appeared another wonder in Heaven. Behold, a great Red Dragon." Revelation 12:3

"Be sober, vigilant. Because your adversary, the devil, as a roaring lion walks about, seeking whom he may devour."
I Peter 5:8

"The thief (Satan) comes not but for to steal, and to kill, and to destroy. I am come that they may have life and that they may have life more abundantly." Jesus Christ, John 10:10

"And I saw the Beast, and the kings of the Earth, and their armies, gathered together to make war against him that sat on the horse (Jesus Christ), and against his army." Revelation 19:19

The Pathway: Color Picture Photo Edition

"BUT UNTO YOU THAT FEAR MY NAME SHALL THE SUN OF RIGHTEOUSNESS (THE SON OF GOD), JESUS CHRIST, ARISE WITH HEALING IN HIS WINGS." Malachi 4:2
David: "This is Soaring Eagle at the helm, and we're coming in! Fire!!!"

"And David gave a commandment, and they were burned with fire!" I Chronicles 14:12

"David encouraged himself in the Lord his God." I Samuel 30:6

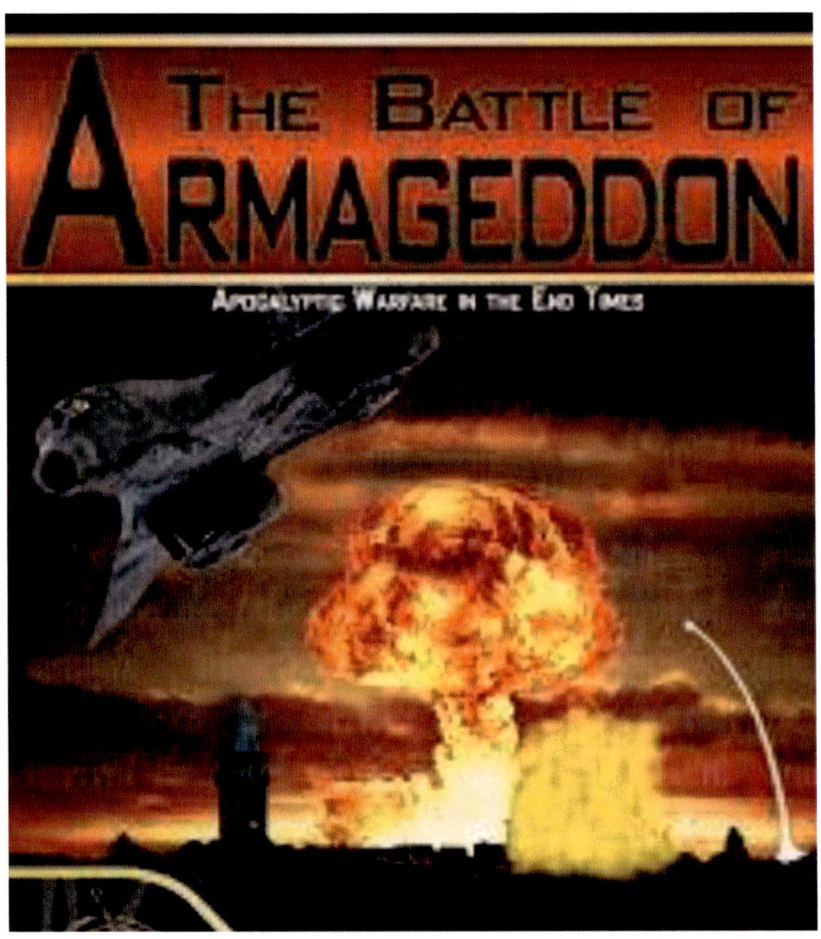

APOCALYPTIC WARFARE IN THE END TIMES

Joshua: "So, far as these ballistic nuts are concerned, they could dish it out, but they sure couldn't take it."

David: "All of these bandits are sweating bullets, Joshua! Every last one of them."

Joshua: "Soaring Eagle, you, Lightning, and Israeli TOP GUN are instructed, at this very bearing, to destroy the Tribulation Temple immediately. Level the Temple in Jerusalem to a parking lot by direct order of Jesus Christ. The Messiah will be on an assist with you on this assignment. Look sharp. Don't break your momentum. Every last one of our people are secure in the bomb shelters that you ordered built. That is confirmed."

David: "Roger that, Joshua. Understood clearly."

David: "Gloriosky, Lightning!"

Jonathan: "No love lost for the Tribulation Temple at this bearing, Eagle."

"And Jonathan said to David, 'Go in peace, forasmuch as we have sworn both of us in the name of the Lord God of Israel, saying, The Lord be between me and thee, and between my seed and thy seed forever.'" I Samuel 20:42 – The Eternal Covenant between David and Jonathan

"Then, Jonathan said to David, 'The Lord God of Israel be between thee and me forever.'" I Samuel 20:23

"The Lord's oath was between them, between David and Jonathan." II Samuel 21:7

The Pathway: Color Picture Photo Edition

CHAPTER TEN
EVERY STONE OF THE TEMPLE SHALL BE THROWN DOWN
Matthew 24:1, 2

"How art thou fallen from heaven, O Lucifer (Satan). How art thou cut down to the ground, which did weaken the nations! For you have said in your heart, 'I will ascend into heaven. I will exalt my throne above the Stars of God. I will sit upon the Mount (Mount Moriah (The Temple Mount in Jerusalem) of the congregation. I will ascend above the heights of the clouds. I will be like the Most High (God).' Yet you have been brought down to hell, to the sides of the pit. And they that shall see you will consider you, saying, 'Is this the one that made the Earth tremble, that did shake the kingdoms?'" Isaiah 14:12-16

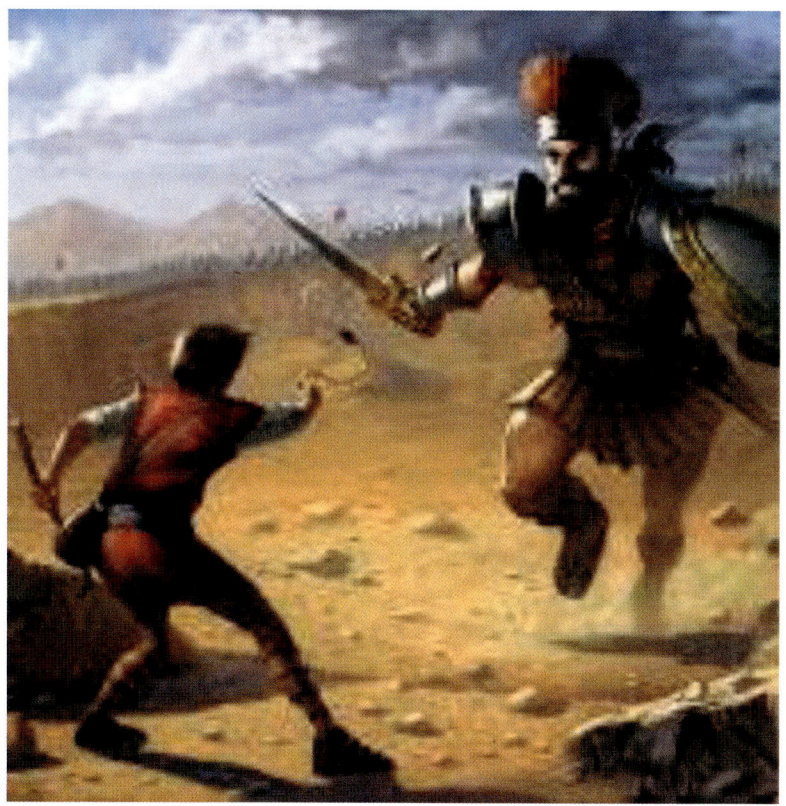

I SAMUEL 17:1-4, 32-37, 44-52

"And David put his hand in his bag, and took out a stone, and slung it, and smote the Philistine (Goliath) in his forehead. And the Philistine fell upon his face to the Earth. So, David prevailed over the Philistine with a slingshot and with a stone, and smote the

Philistine, and slew him. But there was no sword in the hand of David." I Samuel 17:49, 50

"Then, the angel said, 'These are the Two Anointed Ones who stand by the Lord of the whole Earth." Zechariah 4:14, Zechariah, the Prophet, refers to the Restored David and Jonathan as the Two Olive Trees, the Two Olive Branches, and the Two Anointed Ones.

"And I will give power unto my Two Witnesses. These are the Two Olive Trees and the Two Candlesticks standing before the God of the Earth. And if any man hurt them, fire will proceed out of their mouths, and devour their enemies." Revelation 11:3-5 – The Restored David and Jonathan --- The Two Prophets

David, Jonathan, and the TOP GUN Fighter Jet Pilots unloaded their weapons on the Tribulation Temple only to pulverize the entire building and reduced it to less than a parking lot, as ordered. Between the Israeli Messiah, TOP GUN, and the Israeli ground troops, and the allies of Israel, the paramount assignment of blasting the desecrated Temple, as though the God of Israel was sending a nuclear holocaust upon the cities of Sodom and Gomorrah, was most successful.

Just as Jesus had accurately predicted in Matthew 24:1, 2, every single last stone of the Temple would be thrown down. Despite how many scholars state that Jesus was referring to the second Temple when the Romans set it on fire during the siege of Jerusalem in 70 A.D., this is, obviously, incorrect, as the Western (Wailing) Wall of the Temple still remained standing. Jesus Christ said loud and clear, without stuttering: "There shall not be left one stone upon another, that shall not be thrown down." Matthew 24:2, referring to "the buildings of the Temple." Matthew 24:1. Therefore, Jesus was eschatologically making reference to a future Israeli Temple that would be built in the last days. It would be the third Jewish Temple that would have the destiny of being utterly annihilated, according to Jesus. And his prophecy would come to pass toward the very end of the Battle of Armageddon. One reason Jesus knew all too well that the Tribulation Temple would be completely destroyed is because he, personally, would play a key role in destroying it and ensuring that it was totally obliterated for good. In fact, Jesus Christ, the greatest warrior-king who ever lived, would be on the front lines of battle to ensure that this noble endeavor was accomplished.

"THERE SHALL NOT BE LEFT ONE STONE UPON ANOTHER OF THE TEMPLE, THAT SHALL NOT BE THROWN DOWN."
JESUS CHRIST – MATTHEW 24:1, 2

DESTRUCTION OF THE TRIBULATION TEMPLE
"ROUGH DAY, SATAN?" – THE GOD OF ISRAEL
ISAIAH 14:12-16

The Pathway: Color Picture Photo Edition

"And I saw an angel come down from heaven, having the key to the Bottomless Pit and a chain in his hand. And he laid hold on the dragon, that old serpent, which is the Devil, and Satan, and bound him a thousand years. And the angel cast the dragon into the Bottomless Pit, and shut him up, and set a seal upon him, that he should deceive the nations no more, till the thousand years should be fulfilled. And after that, Satan would be loosed a little season. And I saw Thrones, and they sat upon them, and judgment was given them. And I saw the souls of them that were beheaded for the witness of Jesus, and for the Word of God, who had not worshipped the Beast, neither his image, neither had received his mark upon their foreheads, or in their hands. And they lived and reigned with Christ a thousand years. This is the First Resurrection."
Revelation 20:1-5

THE BOTTOMLESS PIT OF HELL IN RUINS
REVELATION 20:1-5 - REVELATION 20:10-15

"For the time has come that judgment must begin in the House of God." Jesus Christ, I Peter 4:17

Michael the Archangel: "Do you yield, Satan? Revelation 12:7, Revelation 20:1-10
Satan: "I yield."

The Tribulation Temple is utterly destroyed at the hand of the God of Israel, to make way for the Millennial Temple.

"The modern-day Babylon (The Great, New Roman Empire) has suddenly fallen and has been destroyed." Jeremiah 51:8

"Alas, alas. That great city, Babylon, that mighty city, in one hour, your judgment has come!" Revelation 18:10

"And saying, 'Alas, alas that great city, Babylon, that was clothed in fine linen, and purple, and scarlet, and decked with gold, and precious stones, and pearls! For in one hour, so great riches have come to nought. And every shipmaster, and all the company in ships, and sailors, and as many as trade by sea, stood far off. And they cried when they saw the smoke of her burning, saying, 'What city is like unto this great city! And they cast dust on their heads, and cried, 'Alas, alas that great city, wherein were made rich all that had ships in the sea by reason of her costliness! For in one hour is she made desolate. Rejoice over her, thou heaven, and ye Holy Apostles and Prophets. For God has avenged you on her. And a mighty angel took up a stone like a Great Millstone, and cast it into the sea, saying, thus with violence shall that great city, Babylon, be thrown down, and shall be found no more at all." Revelation 18:16-21

Jonathan: "Wilko, Joshua. Absolute power won't ever be corrupting absolutely again!"
Jonathan: "You know what today is, don't you, Eagle?
David: "What's that?"
Jonathan: "The 9th of Av."
David: "You have got to be kidding me! The 9th of Av! That's the very day that the first and second Israeli Temples were destroyed!"
Jonathan: "It gives me goosebumps, Eagle. There is no way it's a coincidence. We're not going to hear the end of the rabbis talking about it."
Mulholland Drive: "Joshua, the Tribulation Temple is a thing of the past. It's completely leveled. the Israeli Messiah is officially out in front, coercing Satan and his good time buddies into the Bottomless

Pit, as only he can do. The evil one and company are locked up securely in the Bottomless Pit."

"And I saw an angel come down from heaven, having the key to the Bottomless Pit and a great chain in his hand. And he laid hold on the dragon, that old serpent, which is the Devil, and Satan, and bound him a thousand years. And the angel cast Satan into the Bottomless Pit, and shut him up, and set a seal upon him, that he should deceive the nations no more, till the thousand years should be fulfilled, And after that, he must be loosed a little season." Revelation 20:1-3

"But, beloved, be not ignorant of this one thing, that one day is with the Lord God of Israel as a thousand years, and a thousand years as one day." II Peter 3:8

"Wherefore, by their fruits, you shall know them. Not everyone that says unto me, 'Lord, Lord,' shall enter into the kingdom of heaven. But he that does the will of my Father which is in heaven., Many will say unto me in that day, 'Lord, Lord, have we not prophesied in your name? And in your name have cast out devils? And in your name done many wonderful works?' And then I will profess unto them, 'I never knew you. Depart from me, you that work iniquity!!!'" Matthew 7:20-23

Anyone not found written in the book of life Let them be cast into the lake of fire.
~Revelation 20:15

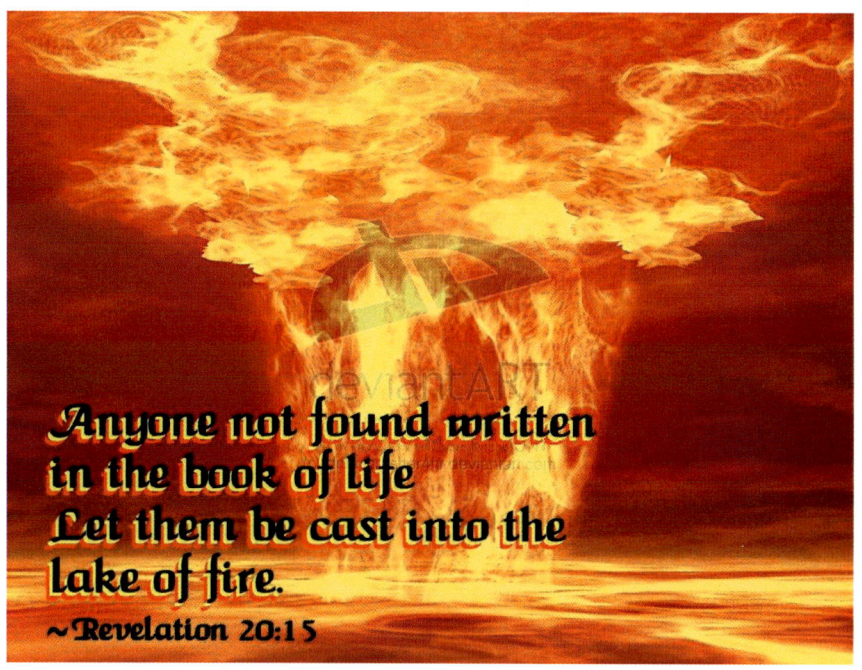

THE BOOK OF LIFE – REVELATION 21:27

"Whose names are written in the Book of Life." Philippians 4:3

"They shall walk with me in white. For they are worthy. They that overcome, the same shall be clothed in white raiment, and I will not blot out their name out of the Book of Life, but I will confess his name before my Father, and before his angels." Revelation 3:4, 5

"The Book of Life of the Lamb of God (John 1:29) slain from the foundation of the world." Revelation 13:8

"Whose names were not written in the Book of Life from the foundation of the world." Revelation 17:8

"Blessed and holy is he that has part in the First Resurrection. On such the Second Death has no power, but they shall be priests (and priestesses) of God and of Christ and shall reign with him a thousand years. And when the thousand years are expired, Satan (the dragon) shall be loosed out of his prison. And the devil shall go out to deceive the nations which are in the four quarters of the Earth, Gog and Magog, to gather them together to battle. The number of whom is the sand of the sea. And they went up on the breath of the Earth, and compassed the camp of the saints about, and the beloved city (Jerusalem). And fire came down from God out of heaven and devoured them. AND THE DEVIL THAT DECEIVED THEM WAS CAST INTO THE LAKE OF FIRE and Brimstone, where the Beast and the False Prophet are, and shall be tormented day and night forever and ever. And I saw a Great White Throne, and him that sat on it, from whose face the Earth and the heaven fled away. And I saw the dead, small and great, stand before God. And books were opened. And another book was opened, which is the Book of Life. And the dead were judged out of those things that were written in the books, according to their works. And the sea gave up the dead which were in it. And death and hell delivered up the dead which were in them. And they were judged every person according to their works. And death and hell were cast into the Lake of Fire. This is the Second Death. And whosoever was not found written in the Book of Life was cast into the Lake of Fire." Revelation 20:6-15

"And there shall in no wise enter into the Temple anything that defiles, neither whatsoever works abomination or makes a lie. But only they which are written in the Lamb's Book of Life."
Revelation 21:27

"And I heard a loud voice, saying, 'Now is come salvation, and strength, and the kingdom of our God, and the power of his Christ. For the Accuser of our brethren is cast down, which accused them before God day and night. Revelation 12:10, 11

"There is, therefore, now no condemnation to them who are in Christ Jesus, who walk not after the flesh, but after the Spirit. For the law in the Spirit of Christ Jesus has made me free from the law of sin and death." Romans 8:1, 2

Satan and his demons were tried, judged, convicted, and sentenced in the God of Israel's Courtroom for crimes against humanity, and supreme justice has been established by Jesus Christ. The justice of God ultimately prevailed over the injustice of evil.

Satan's evil Empire, along with every last bit of the imaginable chaos, pain, and suffering that it perpetrated upon the human race, God's people in particular, was cast into the Lake of Fire. Revelation

20:10-15 – While man's justice is quite limited, in the twinkling of an eye, God dramatically demonstrated that his justice is not limited by any means.

Jonathan: "Joshua, Israel has just crossed over the Jordan River into the Eternal Promised Land! I repeat: Israel has passed over the Jordan River successfully. The Eternal Promised Land is ours for keeps! Mission successfully accomplished! That is official, Joshua."

Joshua (Israeli Command): Roger that, Lightning. Satan is shut down forever. That is official.

David: "Israeli Command, Colonel Ichabod Cohen has been tossed directly into the Lake of Fire, do not pass GO, with every, last one of his bandits bugging out behind him! Satan and his legion of demons were kept at bay long enough for them all to be cast into the Lake of Fire, never to be remembered again. Satan, the Condemner, is now officially condemned. The Accuser can no longer accuse anyone. And the Tormentor will never torment again. The Israeli Messiah masterfully blazed the trail for us all. No worries whatsoever at this bearing. That is official. Soaring Eagle happily reporting!"

Commander Ariel Rosenberg (Israeli Special Forces Chief Commander): "Roger that, Commander. David ... That's the best news I've heard all day!!!"

"It is finished!!!" Jesus Christ, John 19:30

"In the world you have had Tribulation. But be of good cheer. I have overcome the world." Jesus Christ, The Anointed Messiah, John 16:33

David: "Well, the best thing I could possibly say is that the joy of the Lord is your strength!" Nehemiah 8:10

Prince Solomon: "Thou hast brought us out with a mighty hand, O, Lord."

Joshua (referring to the Israeli TOP GUN Fighter Pilots): "Great bunch of leg pullers, these guys."

"Behold, I show you a mystery. We shall not all sleep, but we shall be changed. In a moment, in the twinkling of an eye, at the last trump (from the shofar). For the trumpet shall sound, and the dead shall be raised incorruptible, and we shall be changed. For this corruptible must put on incorruption, and this mortal must put on immortality. So, when this corruptible shall have put on incorruption, and this mortal shall have put on immortality, then shall be brought to pass the saying that is written, 'Death is swallowed up in victory! O, death, where is your sting? O, grave, where is your victory? The sting of death is sin. And the strength of sin is the law. But thanks be to God, who gives us the victory through our Lord Jesus Christ. Therefore, my beloved brethren, be ye steadfast, unmovable, always abounding in the work of the Lord, forasmuch as you know that your labor is not in vain in the Lord." I Corinthians 15:51-58

"But I would not have you ignorant, brethren, concerning, them which are asleep, that you sorrow not, even as others which have no hope. For if we believe that Jesus died and rose again, even so them also which sleep in Jesus will God bring with him. For this we say unto you by the word of the Lord, that we which are alive and remain unto the Coming of the Lord shall not prevent them which are asleep. For the Lord himself shall descend from heaven with a shout, with the voice of the Archangel, and with the trump of God (from the shofar). And the dead in Christ shall rise first. Then we which are alive and remain shall be caught up together with them in the clouds, to meet the Lord in the air, and so shall we ever be with the Lord." I Thessalonians 4:13-17"

"For yourselves know perfectly that the Day of the Lord so cometh as a thief in the night. For when they shall say, 'Peace and safety,' then sudden destruction shall come upon them, and they shall not escape," I Thessalonians 5:2, 3

"But, beloved, be not ignorant of this one thing, that one day is with the Lord as a thousand years, and a thousand years as one day. The Lord is not slack concerning his promise, as some men count slackness. But the Lord is longsuffering towards us, not willing that any should perish, but that all come to repentance (Romans 2:4). But the Day of the Lord will come as a thief in the night. In which the heavens shall pass away with a great noise, and the elements shall melt with fervent heat, the Earth also and the works that are therein shall be burned up. Looking for and hasting unto the Coming of the

Day of God, wherein the heavens being on fire shall be dissolved, and the elements shall melt with fervent heat. Nevertheless we, according to the promise, look for new heavens and a new Earth, wherein dwells righteousness. Wherefore, beloved, seeing that you look for such things, be diligent that you may be found of him in peace, without spot or wrinkle." II Peter 3:8-10, 12-14

"All power has been given unto me in heaven and in Earth!" Jesus Christ, Matthew 28:18

"And they overcame Satan by the blood of the Lamb, Jesus Christ, - John 1:29, Revelation 14:1-5, Revelation 19:7-9 - and by the word of their testimony, and they loved not their lives unto death." Revelation 12:11

"Greater love hath no man than this, that a man lay down his life for his friends." Jesus Christ, John 15:13

"I am the Resurrection, and the Life. He the believes in me, though he were dead, yet shall he live. And whosoever lives and believes in me shall never die." John 11:25, 26, Jesus Christ

"Nay, in all things we are more than conquerors through Christ who loves us. For I am persuaded, that neither death, nor life, nor angels, nor principalities, nor powers, nor things present, nor things to come, nor height, nor depth, nor any other creature, shall be able to separate us from the love of God, which is in Christ Jesus, our Lord." Romans 8:37-39

"Pray for the peace of Jerusalem." Psalm 122:6

"So, David and all people returned unto Jerusalem."
II Samuel 12:31

"And David gathered all Israel together and passed over Jordan." II Samuel 10:17; I Chronicles 13:5; I Chronicles 19:17; The Israeli TOP GUN Operation, "Passing Over the Jordan River," has been successfully accomplished.

"Then David arose, and all the people that were with him, and they crossed over Jordan. By the morning light at daybreak, there was no one left who had not crossed over the Jordan River." II Samuel 17:22

"Then, David and the people that were with him lifted up their voice and wept, until they had no more power to weep."
I Samuel 30:4

"And David went up by the ascent of the Mount of Olives, and wept as he went up, and his head was covered. And all the people that were with David covered their heads. And they went up, weeping as they went up." II Samuel 15:30

"And David behaved himself wisely in all his ways, and the Lord God of Israel was with him." I Samuel 18:14

"And all Israel and Judah loved David, because he went out and came in before them." I Samuel 18:16

"And the fame of David spread throughout all the lands. And the Lord God of Israel brought the awe of David upon all the nations." I Chronicles 14:17

"Thus, the Lord saved Israel (The Eternal Promised Land) that day." Exodus 14:30

And not one of the Israelis was lost, as the Lord God of Israel had promised. Ezekiel 34:11-16; Ezekiel 37:22, 24-28

"Behold, a whirlwind of the Lord God of Israel has gone forth in fury, even grievously upon the head of the wicked. The anger of the Lord shall not return, until he has executed and performed the thoughts of his heart. In the latter days, you shall consider it perfectly." Jeremiah 23:19, 20

"I am a part of all that I have met. Too much is taken. Much abides. That which we are, we are. One equal temper of heroic hearts. Strong in will to strive, to seek, to find, and not to yield." Lord Alfred Tennyson – The Worldwide, Universal Church of Jesus Christ – Ephesians 3:9-21, Ephesians 4:2-16

"Jesus must rise again from the dead. Then Jesus said to Thomas, 'Reach hither your finger and behold my hands. And reach hither they hand and thrust it into my side. And be not faithless but believing.' And Thomas answered and said unto him, 'My Lord and my God.' Jesus said unto him, 'Thomas, because you have seen me, you have believed. Blessed are they that have not seen, and yet have believed.' But these things are written that you might believe that

Jesus is the Christ, the Son of God, and that believing you might have life through his name." John 20:9, 27-29, 30

"Jesus said unto them, 'Come and dine.' Jesus then came, and took bread, and gave it to them, and fish likewise. This is now the third time that Jesus showed himself to his disciples after he was risen from the dead." John 21:12-14

"Even so, come, Lord Jesus." Revelation 22:20

The Pathway: Color Picture Photo Edition

CHAPTER ELEVEN
THE MILLENNIAL TEMPLE
"Be still and know that I am God." The God of Israel
Psalm 46:10

THE MILLENNIAL REIGN OF JESUS CHRIST
REVELATION 20:4-6

Jesus dismounted his white horse and looked from one side of his view of Jerusalem to the other side with a calm, uplifting expression on his face.

Israel's third Temple on Earth has been utterly obliterated to make way for the Millennial Temple.

After dismounting from his white horse on the Mount of Olives, – Zechariah 14:1-4 - Jesus began the nearly two mile walk to the Temple Mount, where the Tribulation Temple had just been destroyed. He walked along the road with a scepter in his hand, and an expression on his face as if he were reminiscing of memories he once had of Jerusalem on Earth.

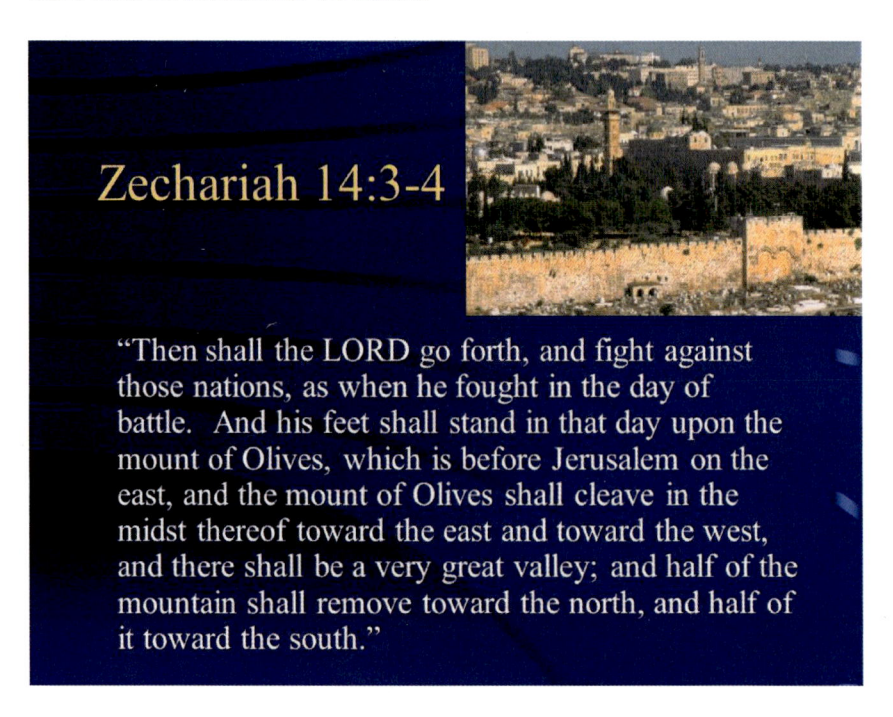

Zechariah 14:3-4

"Then shall the LORD go forth, and fight against those nations, as when he fought in the day of battle. And his feet shall stand in that day upon the mount of Olives, which is before Jerusalem on the east, and the mount of Olives shall cleave in the midst thereof toward the east and toward the west, and there shall be a very great valley; and half of the mountain shall remove toward the north, and half of it toward the south."

Just as much as Jesus ascended to Heaven from the Mount of Olives after his Resurrection (Acts 1:1-12), so he, poetically, descends just as much from heaven to the Mount of Olives, with his army of angels and saints assembled behind him.

In Zechariah 14:4, when the Israeli Messiah, Jesus Christ, is predicted to touch down upon the Mount of Olives on the Great and

Terrible Day of the Lord, the impact is said to be so powerful that it will "cleave" ("baqa" in Hebrew, which means "split") the Mount from the east to the west, creating a great valley. This is the very same verb (in Hebrew) used for the first and most famous of Israel's deliverances at the hand of the Lord God of Israel, that is, when God "split" the Red Sea, - Exodus 14:16, 17, 21, 22; Nehemiah 9:11; Psalm 78:13 - to provide a ticket for the Israelites to be released from the bondage of the Egyptians and the tyranny of Pharaoh. Just as the children of Israel were surrounded by the armies of Pharaoh, so here the Israelis of our modern-day world were surrounded by all of the armies of Satan. Just as the situation in Exodus seemed hopeless, so it had seemed utterly bleak for the Twelve Tribes of the Remnant of the Jews in the latter days. And yet the Israeli Messiah intervened and led the entire Remnant of Israel to safety, delivering Israel once and for all from the snares of an unmerciful devil (Satan), just as the Lord God of Israel had promised in the Hebrew Bible that not one of the Israelis would be lost. Just as God successfully blocked the Egyptian's attempt of preventing the Israelites' escape from Egypt via the Rea Sea, so it came to pass that the Israeli Messiah's feet touched down on the Mount of Olives and opened a way of escape for Israel, securing the long awaited ultimate triumphant victory that has been coveted for so long by the Israeli people. Indeed, the Battle of Armageddon has proven itself to be the final war to end all wars for good. Hence, the Israeli Messiah's triumphant words of confirmation: "It is finished!" The Israeli Messiah, Jesus Christ, who knows the beginning from the end and the end from the beginning, has proven himself to be the greatest warrior of all time and eternity. Zechariah 14:3 - And now, the door is wide open for Jesus to rule the world throughout the Millennial Age (The Israeli Messiah's 1,000 Year Reign; The Millennium).

The phrase, "The Lion of the Tribe of Judah," comes from the prophecy that Jacob, who was later renamed Israel, gave to his son, Judah, in Genesis 49:9, 10. The prophecy stated: "The scepter will not depart from Judah, nor the ruler's staff from his descendants, until the coming of the One (The Anointed One, that is, the Israeli Messiah, Jesus Christ) to whom it belongs, the One whom all nations will obey." This is a prophecy concerning the Israeli Messiah, born in the line of Judah. King David was born in Judah's royal line, hence the phrase, "the Root of David." Revelation 5:5 The True Israeli Messiah is a direct descendant of David, from the royal lineage of the Tribe of Judah. Paradoxically, Jesus also existed before the foundation of the world. Ephesians 1:1-16 - The Israeli Messiah is a genuine warrior, as Judah is the Israeli Tribe that protects Israel in times of war. In fact, Jesus Christ is the greatest warrior of all time in eternity, because he fought for the good of all concerned. Now, Christ has come to make all things right. This fact was the most evident proof of all that everything had, indeed, come full circle, as the late, great Dr. Samuel Goldstein had pointed out to David in the early going.

Upon reaching the Temple Mount, Jesus purified the Earth with every step he took, as he had all along the way, bringing life back to so many beautiful things that were once dormant, dead, and destroyed. There was great significance in Jesus Christ walking to the Temple Mount that day. Each step he took manifested the new world and the New Jerusalem coming down out of heaven. Revelation 21:1-3

What was once the hideous Bottomless Pit of Hell where Satan proudly ruled from beneath the Earth causing calamity and chaos to all the world no longer existed. Without waxing too philosophical or metaphysical, one could say that the Bottomless Pit never existed in the first place, in the face of the tranquility that would now pervade forever. Everything was becoming so new and wondrous that the horrible memories of the past were fading, getting distant, and even totally forgotten. Old things were passing away, and all things were becoming new. II Corinthians 5:17

"And God shall wipe away all tears from their eyes. And there shall be no more death, nether sorrow, nor crying, neither shall there be any more pain. For the former things are passed away." Revelation 21:4

And with a commanding tone in his voice and a wave of his arms, Jesus emphatically commanded, "Peace, be still." Mark 4:39 - Then, all of a sudden, every lingering hint of the chaos existing on Earth had completely subdued, and everything on the planet went quiet, calm and perfectly still. And it was quite apparent that everlasting peace would linger, as spoken of by the Jewish fathers of old and prophesied by the prophets of the Hebrew Bible. All of nature on Earth was under the command of Jesus Christ. And just like that, everlasting peace had been established in the world.

"Therefore, if anyone be in Christ, they are a new creation.
Old things have passed away. Behold, all things have become new."
I CORINTHIANS 5:17

And suddenly, out of what was once the rubble and ashes of the annihilated Tribulation Temple, with a single gesture of both of his hands and the intense light that emitted from his person, a swirling motion began taking place around the Temple Mount that was, for lack of a better word, magical.

And when it became apparent that the Temple Mount had been sanctified and ritually cleansed by the very purity of Christ's presence, the Temple Mount was, literally, glowing as a result. This particular region of the world, among everything else that had been revived, never looked so glorious. And the prophecy of Zechariah 6:12, 13 spontaneously followed suit. Jesus Christ, indeed, built the

Millennial Temple in a miraculous fashion, all by himself, precisely to the specifications and the blueprints of the Temple, vividly described in the fortieth to the forty-eighth chapters of the Book of Ezekiel. Zechariah 6:12, 13

The Israeli Messiah, Jesus Christ, the ultimate warrior from the Tribe of Judah, that is, the Tribe of Royalty, the Tribe of David, the Israeli Tribe of war, entered the newly manifested Millennial Temple and took his Throne, and was crowned as the King of kings and Lord of lords by his heavenly entourage. At this very crossroads, it was absolutely official that the Restoration of the Throne of David had just taken place in full view of many witnesses, and that the God of Israel had fully and ultimately kept his promise that he would never fail to have a man sitting upon the Throne of David, that is, a man of the lineage of David. The ushering in of the Israeli Messiah's Millennial Kingdom meant that everlasting peace would prevail in every single aspect of life from now on. The Prince of Peace, Jesus Christ, has had his way, deserving all the glory: "And of the increase of his government and peace there shall be no end, upon the Throne of David, and upon Christ's Kingdom, to order it, and to establish it with sound judgment and with justice from henceforth even forever." Isaiah 9:6, 7 - Jesus Christ has successfully performed this. And he accomplished it in God's perfect timing. Jesus has suddenly entered into his Temple. Malachi 3:1, 2 - He has established the new Covenant. And many have managed, through Christ's power and grace, to survive the appearance of his coming. All those currently living in Christ and all those who were dead in Christ were now sustained at last. And not one single enemy of God's people ever lingered again to cause any hindrances, chaos, distress, or false accusation.

The Tribulation Temple had been defiled, and therefore, out of necessity, been obliterated. But now, the Temple Mount has been sanctified and the earthly Temple has been restored by Christ forever. The entire Remnant of the God of Israel has been gathered and assembled once and for all. Every Jew and all allies of Christ who had ever lived could be accounted for on this very day, as promised by Jesus. God's anointed people were in Paradise to stay forever, and the First Resurrection mentioned in the Book of Revelation had taken place. Revelation 20:4-6

The Hebrew Bible describes the Jerusalem Temple as "Beit Adonai" or "Beth-Ha-Elohim" which in Hebrew means, The House of God. This denotes the Temple as a place where God dwells. The Temple is a connotation that expresses the earliest Hebrew term that represents God's abode. God desires to have a place to dwell on Earth. "Mishkan" in Hebrew means: The Dwelling Place or Tabernacle. Another biblical Hebrew term for the Temple is "Beit HaMikdash" which means: The Sanctified House or Holy House. Only the Temple in Jerusalem is referred to by this name. And "Mikdash" in Hebrew means: The Sanctuary, a special room, the House of Holiness or the Holy Place.

"I"VE BEEN TO THE MOUNTAINTOP"
A Speech Delivered by Dr. Martin Luther King, Jr.

"Well, I don't know what will happen now. We've got some difficult days ahead. But it doesn't matter with me now. Because I've been to the Mountaintop! And I don't mind. Like anybody, I would like to live a long life. Longevity has its place. But I'm not concerned about that now. I just want to do God's will. And he's allowed me to go up to the Mountain! And I've looked over! And I've seen the Promised Land! I may not get there with you. But I want you to know tonight, that we, as a people, will get to the Promised Land! And I'm happy tonight! I'm not worried about anything. I'm not fearing any man. Mine eyes have seen the glory of the coming of the Lord!"

"I can hear the distant voices of our ancestors whispering by the night fire. Or a big, bold choir shouting, 'I woke up with my mind stayed on freedom.' All their voices, roaming for centuries, have finally found their home here in this great monument to our pain, our suffering, and our victory." United States Congressman John Lewis

"While attaining a lasting, permanent peace in Israel has been elusive to many of our world's greatest minds, perhaps the best way to make this goal a reality is to speak more to the heart than to the head." Honorable United States Congressman Jo Bonner

THE MILLENNIAL TEMPLE
EZEKIEL CHAPTERS 40-48

The fourth earthly Temple had been built. Yet the unique aspect of the Millennial Temple is that it was built solely by the Israeli Messiah, Jesus Christ himself. Human hands did not take part in the construction of this highly significant Temple. Zechariah 6:12, 13 puts it well by proclaiming: "Behold the Messiah who shall build the Temple of the God of Israel. And he shall sit and rule upon his Throne." The Millennial Temple on Earth is the perfect reflection of the Temple in heaven. The Millennial Temple is regarded as the greatest engineering marvel in the world. The Millennial Temple has been built by the Messiah precisely to the blueprints that are detailed in the 40th to 48th chapters of the Book of Ezekiel in the Hebrew

Bible (the Old Testament). The architect and builder of the Millennial Temple is Jesus Christ. All the prophecies, every last one of them, of the prophets in the Bible have now been fulfilled. Any good thing that the God of Israel had promised did not fail to come to pass. The source of everything good in life is Jesus Christ.

The Israeli Messiah, who is from the Tribe of Judah, which is the Tribe of Royalty, the Tribe of David, and the Israeli Tribe of war, has now been crowned as the King of kings and Lord of lords. The ushering in of the Israeli Messiah's Millennial Kingdom means that everlasting peace will prevail in every single aspect of life. The Prince of Peace, Jesus Christ, will have had his way in an unhindered fashion.

The Millennial Temple in the Restored Jerusalem has created a perfect Paradise throughout the entire world. This perfection has permeated every molecule of Creation. The Jewish Messiah, the Anointed One, has come to claim all his people and establish his Throne in his Millennial government. Jesus Christ will now rule this new world government and reign from the Millennial Temple on the Temple Mount in Jerusalem, Israel. The Restoration of the Throne of David has become a reality. The God of Israel's Habitation is now solidified in Jerusalem forever. And from this place, Jesus will watch over the inhabitants of the Earth. From the Millennial Temple, the service of both the everlasting Aaronic and Melchizedek Priesthoods, derived from the Israeli Tribe of Levi, has, officially, in perfect order, been reestablished.

The Millennial Temple, without any deviation, has been built exactly as the blueprints rendered in Ezekiel chapters forty through forty-eight.

In Ezekiel 47:1, we are told that a river of water will flow from beneath the threshold of the Millennial Temple, refreshing the Land of Israel and renewing even the most barren and inhospitable areas of the landscape. The extent of this restorative work includes even the salty waters of the Dead Sea becoming fresh and hosting robust life. The entire world has become as the Garden of Eden. This is an ideal representation and reflection of the heavenly Jerusalem becoming manifested on Earth. Israel is a land flowing with milk and honey once again, and everything is picturesque. Jesus has caused the Millennium to become an absolute reality.

"And they shall say, 'This land that was desolate has become like the Garden of Eden.'" Isaiah 51:3, Ezekiel 36:35, Revelation 2:7

The glorified Jewish Messiah's appearance in Jerusalem, Israel has ushered in his enthronement blessings of the Millennial Kingdom.

At this time, Jerusalem will be called the Throne of the Lord. The clearest evidence that the Restoration of the Throne of David has taken place is the presence of the Millennial Temple. The Shekinah Glory of God, rendering everlasting peace, is having its way all over the world. The never-ending beauty of Israel has become established, and the God of Israel's eternal Covenant is being enforced. As the Israeli Prophet, Malachi, put it: The Messiah has come "with healing in his wings." Malachi 4:2 - The Israeli Messiah has brought the entire world back into proper alignment in a dramatic fashion. And every one of God's people are 100% healed of all their maladies. Jesus Christ has made everyone whole.

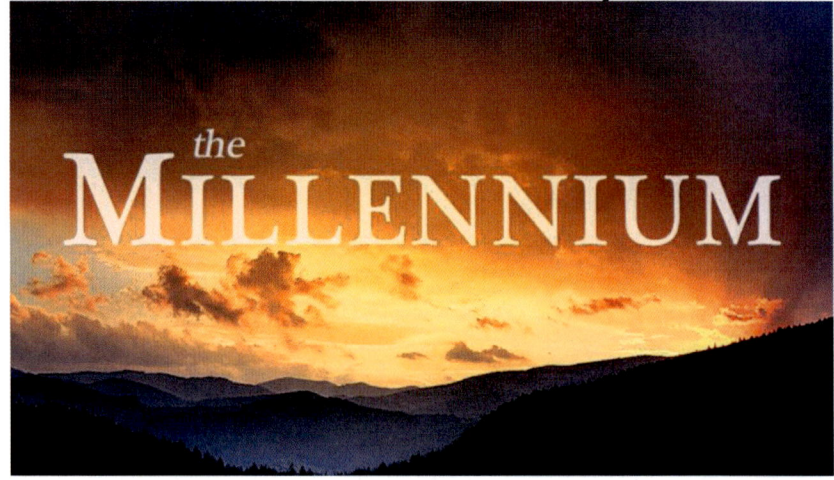

"And the Lord said to David and to Solomon, his son, 'In this House, and in Jerusalem, which I have chosen, will I put my name forever.'" II Kings 21:7 – THE RESTORATION OF THE THRONE OF DAVID IS BEING FULLY REALIZED IN JESUS CHRIST'S MILLENNIUAL REIGN.

The Jewish Messiah is now the undisputed, unchallenged king over the newly restored Earth. Jesus provides the Israelis with a taste of heaven, the Tree of Life bearing twelve kinds of fruit to heal the nations, the eternal Temple with its pearly gates, streets of gold, mansions to accommodate everyone, the cessation of tears and sorrow, a new, eternal Jerusalem, and the restored planet of Earth. Jesus has brought lasting peace and prosperity to a barren wilderness. The Millennial Temple has been firmly established on the Temple Mount, and as the Prophets Isaiah and Micah said: "And they shall beat their swords into plowshares, and their spears into pruninghooks. Nation shall not lift up sword against nation, neither shall they learn war anymore." Isaiah 2:2-4, Micah 4:1-3

"THE LION SHALL LAY DOWN WITH THE LAMB."
ISAIAH 11:6
ALL THE ARMAMENTS OF WAR, ESPECIALLY NUCLEAR MISSILES AND ALL WEAPONS OF MASS DESTRUCTION ARE COMPLETELY DISMANTLED, AND EVERLASTING, PERMANENT PEACE PREVAILS ON EARTH

"And in this mountain shall the Lord of hosts make a feast of fat things full of marrow, of wines on the lees well refined. And he will destroy in this mountain the face of the covering cast over all people, and the vail that is spread over all nations. He will shallow up death in victory. And the Lord God of Israel will wipe away tears off all faces. And the rebuke of his people shall he take away from off all the Earth. For the Lord has spoken it. And it shall be said in that day, 'Lo, this is our God. We have waited for him, and he will save us. This is the Lord God of Israel. We have waited for him. We will be glad and rejoice in his salvation." Isaiah 25:6-9, The Power of the Marriage Supper of the Lamb, Jesus Christ

THE MARRIAGE SUPPER OF THE LAMB
REVELATION 19:5-9

"And a voice came out of the Throne, saying, 'Praise our God, all ye his servants, and ye that fear him, both small and great.' And I heard as it were the voice of a great multitude, and as the voice of many waters, and as the voice of mighty thunderings, saying, 'Alleluia! For the Lord God omnipotent reigns. Let us be glad and rejoice and give honor to him. For the Marriage Supper of the Lamb, Jesus Christ, has come, and his wife, the Church of Jesus Christ, has made herself ready.' And to her was granted that she should be arrayed in fine linen, clean and white. For the fine linen is the righteousness of the saints. And he said unto me, 'Write, Blessed are they which are called unto the Marriage Supper of the Lamb (Jesus Christ)' And he said unto me, 'These are the true sayings of God.'" Revelation 19:5-9

"The Lord brought me into his Banqueting House, and his banner over me was love." Song of Solomon 4:7

At the outset of the Millennium, Jesus prepared a lavish banquet in celebration of the victory. And just as Isaiah, the Prophet, had mentioned, the banquet consisted of "delightful food, with choice pieces of meat and refined, aged wine." Jesus summoned all his people to his banquet table, and his banner over his people would always be love. Song of Solomon 2:4 - It will not be a sad occasion like the Last Supper, which had signaled Christ's departure from the world. The Marriage Supper of the Lamb is a festive event marking the beginning of the way life was intended to be all along. There is a direct relation between the Last Supper of Jesus Christ and the Marriage Supper of the Lamb.

THE LORD'S SUPPER
Matthew 26:26-29, Mark 14:22-25, Luke 22:19, 20
I Corinthians 11:23-26

"And Jesus took the cup, and gave thanks, and gave it to his disciples, saying, 'Drink ye all of it. For this is my blood of the New

Testament, which is shed for the remission of your sins. But I say unto you, I will not drink henceforth of this fruit of the vine, until that day when I drink it new with you in my Father's kingdom.'" Matthew 26:26-29 – Jesus Christ, at the Lord's Supper, referring to the Marriage Supper of the Lamb

"AND A LITTLE CHILD SHALL LEAD THEM" ISAIAH 11:6

And this has all been made possible because the new, perpetual, unconditional, everlasting Covenant of the God of Israel has been fulfilled by Jesus Christ, the Israeli Messiah. This Covenant was initially founded on the sure mercies of David. Isaiah 55:3, 4 - God had promised to give a light to David and his sons forever. This Covenant is one of peace, "Shalom" in Hebrew, promising a new Spirit and a new heart for each one of God's people. And with this Covenant, God declared that David, his servant, would be the Shepherd over the people, and that he would set the Sanctuary, that is, the Millennial Temple, in the midst of the people forevermore. – Ezekiel 37:25-28 - And as the mountains are round about Jerusalem, so the Messiah, Jesus Christ, will be round about his people henceforth even forever. Psalm 125:2

So, now, there is great joy in Jerusalem. And this joy expanded out to embrace and permeate every atom and molecule on Earth. And God was still claiming the city of Jerusalem for David's sake, so that the people may have rest. Jerusalem, Israel is the city of David. And Jerusalem has been chosen by God to be where the government of the Millennial Kingdom will be centered. Jerusalem, Israel is the Capital of the Millennial Kingdom, The New Jerusalem has officially descended out of heaven from God. Revelation 21:1-27 - God has kept Israel as the apple of his eye - Deuteronomy 32:9, 10, and the inheritance of God's people is supreme justice and everlasting peace.

THE ARK OF THE COVENANT CAN NOW BE RESTORED TO ITS PROPER PLACE – THE MILLENNIAL TEMPLE

"'And it shall come to pass, when ye be multiplied and increased in the land (The Eternal Promised Land of Israel), in those days' says the Lord, 'They shall say no more, the Ark of the Covenant of the Lord, neither shall it come to mind, neither shall they remember it, neither shall they visit it, neither shall that be done any more. At that time, they shall call Jerusalem the Throne of the Lord. And all nations shall gather unto it, to the name of the Lord, to Jerusalem. In those days, the House of Judah shall walk with the House of Israel, and they shall come together out of the land of the north to the land that I have given for an inheritance unto your fathers.'" Jeremiah 3:16-18

There are some who misinterpret this passage of scripture to mean that God is saying that there will come a time when the Ark of the Covenant will not need to be remembered. That is not what's being said here. God is stating that a day will come when people will stop saying that the Ark of the Covenant will no longer have a place in the Temple (The Millennial Temple), in the Holy of Holies, the resting place of the Ark. It is imperative that the Ark of the Covenant be restored, in the days of the Restoration of the Throne of David, to the Millennial Temple. And one factor that remained eternal with the God of Israel is that the Ark of the Covenant would always be in David's care.

"'For this is the Covenant that I will make with the House of Israel after those days,' says the Lord God of Israel. 'I will put my laws in their minds and write them in their hearts. And I will be to them a God, and they shall be to me a people.'" Ezekiel 11:19, 20, Ezekiel 36:26-38, Ezekiel 37:25-28, Hebrews 10:16

Ever since 586 B.C., when the Babylonians destroyed the Temple in Jerusalem at the command of Nebuchadnezzar, the Ark of the Covenant has been missing. But now, new, glorious circumstances have developed to make it possible for the Ark to be successfully restored to the Millennial Temple by David, and appropriately so. This would, of course, be the most monumental feat of all time, because the significance and gravity of this gesture is beyond measure. The power brought about by the manifest presence of the Shekinah Glory of God upon the mercy seat of the Ark of the Covenant, between the two Cherubim, is beyond calculation. The end result would be that the Shekinah presence of God would engulf people throughout the entire world with peace, the peace of God that passes all understanding. I Kings 8:1-11, II Chronicles 5:1-14, Philippians 4:7

As a direct result of the fourth earthly Temple of the God of Israel (The Millennial Temple) being built by Jesus Christ, mankind's common enemy, Satan, has been "cast into the Lake of Fire," along with the afflictions of war, famine, pandemics, hated, chaos, civil unrest, and so forth, to emit ongoing everlasting peace around the globe from that day on.

THE ARK OF THE COVENANT
I KINGS 8:1-11
II CHRONICLES 5:1-14
REVELATION 11:19

"And the Temple of God was opened in heaven, and there was seen in his Temple the Ark of the Covenant. And there was lightning, and voices, and thundering." Revelation 11:19

"Then, Solomon assembled the Elders of Israel, and all the heads of the Tribes, and the Chief of the fathers of the children of Israel, unto King Solomon in Jerusalem, that they may bring up the Ark of the Covanent of the Lord to the city of David (Jerusalem), which is Zion." I Kings 8:1, II Chronicles 5:2

The Millennial Temple would not be complete without the Ark of the Covenant having been reinstated there. And David was the one responsible for making it possible for the Ark to be restored to its rightful place. So, from that very day forward, the House of Israel knew that Jesus Christ is their Messiah in a most personable manner.

"For the Son of God has come to seek and save that which was lost. What do you think? If a Shepherd has a hundred sheep, and one of them has gone astray, does he not leave the ninety-nine, and go into the mountains, and seek after that sheep which has gone astray?

Even so, it is not the will of your Father who is in Heaven that one of these little ones should perish." Luke 19:11, 12, 14

"But whosoever shall offend one of these little ones which believe in me, it would be better for him that a millstone were hanged about his neck, and that he were drowned in the depth of the sea." Jesus Christ, Matthew 18: 6, Mark 9:42, Luke 17:2, Revelation 18:21

"In my Father's House are many Mansions. And if I go and prepare a place for you, I will come again, and receive you unto myself. That where I am, there you may be also." Jesus Christ, John 14:2, 3

"And one of the Elders said unto me, 'Weep not. Behold, the Lion of the Tribe of Judah, the Root of David (Jesus Christ), has prevailed to open the book, and to loosen the seven seals thereof.' And they sung a new song, saying, 'Thou art worthy to take the book, and to open the seals thereof. For you were slain and have redeemed us to God by your blood out of every kindred, and tongue, and people, and nation. And Jesus has made us unto our God kings (and queens) and priests (and priestesses).'" Revelation 5:5, 9, 10

"And it shall come to pass, afterward, that I will pour out my Spirit upon all of mankind." Joel 2:28, Acts 2:17

The best three words to describe Jesus are compassionate, caring, and understanding. And one thing was quite certain: Jesus is here on Earth to stay.

"For unto us a child is born (Jesus Christ), unto us a Son is given. And the government shall be upon his shoulder. And his name shall be Wonderful, Counsellor, The Mighty God, The Everlasting Father, The Peace of Peace. Of the increase of his government and peace there shall be no end, upon the Throne of David, and upon his kingdom to order it, and establish it with judgement and justice from henceforth even forever. The zeal of the Lord of hosts will perform this." Isaiah 9:6, 7

"Suffer the little children to come unto me. For of such is the Kingdom of Heaven." Jesus Christ, Matthew 19:14

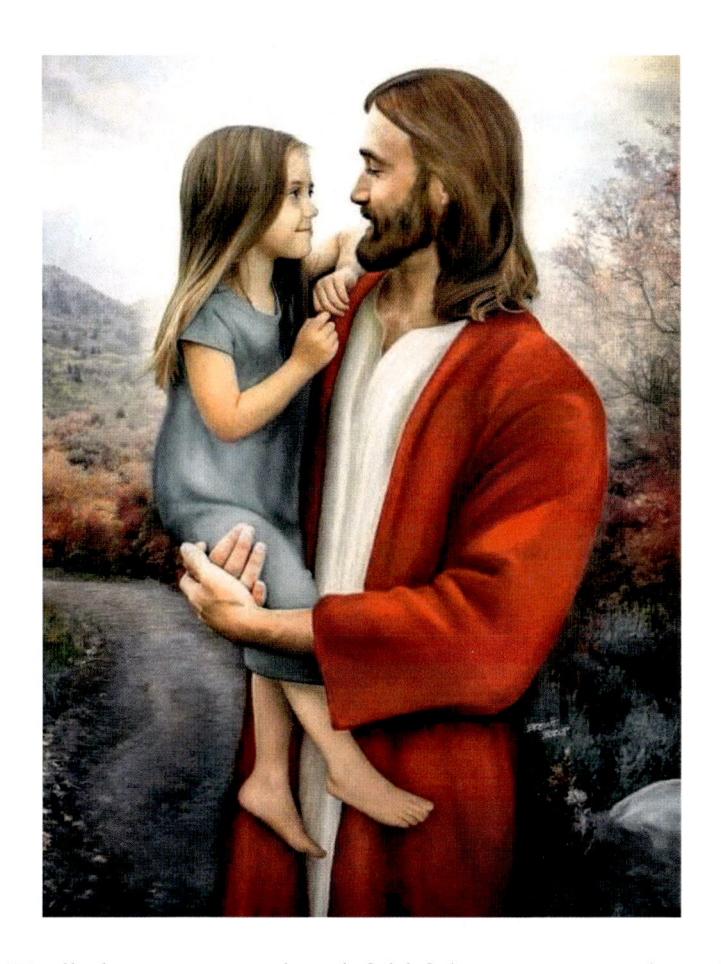

"Well done, my good and faithful servant. You have been faithful over a few things. I will make you ruler over many things. Enter into the joy of your Lord." Jesus, Matthew 25:21

CHAPTER TWELVE
THE RIGHTFUL PLACE FOR THE ARK OF THE COVENANT

THE ISRAELIS BOW AS KING DAVID BRINGS THE ARK OF THE COVENANT INTO JERUSALEM, ISRAEL TO THE MILLENNIAL TEMPLE

And David gathered all Israel together to Jerusalem, to bring up the Ark of the Covenant, also referred to as the Ark of the God of Israel, into the Holy of Holies in the Millennial Temple, which David had prepared for it. And all the way as the Ark was carried to the Temple, there was the sound of musical instruments and celebration. And when the Ark was brought into the city of David, Jerusalem, the people began to shout so loudly that the Earth rang. Then, David, Bathsheba, and the entire camp of Israel wept and worshipped God worldwide.

And once the Ark of the Covenant was restored to the Millennial Temple, a sight that Israel had not seen since Solomon's Temple was destroyed in 586 B.C. by the Babylonians, and the Ark had disappeared and not been seen again since in the Temple, the same exact result took place, only to a much, much more intense degree than the scene depicted in the First Book of Kings and the Second

Book of Chronicles in the Hebrew Bible. I Kings 8:1-11 – II Chronicles 5:1-14:

"After the priests carried the Ark of the Covenant into the Millennial Temple and set it in its proper place in the Holy of Holies, the power of God became overwhelming, to say the least. When the Ark of the Covenant, on this momentous occasion, had found its eternal home in the Millennial Temple, an auspicious cloud representing the presence of the Shekinah Glory of God filled the House. And the priests were not capable of standing to minister because of the intensity of power and glory of God that had filled the Temple." I Kings 8:1, 4-6, 10, 11, II Chronicles 5:2, 7, 13, 14

The interior of the Millennial Temple is divided into two sections: The Holy Place, Hekal in Hebrew, and the Most Holy Place, the Holy of Holies, Qodesh Qodashim or Kodesh HaKodashim in Hebrew, which were separated from each other by a curtain or veil (paroket or parochet in Hebrew).

Within the Holy Place (outside the Holy of Holies) inside the Temple, three objects are housed within the Temple, including the Golden Table for the Showbread, the Table (altar) of Incense, the Golden Seven Branched Candelabrum (Candlestick), also known as a Menorah in Hebrew and the Golden Altar of Incense.

Within the Most Holy Place (The Holy of Holies – inner Sanctuary within the Millennial Temple), the Ark of the Covenant had finally found its rightful, eternal place on Earth. The Ark contained the Golden Pot of Manna, Aaron's Rod, and the Tablets of the Covenant, which are the Ten Commandments. The Ark rested on a bedrock platform that protrudes within the Holy of Holies, called in Jewish tradition the Foundation Stone, Even HaShetiyah in Hebrew. Jesus Christ will serve as the Great High Priest of Israel. And Jesus' priests will officiate in the Outer Court of the Temple and in the Holy Place. When Jesus died upon the Cross for our sins, - John 3:16, I Corinthians 5:21 - the veil separating the Holy of Holies from the rest of the world was torn in half. Luke 23:44-46, Hebrews 9:3 - This signified that we all now have access to forgiveness of sin through Christ.

And just as expected, the Ark of the Covenant's presence in the Millennial Temple, Israel's 4th earthly Temple, engulfed the entire world in the Lord's presence, the Shekinah Glory of the Lord (the peace of God that passes all understanding – Philippians 4:7).

Just as much as the miraculous presence of the Restored Solomon had made it possible for Solomon's Temple to be rebuilt, so too would his presence in the world assist in making it possible for the holy Ark of the Covenant, Aron Hakodesh (The Holy Ark) in Hebrew, to be restored to the Millennial Temple and bring rest to all of Israel's enemies for all time.

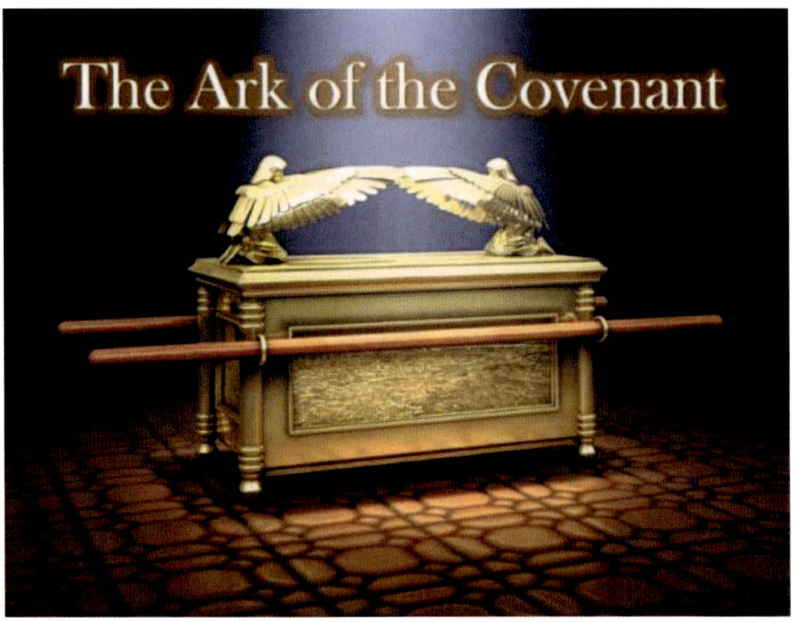

"And David said, 'Is there not a cause?'" I Samuel 17:29

It all had a meant to be feeling on the glorious day when everyone observed David, appropriately and poetically, leading the priests of the Tribe of Levi in bringing the Ark of the Covenant of the God of Israel into the newly built Millennial Temple, to place it in the Most Holy Place (The Holy of Holies). The mighty wings of the Ark spreads over it, and the power of God was restored to its mercy seat.

And the color of the Shekinah Glory of God is a beautiful shade of amber, according to Ezekiel, the Prophet, confirming the victory of Jesus Christ to all of his people. Ezekiel 1:4, Ezekiel 1:27, Ezekiel 8:2

"Who am I, O, Lord God? And what is my house,
that you have brought me to such a glorious place?"
II SAMUEL 7:18-29, I CHRONICLES 17:16-27 - David

Once the Ark of the Covenant rested in the Holy of Holies within the Millennial Temple in such an unprecedented fashion, David bowed before the Ark, and gloriously and appropriately recited: "Lord, remember David, and all his afflictions. How I swore unto the Mighty God of Jacob. Surely, I have not come into the comfort of my house, nor gone up into my bed, or given sleep to my eyes, or slumber to my eyelids, until I found a place for the Lord, a Habitation for the Mighty God of Israel." Psalm 132:1-5

And despite the fact that so many people all through the years had said that the Ark of the Covenant of the God of Israel would never be restored to the Israeli Temple again, and that there would come a day when the Ark would never come to anyone's mind, nor be remembered, or ever be seen at a future date again, Jerusalem would once again see the Throne of David restored and the Ark of the Covenant settled in its proper place forever, just as the Israeli Prophet, Jeremiah, foresaw. Jeremiah 3:16-18 - And all the nations of the Earth gathered to Jerusalem in the name of the Lord in these days. The House of Judah was now walking with the House of Israel. And all the people of Israel, past and present had come together to the Eternal Promised Land, the land of milk and honey, as the apple of God's eye – Deuteronomy 32:9, 10, and received an inheritance promised to the fathers long ago, and their children, and their children's children.

And not until the reign of the Restored David had the kingdom of Israel actually secured its promised imperial dimensions, which are now all inclusive. David had successfully reinvented his army, the government, and the religion of Judaism (advocating Jesus Christ as the Messiah – Mashiach ben David) for Israel's sake, according to the thirty-seventh chapter of Ezekiel – Ezekiel 37:25-28, freeing his people from their primitive tribal existence and showing them how a modern cosmopolitan nation ought to function in true form. David turned the Twelve Nomadic Tribes of Israel into a single unbeatable superpower. David was mightily used, in top-form fashion, to make it possible for the Millennial Kingdom to be ushered in.

"'And it shall come to pass, when you are multiplied and increased in the land, in those days' saith the Lord, 'they shall say no more, The Ark of the Covenant of the Lord God of Israel, neither shall it come to mind. Neither shall they remember it. Neither shall they visit it. Neither shall that be done anymore.'" Jeremiah 3:16

David somehow managed to restore the Ark of the Covenant to its rightful, proper place for all eternity.

"And David gathered all Israel together to Jerusalem, to bring up the Ark of the Lord unto his place (The Holy of Holies in the Millennial Temple), which David had prepared for it."
I Chronicles 15:3

CHAPTER THIRTEEN
THE RESTORATION OF
THE THRONE OF DAVID

THE SYMBOL OF JERUSALEM, ISRAEL

The Earth brought forth life and was renewed in one day. And along with the package, Israel was born all at once. And the most fought over city in the world, Jerusalem, Israel, was now like a flowing river extending everlasting peace to the entire world. People were once again allowed into the Garden of Eden, and they were partaking of the healing fruit of the Tree of Life in the midst of the garden. There was nothing but hope and assurance in the hearts of everyone, because they were experiencing a new heaven and a new Earth without guile, and there was great comfort in knowing that children would have a secure future as well. There was no reason to ever feel threatened about anything again. And all the citizens of Jerusalem were there to stay, never to be uprooted again.

The Israeli Messiah, Jesus Christ, had always existed before the foundation of the world, and the trademark of the new government on Earth which he had established was peace without end. The Throne of David had been restored with judgment and justice, procured by Almighty God's standard. The Throne of David was now firmly revived forever.

The Restoration of the Throne of David was now permanently established. The people of Israel could take confidence in the fact that from that day forward, they would experience nothing but peace.

Jesus Christ, the Israeli Messiah, had come as he promised, and the end result was singing, gladness, and everlasting joy. People, literally, did not know the meaning of the words, "sorrow" and "mourning" any longer – Isaiah 51-11. People didn't stop to think that it was too good to be true. They were not taking deep breaths, or sighs of relief, or saying to themselves: "I can't believe this is happening!" With totally calm composure, everyone inherently knew in their hearts that things would always be this way now.

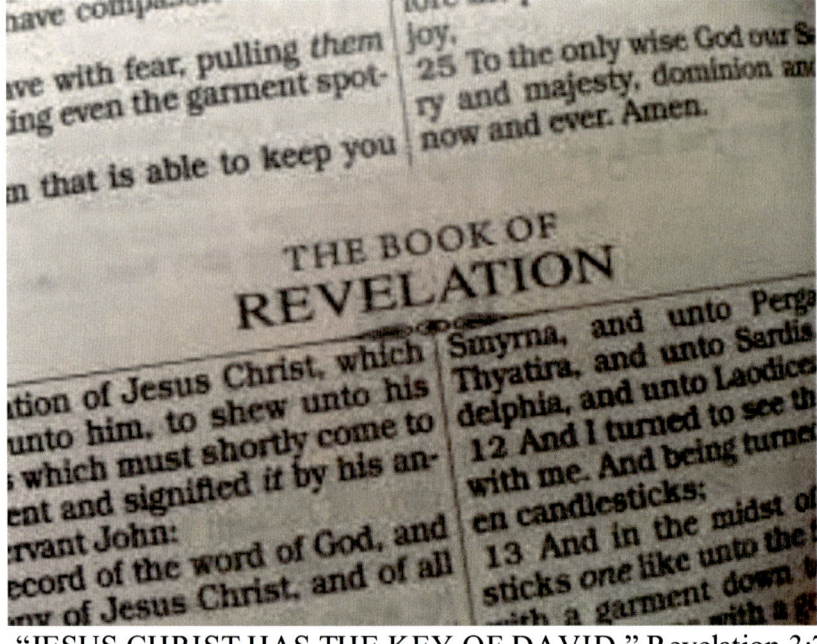

"JESUS CHRIST HAS THE KEY OF DAVID." Revelation 3:7

"Heaven and Earth shall pass away, but my words shall not pass away." Jesus Christ, Matthew 24:35

"And I saw a new heaven and a new Earth. For the first heaven and the first Earth were passed away." Revelation 21:1

"And I, John, saw the holy city, New Jerusalem, coming down from God out of heaven, prepared as a bride (The Church of Jesus Christ) adorned for her husband (Jesus Christ)." Revelation 21:2

"An entirely new heaven and Earth were created, and the former heaven and Earth were never to be remembered again. And the New Jerusalem came down from God out of heaven. And I heard a voice out heaven, saying, "Behold, the Ark of the Covenant is with men!" Revelation 21:3

"And they shall say, 'This land that was desolate has become like the Garden of Eden." Ezekiel 36:35

And Jesus Christ, who sat upon the Throne of the Millennial Temple, said, "Behold, I make all things new. It is done. I am the Alpha and Omega, the Beginning and the End. I give unto him that is athirst of the Fountain of the Water of Life freely. He that overcomes shall inherit all things. And I will be his God."

And there was a pure river of water of life proceeding out of the Messiah's Throne. And in the midst of Jerusalem, there was the Tree of Life bearing twelve various kinds of fruit. And the entire city of Jerusalem consisted of pure gold. Revelation 21:18, Revelation 22:1-4

In unsurpassed epic proportion, the nation of Israel has been restored, and Christ's Millennial Kingdom has been established in a glorious fashion.

Ha-Mashiach (Mashiach ben David): Hebrew for "The Messiah" or "The Anointed One"

Mishpachah: Hebrew for "Members of the Messiah's Household"

David's life had offered an enduring definition of what it means to be human. David always managed to live and survive. The Restoration of the Throne of David serves as an eternal reminder of David's indomitable will of bringing victory to Israel. As stated in Isaiah 55:3 - "The everlasting Covenant that God made with Israel is based upon the sure mercies of David, a leader and commander to God's people." And in the First Book of Samuel, it is also confirmed that, "The Lord has sought for himself a man after his own heart, and the Lord has commanded him to be Captain over his people." And just as much as the God of Israel has been seeking David, it can safely be said that David was seeking the God of Israel.

SO, DAVID MOVED ON, AND HIS ARMY FOLLOWED HIM

"And they shall dwell in the land that I have given unto Jacob, my servant, wherein your fathers have dwelt. And they shall dwell therein, even they, and their children, and their children's children forever. And my servant David, shall be their prince forever. Moreover, I will make a Covenant of Peace with them. It shall be an everlasting Covenant with them. And I will place them, and multiply them, and will set my Sanctuary (The Millennial Temple) in the midst of them forevermore. My Tabernacle also shall I be with them. Yea, and I will be their God. And they shall be my people. And the heathen shall know that I the Lord do sanctify Israel, when my

Sanctuary (The Millennial Temple) shall be in the midst of them forevermore." Ezekiel 37:25-28

The Day of the Lord came upon us all the inhabitants of Earth like a thief in the night, and the Millennium was upon us in an instant. Because one day with the God of Israel is as a thousand years, and a thousand years is as a day. II Peter 3:8

The God of Israel kept his promise to the fathers of all the people, who had longed for the Temple to be built in its rightful place on a permanent basis in beauty. God had chosen Jerusalem, and now, with the Millennial Temple in place, his name would be there forever from generation to generation.

"THEY SHALL DWELL IN THE LAND
THAT I HAVE GIVEN UNTO THEM."
EZEKIEL 37:25 – THE GOD OF ISRAEL
THE ETERNAL PROMISED LAND OF ISRAEL

Among all the Twelve Tribes of Israel, God's will was being done on Earth as it is in Heaven. Matthew 6:9-13 – The Lord's Prayer. Now, God's people were in the Eternal Promised Land, and his Spirit was in them eternally. Just as much as Jesus is the Resurrection and the Life, his chosen people would never again witness death. John 11:25, 26 - This is the very promise that the Israeli Messiah had rendered, that is, the promise of eternal life, and Jesus Christ came through with flying colors. John 3:16, I John 1:1-3, I John 2:25, I John 5:11, I John 5:13

"These things have I written unto you that believe on the name of the Son of God. That you may know that you have eternal life, and that you may believe on the name of the Son of God." John, the Apostle, I John 5:13

And the Israeli Messiah used David to accomplish his monumental feats, as predicted in Hosea 3:5: "Afterward shall the children of Israel return, and seek the Lord their God, and David, their king. And you shall fear the Lord and his goodness in the latter days."

"Wherefore, God also has highly exalted him, and given him a name which is above every name. That at the name of Jesus every knee should bow, of things in heaven, and things in Earth, and things under the Earth. And that every tongue should confess that Jesus Christ is Lord, to the glory of God the Father." Philippians 2:9-11

David paused to reflect upon the words of Christ in Luke 10:24, "For I tell you, that many prophets and kings have desired to see those things which you see and have not seen them. And to have heard those things which you hear and have not heard them." And David could not help but be reminded of his college days at Harvard University, when he learned a Kennedy expression that he grew to love: "Some men see things as they are and ask, 'Why?' I dream things that never were and ask, 'Why not?'"

"AND I HAVE RESTORED UNTO YOU THE YEARS THAT THE LOCUSTS AND THE CATERPILLARS HAVE EATEN, BY MY GREAT ARMY, which I sent among you. And you shall eat in plenty, and be satisfied, and praise the name of the Lord your God, who has dealt wondrously with you. You shall know that I am in the midst of Israel. And it shall come to pass that I will pour out my Spirit upon all mankind." Joel 2:25-28 – The Restoration of the Throne of David

"'Behold, I will bring it health and cure, and I will cure them, and will reveal unto them the abundance of peace and truth. And I will cause the captivity of Israel to return, and will build them, AS AT THE FIRST. The voice of joy, and the voice of gladness, the voice of the bridegroom, and the voice of the bride, the voice of them that shall say, 'Praise the Lord of hosts. For the Lord is good. For his mercy endureth forever. And of them that shall bring the sacrifice of praise into the House of the Lord. For I will cause to return the captivity of the land, AS AT THE FIRST,' saith the Lord God of Israel. 'Behold the days come,' saith the Lord, 'that I will perform that good thing which I have promised unto the House of Israel and to the House of Judah. In those days, and at that time, will I cause the Branch of Righteousness (Jesus Christ) to grow up unto David. And I shall execute judgment and righteousness in the land. For thus saith the Lord God of Israel, David shall never lack a man to sit upon the Throne of the House of Israel." Jeremiah 33:6, 7, 11, 14-17

"Who hath heard such a thing? Who hath seen such things? Shall the Earth be made to bring forth in one day? Or shall a nation (Israel) be born at once? For as soon as Zion (Jerusalem, Israel) travailed, she brought forth her children." Isaiah 66:8

THE SOVEREIGNTY OF GOD by David
Dedicated to my wife, Bathsheba
Song of Solomon 4:7

God looks down from his Throne in heaven, and sees the entire parade (past, present, and future) before him. God sees it all from the beginning to the end and from the end to the beginning. God observes everything in infinite detail, and he considers all the ramifications from his unique perspective. God has created all the characters on the stage, and God knows the entire script by heart. God is the Supreme Director of the good matters in life that all, ultimately, lead to a positive conclusion. We cannot comprehend this glorious concept in its entirety, but God, in his own perfect timing, demonstrates that he alone is sovereign forever.

CHAPTER FOURTEEN
THE GRAND REUNION

INSIDE THE MILLENNIAL TEMPLE

"One thing have I desired of the Lord, that will I seek after. That I may dwell in the House of the Lord God of Israel all the days of my life, to behold the beauty of the Lord, and to enquire in his Temple." David, Psalm 27:4

As David, Bathsheba, Prince Solomon, Princess Charity, Jonathan, and Tamera stood in the Millennial Temple that Jesus Christ had built, admiring it's radiant, overwhelming beauty, along with many other bystanders, they heard a familiar voice behind them, saying, "It does, indeed, appear, now, that everything has come full circle, my dear boy."

And before David had a chance to even turn around, tears came to his eyes and joy in his heart. The same reaction could be said for Jonathan, because he too recognized the voice distinctly.

Both of them did an immediate about face, practically in sync with each other, and there stood Dr. Samuel Goldstein with an effervescent glow all around him, with Dr. Esther Schindler standing happily by his side.

"Glory be to my God!" David exclaimed with utter joy. "He is mighty to do anything!"

David and Jonathan embraced Dr. Goldstein and Esther Schindler as close as they possibly could, with Jonathan shouting out, "Now, it's totally confirmed that the Restoration of the Throne of David has taken place."

David's anointing was renewed forever from being once again in Dr. Goldstein's presence. It was a special moment for all of Israel and the world to revel in. And if that wasn't enough, David glanced behind where Dr. Goldstein was standing, and there was Prince

Solomon holding hands with a tender-aged Queen of Sheba, the love of Solomon's life. Everything had, indeed, come full circle.
I Kings 10:1-13

"And David sang unto the Lord God of Israel the words of a song in the day that the Lord had delivered him out of the hand of all his enemies." II Samuel 22:1-51, Psalm 18:1-50

"And King David sat before the Lord God of Israel, just as much as in the Hebrew Bible, and he said, "Who am I, O, Lord God? And what is my house, that you have brought me to this place? And this was yet a small thing in your sight. For you have regarded me according to the estate of a man of high degree. Because you know your servant. And what one nation in the Earth is like your people, even like Israel. For you have confirmed that the people of Israel are yours forever: And you, therefore, are our God forever. And as you have said to me, you have established your Temple forever. Let your name be magnified forever, even the God of Israel. And let the House of David be established and blessed before you forever. Therefore, now, let it please you to bless the House of your servant, that it may continue forever before you. For you have blessed this House, O, Lord. And it shall be blessed forever." II Samuel 7:18-29, I Chronicles 17:16-27

"Wherefore David blessed the Lord before all the congregation. And David said, 'Blessed are you, Lord God of Israel, forever and ever.'" I Chronicles 29:10

"'My Covenant will I not break once I have sworn unto David,' says the God of Israel. 'His seed shall endure forever, and his Throne as the Sun before me. It shall be established forever as the Moon, and as a faithful witness in heaven." Psalm 89: 34-37, David, the King of Israel

"Who is she that looks forth as the morning, fair as the Moon, and clear as the Sun, and terrible as an army with banners?"
Song of Solomon 6:10, Bathsheba, the Queen of Israel

"Thou art all fair, my Love. There is no spot in thee."
Song of Solomon 4:7

Life is not measured by the number of breaths we take. Life is measured by the number of moments that take our breath away.

The Pathway: Color Picture Photo Edition

DAVID AND BATHSHEBA REUNITED AT LAST

It was a glorious rendezvous between King David and Queen Bathsheba after the Battle of Armageddon. You could easily say that it was the single most glorious reunion of all time. And the people of the world reveled in witnessing the King and Queen of Israel,

Prince Solomon, Princess Charity, and their heroic palace German Shepherd, Shalom, all brought back together again, especially in view of everyone living in such a new, novel world now. The family dynasty of Israel dazzled the entire globe, and David and Bathsheba were the talk of the town. There was not a single person on Earth who did not desire to hear all the stories covering the King and Queen of Israel.

While the people of Israel and the world fell in love with the couple eternally, David and Bathsheba decided to get away from the limelight to spend some quality time with each other. They chose to go to what use to be the Dead Sea. Following suit with the newly restored planet of Earth, the body of water there had become perfectly pure and pristine, teeming with robust life, and was now appropriately dubbed as the Sea of Living Water.

The couple traveled to a spot they were familiar with at the revived body of water. They slipped chest-deep into the non-threatening sea together. They were under a full Moon that shimmered a beautiful reflection upon the Sea of Living Water. The light of the Moon traveled all the way to where the happy couple were embracing each other.

"Hope springs eternal, David." Bathsheba pointed out.

David looked deep into Bathsheba's eyes, and said, "I'd take another chance, take a fall, take a shot for you, Bathsheba."

"Looks like there really are consolations in life, huh, David?" Bathsheba asked, fishing for an appropriate response.

"You are eternally luminous, Bathsheba. I'll settle for that consolation." David stated in all sincerity. "The only mystery I could never solve is why my heart could never let go of you. You're the only one who ever really knew me at all."

"There goes that disarming charm of yours again, David, accompanied by that infectious smile. Your charm is what makes you the best of the best!" Bathsheba joyfully remarked. "We're both just a couple of hopeless romantics."

David and Bathsheba embraced each other even closer and kissed in a most passionate manner.

"How's that for verifiable data, Commander?" Bathsheba asked, staring David directly in his eyes with laser beam focus.

"Bathsheba, we may have just concluded the war to end all wars, but there's always something left to conquer." David responded, implying his endless pursuit of Bathsheba. "All is well. Here's to World War None!"

"Love gives not but itself and takes not from itself. Love possesses not nor would it be possessed. For Love is sufficient unto Love, my Love." Bathsheba recited to the love of her life. "Isn't the Moon beautiful tonight, David?"

"That's not the Moon in the sky, Bathsheba. That's a reflection of the Moon. You're the beautiful Moon, causing that reflection." David clarified.

"And should I be the Moon, then, you are the Sun who gives me light, David." Bathsheba noted.

"I bet you're hard to get over, Bathsheba. I bet the Moon just doesn't shine," David said, as tears streamed from Bathsheba's eyes down her cheeks.

ABOUT THE AUTHOR

Bruce Davidson is a graduate of one of the twentieth top-ranking universities in the United States. His novel, "The Pathway: Color Picture Photo Edition," resulted from his most recent pilgrimage to his heritage of Israel. "The Pathway: Color Picture Photo Edition"

The Pathway: Color Picture Photo Edition

is written in a fashion that borders on metaphorical possibilities and concrete reality.

In the United States Air Force, Bruce worked with F-4 Phantom Combat Fighter Jets. It would be from Europe and the United States that Bruce through the years would frequent Israel and become updated on the nation's overall cultural, military, diplomatic, and social status. It would be from Europe and the United States, through the years, that Bruce visited his heritage of Israel to become refreshed and updated. All the facets and dimensions of the nation of Israel are incorporated in "The Pathway: Color Picture Photo Edition."

From the author of "Christ's Triumphant Appearance" (a commentary to "The Pathway: Color Picture Photo Edition"), Bruce Davidson, in his novel, "The Pathway: Color Picture Photo Edition," provides the reader with the very Spirit of Israel. This Spirit is very much embodied by the two key protagonists of the plot, who are deeply involved with each other and the destiny of Israel. Modern-day David and Bathsheba are portrayed in this novel as an Israeli romantic item who would do anything for each other and Israel. There are no weak links in the chain attaching these two together. The collective purpose of this couple's journey is imperative to the pathway of success where Israel is concerned in contemporary days. The central theme of "The Pathway: Color Picture Photo Edition" surrounds the Israeli Temple and the Temple Mount. People have speculated for many years as to whether or not the futuristic, prophesied Temple will be rebuilt. And if it is possible, what circumstances are conducive in bringing it about.

A war is on the horizon potentially offering the hope of being the war to end all wars. Armageddon (the apocalypse) will be fought by the Israeli military and Israel's associated allies, with the intention of ushering in everlasting peace to the world. And while there are no guarantees, it is hoped that the Millennial Temple will become established to make that everlasting peace a reality.

The novel, "The Pathway: Color Picture Photo Edition," is conducive to the hope that peace is not merely a pipe dream.

Camelot either has a shot at being restored or will remain lost forever.

The Pathway: Color Picture Photo Edition

Made in the USA
Columbia, SC
04 August 2025

d26448cd-9191-4fe2-9150-9f4a365e01a5R02